'This book neatly juxtaposes the search for sources of solidarity in the West, not in a return to Christianity, as some have proposed, but in innovative movements and initiatives emerging out of a diversity of religion, belief and non-belief. The concept of myth is borrowed from religion and deployed in empirical investigations of both religious and non-religious settings. This opens up a valuable space for thinking again about categories and sources of solidarity in the public realm which for a while had gone missing, and will allow scholars, students and interested activists to think deeply about the possibilities.'

Adam Dinham, Professor of Faith and Public Policy
and Director of the Faiths and Civil Society Unit,
Goldsmiths, University of London, UK

'This book addresses head-on the peculiar situation of the current west. We now see that even our replacements for religion, capitalism and libertarianism, are dubious and damaging myths. Yet with their demise, our sense of the emptiness left by the absence of real faith merely intensifies. Tim Stacey's modest proposal is that we try to link some renewed sense of transcendence to local practices of mutual support, respecting human dignity and the natural world. It is not a bad starting-place for renewal.'

John Milbank, Research Professor of Religion, Politics
and Ethics and President of the Centre of Theology
and Philosophy, University of Nottingham, UK

Myth and Solidarity in the Modern World

In the context of the rise of reactionary politics across the globe, this book seeks new ways of developing solidarity across religious, political and economic differences. Drawing on an increasingly influential Christian theological movement, postliberalism, it claims that the dominance of liberal, secular rationality has blinded people to the fundamental role of transcendence and myth in developing solidarity. The result is either atrophy, or a retrenching in divisive myths of faith, race, nation or economic status.

Liberalism is now a dominant force across the globe. But its resonance in the Anglo-Saxon West, from which it originates and has been most fully realized, is relatively underexplored. The book thus follows two simultaneous lines of enquiry. Firstly, a genealogical study of social scientific and policy iterations of the relationship between belief and solidarity in the Anglo-Saxon West, placing postliberal theory into dialogue with the sociology and anthropology of religion, politics and economics. Secondly, it draws from original ethnographic research with groups in London, UK, that seek to develop solidarity in the face of deep-seated difference.

By bringing a new way of framing these contentious debates about contemporary society, this research offers tools for more productive conversations around religious and political topics, in particular concluding with a clear policy proposal. It is, therefore, a useful resource for both academics of theology and religious studies, political philosophy, sociology and anthropology, and politicians, policy makers and practitioners hoping to develop solidarity in the modern world.

Timothy Stacey is a Postdoctoral Fellow at both the Religion and Diversity Project, University of Ottawa, Canada and the Faiths and Civil Society Unit, Goldsmiths, University of London, UK. He is interested in the role of religion and belief, or 'myth' as he prefers, in developing solidarity, with special attention to the implications for politics, public policy and practice. He has developed successful funding bids both internally and with a range of funders, including the Arts and Humanities Research Council (AHRC).

Routledge New Critical Thinking in Religion, Theology and Biblical Studies

The *Routledge New Critical Thinking in Religion, Theology and Biblical Studies* series brings high-quality research monograph publishing back into focus for authors, international libraries and student, academic and research readers. This open-ended monograph series presents cutting-edge research from both established and new authors in the field. With specialist focus yet clear contextual presentation of contemporary research, books in the series take research into important new directions and open the field to new critical debate within the discipline, in areas of related study, and in key areas for contemporary society.

For a full list of titles in this series, please visit www.routledge.com/religion/series/RCRITREL

Myth and Solidarity in the Modern World

Beyond Religious and Political Division

Timothy Stacey

Routledge
Taylor & Francis Group

LONDON AND NEW YORK

First published 2018
by Routledge
2 Park Square, Milton Park, Abingdon, Oxon OX14 4RN

and by Routledge
711 Third Avenue, New York, NY 10017

Routledge is an imprint of the Taylor & Francis Group, an informa business

British Library Cataloguing-in-Publication Data
A catalogue record for this book is available from the British Library

Library of Congress Cataloging-in-Publication Data
Names: Stacey, Timothy, author.
Title: Myth and solidarity in the modern world : beyond religious
    and political division / Timothy Stacey.
Description: New York : Routledge, 2018. | Series: Routledge new
    critical thinking in religion, theology, and biblical studies | Includes
    bibliographical references and index.
Identifiers: LCCN 2017052129 | ISBN 9780815348160 (hardback :
    alk. paper) | ISBN 9781351167840 (ebook)
Subjects: LCSH: Religion and sociology. | Cooperation—Religious
    aspects. | Solidarity—Religious aspects. | Postliberal theology. |
    Religion and politics.
Classification: LCC BL60 .S668 2018 | DDC 201/.7—dc23
LC record available at https://lccn.loc.gov/2017052129

ISBN: 978-0-8153-4816-0 (hbk)
ISBN: 978-1-351-16784-0 (ebk)

Typeset in Sabon
by Apex CoVantage, LLC

MIX
Paper from
responsible sources
FSC
www.fsc.org   FSC® C013604

Printed and bound by CPI Group (UK) Ltd, Croydon, CR0 4YY

Contents

Acknowledgements

I am grateful to my dad, who has spent the last 35 years working in an unfulfilling job, thus affording his children the stability to undertake more creative pursuits. Academia remains a largely middle-class pursuit. I am grateful to have been among the lucky few who could pursue their interests to this level. My grandma also offered me financial support in the early years of my PhD. Thank you.

I am grateful to both my dad and my mum for offering us love on the basis of the kinds of characters we become rather than on the basis of worldly success. I am especially thankful to my mum for the gift of attention over time that ingrained this sense in us every day. The resultant self-worth has meant that for me academia can and has always been a pursuit of passion rather than of success. I see many young scholars around me who are deeply stressed by a relentless need for affirmation.

Thank you to John Milbank and Adrian Pabst for inspiring my interest in postliberalism. Thank you to Adam Dinham for dragging me kicking and screaming into the world of social science. Thank you to Abby Day and Chris Baker, whose vital comments on my PhD helped to inspire this book.

Most of all I am grateful to Fernande Pool. After meeting at a conference in Bern, where we bonded over a shared love of virtue ethics, beer and silliness, she soon became my best friend, worst critic and the love of my life. Thank you for introducing me to anthropology. Thank you for whisking me off to India where most of this book was written. Thank you for coming with me to Canada where this book was finished. Thank you for reading every chapter over and over with the kind of dedication only a lover can offer. Thank you for crying with me over every pitfall, celebrating every achievement and helping to make the myths we live by together. With your help, I aim to be the change I want to see the world.

Finally, thank you to all of those who agreed to participate in this study, without whom it would not have been possible. This book suggests that people find moral strength in remembering and emulating their heroes. Many of you are mine. I hope I have done you justice in what follows.

Introduction

We live in a time of turmoil and paradox. Radical diversity of ideas of how we ought to live seems to increasingly threaten possibilities of living well together. Purportedly democratic countries are in reality ruled by technocratic elites that neglect to empower the majority of people in the politics of how we ought to live. Global capitalism squeezes all but the wealthiest and most privileged for time and resources, leaving ever less time and creative energy to question how we ought to live. In the wake of these pressures, reactionary movements that retrench themselves in faith, race, nation and protectionist economics are gaining traction across the globe, from Europe to the United States, from India to the Philippines, from North Africa to the Middle East. What recourse is left for those who hope to live well together? This book is a small contribution to the quest for a new hope. It asks how we can begin to imagine a different way of living together. It asks how we can begin to imagine solidarity in the modern world.

The reactionary movements pervading the world at the moment are neither of the left nor the right, but of both simultaneously, and thus give the lie to this tired binary. A key thread uniting these disparate movements is the claim that a liberal elite has become disconnected from ordinary people, prioritising diversity of belief and practice over solidarity rooted in shared beliefs and practices; elites over democracy; and economic growth over equality. Liberal elites/ordinary people has become a particularly inflammatory distinction that seems to be reproduced by responses to political developments. The most consistent response on the part of the political establishment to the rise of reactionary politics of left and right has been the reassertion of liberalism: rather than taking reactionary politics as indicative of an underlying issue with liberalism itself, politicians and policy makers treat reactionary politics as indicating that the liberal revolution is not yet finished: another group that needs to be educated in the inevitability of diversity or the economic utility of globalisation. It is this very strategy that creates a vacuum in which reactionary politicians can claim to speak on behalf of ordinary people by doing little more than defaming the establishment. With each victory of reactionary politics, the vitriol of liberals merely increases, and with it the disconnect between the establishment and so-called ordinary people.[1]

There seems to be a lack of awareness of violations of solidarity throughout the world, an awareness of what is missing, of what cries out to heaven, let alone of imagination as to what might fill the void.

'Given the inflammatory nature of the liberal elites/ordinary people distinction, to reproduce this terminology in an academic study might seem unwise. Yet this distinction finds credence in a growing body of research.

Over the last ten years a small but influential Christian theological movement known as postliberalism has slowly been making its way outside of the academy to politics, policy and civic activism. Postliberals regard our current political difficulties as rooted in intellectual shifts emerging from the European Wars of Religion in the 17th century (Michea 2009; Milbank 1990/2006; Taylor 2007). According to the logic of the time, humans were incapable of achieving solidarity rooted in shared beliefs and practices without descending into violence. This pessimistic attitude gave birth to liberal social theory, which claims that a belief-independent rationality is the only basis of political and economic legitimacy. The result is twofold: First, since the only belief-independent needs common to all human beings are improvements in security and wealth spread as widely as possible, these become the sole aim of politics and economics. Second, belief-independent rationality is intellectually complex, requiring logical or empirical evidence rather than achieved consensus. Thus politics and economics become the preserve of an educated elite whose role is to educate, rather than empower, ordinary people. The state-citizen relationship becomes sacrosanct, and no intermediary institutions, from churches to schools, and eventually even families, are to be trusted in curating answers to the question of how we ought to live. So excluded from the political process, ordinary people retrench in divisive categories such as faith, race, nation or economic status.

For postliberals, this lack of trust in ordinary people is evidenced as much by the welfare state, which substitutes a state-citizen, patron-client relationship for organic reciprocity between the advantaged and disadvantaged, as by capitalist economics, which reifies an idea of ordinary people as motivated by greed and competition as opposed to cooperation.

Thus the postliberal analysis suggests there is some heuristic potency in distinguishing between a liberal elite, defined as those in positions of political, cultural or economic power who explicitly or implicitly adopt liberal ideologies and practices, and ordinary people, defined as those whose power is confined primarily to voting, interventions in the public sphere or participation in collective action.

In large part because of its adoption of this discourse, the postliberal analysis proves indispensable in the contemporary political context because it legitimises the complaints of reactionaries while delegitimising their response. A liberal elite has indeed come to regard ordinary people as incapable of achieving solidarity. Yet the appropriate response, rather than rejecting conventional politics altogether, as if the dominance of liberalism reflected a conspiracy of those in power, is to encourage the critical reform of conventional politics. Siding neither with reactionaries, nor with those in power, postliberals seek to make a collective search for solidarity rooted in shared beliefs and practices the central goal of political and economic decision-making.

Over the last four centuries, liberalism has become the dominant political force in the Anglo-Saxon West and, through its power, the wider West (Milbank and Pabst 2016).[2] Over the last century, as the latter's ideologies and practices have spread, liberalism has become the dominant force across the globe, reified through multifarious institutions, from the United Nations to the International Monetary Fund, from governmental development aid to non-governmental organisations (NGOs) (Wilson 2012). Liberalism is particularly dominant in former British colonies, and most evident in India, where an educated, rational elite sees its role as benevolently presiding over the lives of the uneducated religious masses (Pool 2016). The postliberal analysis sheds light here too, making sense of the similarities between reactionary movements spread far apart culturally and geographically. It has thus never been more important to question the resonance of liberalism in the settings in which it originates. If liberalism does not have a stable home in the Anglo-Saxon West, its relevance elsewhere must be called into question too.

Yet the central shortcoming of postliberalism is its reliance on Christian theological theory, an influence with waning resonance in the Anglo-Saxon West, let alone the rest of the world. The risk is that this Christian influence will either fail to resonate with the majority of the populace, or, more worrying, that it will further encourage a retrenching into divisive categories. It must be said at this point that postliberalism is by no means intended to be anti-liberal. Postliberals have a deep respect for plurality of beliefs and practices, from religion to sex. Indeed, one of their core arguments is that plurality is actually undermined by liberalism, since it regards plurality as implying irreconcilable differences that must be managed by an elite. On this matter then, it is particularly worth noting that throughout the book when I discuss liberalism, I intend the political theory, and not the notion of plurality.[3] The problem is that the postliberal reliance on Christian theological theory will alienate certain groups and individuals. At times, particularly when speaking to secular institutions and individuals, postliberals have sought to shed this Christian influence. But in so doing, they too often adopt the purportedly belief-independent rationality they set out to challenge. What is required instead is an alternative response that questions how to cultivate solidarity in the context of radical diversity of belief and practice. This book is a search for such an alternative.

This search is assisted by two simultaneous lines of enquiry: first, a genealogical study of academic and policy iterations of the relationship between belief and solidarity in the Anglo-Saxon West, placing postliberal theory into dialogue with the sociology and anthropology of religion, politics and economics, and second, original ethnographic research with groups seeking to develop solidarity in a space of radical diversity of belief and practice in the Anglo-Saxon West, namely, London, UK.

The particular focus on the Anglo-Saxon West generally and London specifically is considered fundamental for three reasons. First, the majority of ethnographic research into liberal ideologies and practices thus far has focused on settings to which these ideologies and practices have spread. While such research usefully demonstrates the unsuitability of these ideologies and practices to colonial and postcolonial contexts, the risk is to reify a distinction between "the West and the rest". A number of scholars have pointed to the detriments of this distinction in understanding those outside of the West. Here I suggest this distinction is problematic for understanding people in the West. The assumption that liberal ideologies and practices resonate or sit well with people in the West and the resultant neglect of ethnographic study in this area is perhaps a chief cause of the disconnect between liberal elites and ordinary people – a problem which is then amplified as these ideologies and practices spread elsewhere. Particularly by exploring the resonance or lack thereof of liberalism in settings in which it has been dominant for decades if not centuries, it may be possible to point to potentially universal findings. And by thus assessing the resonance of liberalism in the West, it may be possible to better predict points of tension that are not resolved merely by time or cultural assimilation – what does not work here, now may well not work anywhere, anytime.

Still, why the "Anglo-Saxon" West? By Anglo-Saxon West I intend Britain, the United States and Canada. To use this designation may seem simultaneously too broad and too limiting: too broad, because religious, political and economic differences will tear at the seams of a project seeking to draw these spaces together into one study; too limiting, because it is unclear how focus on such a limited geographical area could have global resonance. Yet as each empirical chapter will relate in more detail, the Anglo-Saxon world is deemed as having sufficient religious, political and economic parity and, perhaps more significantly, enough mutual influence to deem amalgamating them in this way not merely justified but theoretically prudent. To thus combine these regions is not to deny regional difference between and within Britain, the United States and Canada. Rather, it is to suggest that shared trends within each of these nations demand attention for understanding any religious (particularly Christian and more specifically Protestant influences), political (particularly ideas of the state as maintaining peace between a fragmented populace) and economic (particularly the focus on free markets) developments.

Colonialism, postcolonialism and globalisation have rendered the Anglo-Saxon West the most dominant and influential region in the wider West and across the globe. As already related above, far from its being limiting, targeting the Anglo-Saxon West for empirical research is deemed crucial to critically evaluating the viability of its ideologies and practices as they spread elsewhere. This power and influence has also rendered the Anglo-Saxon West the most attractive destination of education and migration.

Second, as will be elucidated in more detail further down, ethnographic research is deemed essential to the authenticity of this study, and ethnography is necessarily limited in the temporal and geographic scope it can encompass.

Third, London has come to represent the pinnacle of liberal dominance. As much as having an ideology and history, liberalism has a place. Liberal elites are perceived as living in wealthy metropolitan areas. Particularly in the UK, the liberal elite are perceived as living and working primarily in London. This perception has grounding in reality. As the national centre of 'political, bureaucratic and legal administration', as well as a global centre for research, NGOs and commerce, London is a city buzzing with some of the world's most advantaged, talented, wealthy and powerful people (Bretherton 2015: 2012). London has the most highly educated people not only in the UK but in the world (Parr 2014). London has the highest proportion of wealth per capita in the UK and, when compared with other parts of the country, has the highest income disparity in Europe (Kelly 2015). As a result, ever greater levels of immigration are deemed essential for sustaining the services that support a comfortable lifestyle. Amidst so much diversity, London's values on sex, sexuality, welfare and immigration differ greatly from the rest of the country. London remains a stronghold of Labour voters, even when the rest of the country votes Conservative. London voted to remain in the EU when the rest of England voted to leave. And Londoners are far more likely than their UK counterparts to believe that multiculturalism has benefited the country (Mann 2015).

Perhaps partly as a result, London is also the key setting in which postliberalism has gained traction in recent years. Postliberalism has become a key influence of some of London's and by extension the UK's leading think-tanks, including ResPublica, Demos and the Institute for Public Policy Research (IPPR), as well as key political movements and agendas such as Red Tory, Blue Labour, the Big Society and Movement for Change. Given its unique status as a global city, by focusing on London, I do not intend that my findings are generalisable to the world or even to other major cities as they are. Rather, drawn as they are from a time and place in which liberal ideologies and practices are perhaps most dominant, I treat my findings as generalisable to the world as it might become if liberalism is to consolidate its global hegemonic status.

Coming to terms with context (I): liberalism and postliberalism in the Anglo-Saxon West

The first step in exploring the resonance of liberalism and postliberalism in the Anglo-Saxon West is to recognise, to modify Latour (1993), that we have never been liberal. This point extends as much to politicians and policy makers themselves as to ordinary people. It is quite easy to suggest, following the postliberal analysis, that if the first wave of liberalism came in the wake of the European Wars of Religion in the 17th century, finding voice primarily in the works of Hobbes and Locke, then a second, perhaps stronger wave came in the wake of the Second World War. Here, rather than merely reacting against religion, liberal theorists, particularly the likes of Rawls, Dworkin and Habermas reacted against ideology entirely. The very notion of basing politics on anything other than reasoned consensus as to how to spread wealth and security as widely as possible became anathema – a suggestion tantamount to the violence of the holocaust itself. And we could follow this line of analysis further, attributing the global popularity of Fukuyama's (1992) 'end of history' thesis to a desperate yearning for the simplicity of rational consensus alone.

Yet the reality is far more complex. In the wake of the Second World War, ideological and aesthetic unity were developed throughout the nations of Europe and North America to inspire a sense of solidarity that might distil the appeal of fascism and communism (Judt 2010; Wall 2008). In the USA, the pledge of allegiance was formally recognised by Congress and sociologists recognised the implicit development of a civil religion, the darker side of which emerged during the McCarthy-era denouncements of public intellectuals and activists. At the same time, and paradoxically, successive governments coalesced around Roosevelt's New Deal policies. In the UK, where this work is primarily situated, the coronation of Elizabeth II was deliberately designed to be more impressive than the Nuremberg Rallies. Most fundamentally of all, a shared Christian heritage formed the linchpin of a new ideological consensus around the development of the welfare state (Dinham 2014). The welfare state, moreover, was regarded, at least by its progenitors, not merely as a wholesale intervention of the state into all social realms, but rather as supplementing and undergirding charitable activity (Beveridge 1948). Yet the founders of the welfare state could not have known that the Christian underpinning of their project would soon be challenged by rapid religious change.

This emergent religious change notwithstanding, even as the underpinning narrative of the welfare state secularised, partly in line with, partly producing wider social changes, a strong ideological component remained, particularly the focus on 'social justice' (Dinham 2000). This focus on social justice was supplemented by a concern for local control. This dual focus remained under the 'Third Way' socialism of British New Labour. Particularly the New Deal for Communities (NDC) was conceived as belonging to neither the left nor the right, but rather as placing ordinary people at the centre of political and economic activity.

It might be contested that at the same time as the Christian narrative underpinning the welfare state diminished, so the liberal prioritisation of belief-independent rationality as the linchpin of politics and economics crept in. Prochaska (2006) laments the loss of a shared spirit of responsibility, and the rise of the assumption that one's only social duty is to pay tax. Dinham (2005) claims that every attempt of government to empower local people has always ended in government overpowering local people. In the end, ordinary people cannot be trusted to choose what is right. Moreover, NDC in particular was regarded along Hegelian lines as the catalyst and culmination of a long process of transforming politics into rational consensus.

Still, this focus on belief-independent rationality seems to jar with New Labour's other flagship community programme, Face to Face, Side by Side, which placed 'faith groups' at the centre of community development (DCLG 2008). Face to Face, Side by Side was the core of the multi-faith policy paradigm as it became manifest in the UK, and represented an authentic reawakening to the power of religion in the public sphere. Yet combined as it was with the liberal emphasis on the pivotal role of the state on the one hand, and rational consensus on the other, Face to Face, Side by Side was doomed from the beginning to be an act of policy hopefulness, rather than a rediscovery of solidarity in a world of radical diversity of belief and practice.

All of these changes need to be read moreover, in the context of three developments: first, the increasing centralisation of the state from the 1950s to present. It is the greatest trick of neoliberals to present themselves as bucking this trend by selling state assets. At least as far as the UK is concerned, Thatcher governments, through New Labour to the Conservative-led governments since 2010 have combined the championing of free market principles with unprecedented centralisation of state power. Over the last 20 years in particular, it is no longer merely intermediary institutions but local governments that cannot be trusted in curating answers to the question of how we ought to live. The second development, running in parallel, is decreasing engagement with conventional politics, from voting to trade union membership. And alongside these is the emergence of businesses with more resources than states. The turning away from the state must thus be seen not merely as a rejection of its power, but also of its futility.

This history and these three developments taken together garnered much support for postliberal thinking amongst the Conservative opposition on the build-up to the general election of 2010. The Big Society programme in particular seemed to offer hope of a government authentically empowering radical community activists to agitate for change amongst the state and big businesses alike. This programme would be postsecular, encouraging people of all religions and none to work together in developing solidarity. Yet this programme too seemed to diminish within weeks of the Conservative-led government taking office.

It was in light of this complex history, this entangling of liberal and post-liberal ideas in policy and in lived realities, and the clear impossibility of simply reviving a Christian narrative of solidarity in a context of radical diversity of belief and practice, that the idea for this book emerged. Even as I write now, I have no sense of providing a definitive contribution. Rather, my intention then and now remains the same: to reawaken religious and secular subjects to possibilities of solidarity; to refuse the simple answer; to grapple with, embrace complexity; and to provide inklings for imagining a different way of living together.

Coming to terms with context (II): from postliberalism to social science, from theologian to ethnographer

It was never my intention to undertake ethnography. It is only now, looking back that I am able to see how essential it was for the integrity of the *reference wrt my own struggle for research integrity.*

earch to have done so. If it is ordinary people that liberalism purportedly neglects, ordinary people that postliberals purportedly reimbue with
the trust required to collectively and peacefully explore how to live, then it
is with ordinary people that I must critically explore the resonance of liberalism and postliberalism alike.

In fact, my background was in political theology. I had first become
inspired to become an academic sitting in the leather armchairs of the staff
club lounge at the University of Nottingham. It was armchair academia that
I was destined for. The first jolt came when I realised there was a disconnect
between the postliberalism that inspired me and my own identity: I am not
a Christian. It then occurred to me that this disconnect spoke to a larger
problem: like the liberalism it criticises, postliberalism, in method at least,
fails to engage with the lived realities of ordinary people. All I knew as I
left the comfort and simplicity of Nottingham for the chaos of London was
that I wanted to place postliberal theory into dialogue with secular politics
and policy, in such a way as I have above. But as every social scientific PhD
student learns, one must have data. With my background in armchairs, this
'data' seemed as elusive to me as quantum particles or the idea of God: it was
something out there that could not be pinned down. Even as I sat through
numerous quantitative and qualitative research methods classes, it seemed
that unless someone could demonstrate how my particular ideas could be
operationalised and measured, I would be lost forever in a black hole.

It was in a state of liminality between my armchair and this black hole, in
my flat between Finsbury Park and Tottenham, in the summer of 2011, that I
heard over the radio – the irony does not escape me – that riots were breaking
out on Tottenham High Road. Very quickly, these riots spread across London
and then the UK. Not having lived in a single place for more than four years
my entire adolescence and early adulthood, I had always had a yearning to
belong somewhere. This, I thought, was my opportunity. I had to find a way
to get involved in the solution, to live out my duty as someone living locally.

As I became more involved I realised the riots were a perfect concatenation of the theorising that had embattled me: numerous rioters cited the
corruption of government and business and a sense of disempowerment
as enraging them and justifying them in their own corruption (Guardian/
Reading the Riots 2011; LC 2012). Others claimed that the state's deliberate disempowerment of parents had rendered them incapable of controlling
their children (Lammy 2012).

My first thought was to quit my PhD. Why spend my time between an
armchair and a black hole when I could be answering all of my questions
through action? It was only later that I realised I could combine the two: to
explore the resonance of liberalism and postliberalism by working alongside the inspiring people taking direct action to develop solidarity. Thus this
book was conceived.

It was then that the real struggle for research integrity began. I have already
stressed that postliberals regard our current political difficulties as rooted in

the prioritisation of a belief-independent rationality. Yet this belief-independent rationality is itself a core value of social scientific exploration. In the words of Durkheim, a founding father of social science, 'all preconceptions must be eradicated' (Durkheim 1902/1984: 31). Thus by placing postliberalism into dialogue with social science, I was risking nothing less than undermining the entire project. Milbank (1990/2006: 382) puts the point thus:

> Theology has frequently sought to borrow from elsewhere a fundamental account of society or history, and then to see what theological insights will cohere with it. But it has been shown that no such fundamental account, in the sense of something neutral, rational and universal, is really available. It is theology itself that will have to provide its own account of the final causes at work in human history, on the basis of its own particular, and historically specific faith.

Milbank thus sets up an interminable struggle between theology and social science, forcing researchers to choose one or the other.

Yet there are resources, both internal to postliberalism itself, and from social science, that allow us to overcome this bind. In drawing on these resources, I develop my own research approach, which I call the methodological suspension of disbelief.

I draw initially on two points, the first internal to postliberalism, the second from social science. First, from a postliberal point of view, Taylor (2014) explains that theology and social science display very different models of truth. He distinguishes between the Hobbes-Locke-Contiac, or instrumental-designative model of truth, and the Hamann-Herder-Humboldt, or expressive-enactive model of truth – what might be more broadly considered the correspondence and creative models. The first model is that which leads to logical positivism, consisting of a literalist, scientific language in which all words and truths correspond to either a logical or an empirically observable reality. The second model is a metaphorical, poetic model that is aware of the constitutive power of language: language can intervene to change reality. Language is constitutive of reality and shapes the world it describes. So for example, it would make a difference whether policy makers emphasised "solidarity" or "social capital" when commissioning services.

From this perspective, one need not see my project as placing postliberalism into dialogue with belief-independent rationality, but rather as treating postliberalism as an intervention that can be tested in terms of resonance. The research asks less whether postliberalism corresponds to an objective reality than whether it has resonance with ordinary people. For postliberals to assert that this method remains unacceptable is simply to assert that their opinion as experts is more valid than the feelings of ordinary people – that is, to commit the same fault they attribute to liberalism.

The second point, drawn from a social scientific point of view, is that the distinction between theology and social science set out above partly relies on an out-dated construction of the latter. While it is true that for Durkheim, preconceptions had to be eradicated, the second half of the last century saw researchers engaged with lived realities become aware that preconceptions are unavoidable (Geertz 1973; Winch 1958). Not only are beliefs implicit in the way that we relate to the world, forming a habitus, but values are central to one's entire research project, from the topic one chooses to the methods one employs (Du Bois 1979; Flyvbjerg 2001: 53–65; Longino 1990).

Social constructionists in particular pay very little attention to a belief-independent reality, holding that 'our knowledge of the world . . . is not derived from the nature of the world as it really is' but 'through the daily interactions between people in the course of social life . . . especially language' (Burr 2015: 4–5). Social constructionists pay attention to the way that realities change over time according to the way that they are interpreted by social actors, and stress that 'external forces that have no meaning for those involved in [any] social action' are far less important than the ideas and understandings the social actors themselves put forward (Bryman 2004: 13).

By adopting a social constructionist approach, I realised I could treat post-liberalism as an intervention, and derive findings based on open and honest conversations between myself as a researcher-activist and my research participants.

Yet this point notwithstanding, I also had to recognise that as a researcher I was bringing something to the table, namely complex theory and an awareness of ideological and structural influences. If postliberals place too much weight on the thoughts of experts, social constructionists place too little. It was with this thought in mind that I turned to the works of Bhaskar and critical realism (1979, 1986; for an overview see Gorski 2013). What Bhaskar envisages is dialogue between the explanatory theories provided by the researcher, and the lived experience provided by the research participant.

These points have strong implications for how my expertise as a researcher is developed, impinging on my genealogical study of academic and policy iterations of the relationship between belief and solidarity in the Anglo-Saxon West, of which a preliminary history has already been outlined above. I place postliberal theory into dialogue with the sociology and anthropology of religion, politics and economics. I do so not to test postliberalism against belief-independent rationality, but to provide a bridge from normative theory to the lived realities of ordinary people. This said, in each chapter points do arrive at which, in making normative claims, postliberals draw on statements about reality that can and must be operationalised and empirically explored. Where such points arise, I develop triangular dialogue between the generative mechanisms posited by postliberal theory, most significantly the salience of what I have come to call 'transcendent ideals' in sustaining solidarity, the sociology and anthropology of religion, politics and economics, and the testimony and actions of my participants. This approach is particularly significant in engagements with secular people, behind whose actions I observe transcendent ideals. Here my treatment of the research as intervention is deemed crucial, since it is only by pressing my participants to explore their own motivations that these ideals come to the surface.

These points also impinge on how this further exploration will be carried out. In order to treat my research as an intervention, I must be as immersed as possible in the lives of those people I wish to explore, posing questions to myself as well as to my participants from the inside.

I develop these points by use of a third, this time combining insights from postliberalism and social science. MacIntyre (1981/2007: 175) suggests that the only way to understand another tradition is not by judging it according to belief-independent rationality, but by learning its language, immersing oneself fully in its implications, and using one's knowledge from elsewhere to make judgements from the inside.

Davie (2015: 233) contributes to this point, suggesting that 'researchers who "live" in the field (in whatever capacity and in whatever kind of society) are more likely to display a respect for their subjects and the lifestyles they embrace'.

Both MacIntyre and Davie thus prioritise ethnographic research as a means of fully immersing oneself in one's participants' lives. I develop these points by stressing that ethnography is uniquely able to capture four aspects of discourse:

- Discourse in action: the spontaneous, unreflective and unfiltered discourses that arise in the everyday (Hansen 2012: 19). By observing this aspect, ethnographers can cut through even those categories adopted into reflective public parlance.
- Discourse as action: the ways in which discourses are employed as performances to incite a response: chastising, admonishing, inspiring (Hirschkind 2006: 113; Laidlaw 1995: 11). By observing discourse as action, ethnographers can observe how beliefs and practices are shaped by participants' social environment.
- Discourse through action: the use of performance as a way of talking (Stacey 2016: 181). By observing this aspect, ethnographers can explore both the limits of discourse, and how belief manifests itself in performance.
- Ambiguities and contradictions between discourse and action. By observing this aspect, ethnographers can gauge the consistency of and between beliefs and practices.

With these insights in mind, I immerse myself in the beliefs and the practices of those I am exploring with the intention of providing a confessional account that is true to their experiences, incorporates my own perspectives as an outsider engaged reflexively, and engages with lived realities. Special emphasis is placed on the theoretical and experiential learning processes I go through in order to take on these beliefs and practices as my own, and these are conveyed to the reader.

The methodological suspension of disbelief is thus a tripartite process: of treating my role as researcher as an intervention rather than a belief-independent inquirer; of placing my knowledge as a researcher into dialogue with the collaborative constructions between myself as a researcher and my participants; and of grounding these collaborative constructions in a full immersion in my participants' lives.

Coming to terms with context (III): groups seeking to develop solidarity in the UK

It was with this concept of the methodological suspension of disbelief in mind that I returned to ask exactly whose lives I would immerse myself in. Following the history offered above of post-war policy paradigms for developing solidarity in the UK, I chose to work with four organisations indicatively representing these shifting paradigms: Christian, secular, multi-faith and postsecular.

I say that the groups 'indicatively' represented these paradigms for four reasons: first, the history of these shifting paradigms is one I have myself constructed, and participants themselves may not be aware of operating within these paradigms. Second, these paradigms should be considered ideal types, which in reality are operating alongside one another simultaneously, and any organisation may simultaneously draw on any of these paradigms. Third, these paradigms are themselves open to question. They have been constructed from the outside, and my understanding may shift from the inside. Finally, no group can be considered to quantitatively represent these paradigms as if they provided a sample that might be generalised either to the UK or the Anglo-Saxon West as a whole.

In addition to these criteria, I sought groups that seemed to be carrying out in practice what postliberals called for in theory, namely, making a collective search for solidarity rooted in shared beliefs and practices the central goal of political and economic decision-making. In so doing, I hoped to find cases that challenged postliberal theory. By choosing groups with very different ideational underpinnings but very similar practices, I hoped to naturally foreground questions of how to cultivate shared beliefs and practices in spaces of radical diversity of belief and practice.

I chose to work with Christians on the Left (CotL), Hackney Council for Voluntary Service (HCVS), the Faith-based Regeneration Network (FbRN) and London Citizens (LC).

I chose CotL on the basis of their roots in the Christian socialism outlined above. Christian socialism originated in the 19th century. Norman (1987: 16) has said of the Victorian Christian Socialists that the one thread uniting them all is an aversion to competition. I suggest that there is also a positive connection, namely, that they all promote social goals such as human dignity, friendship, reciprocity and empowerment. The Victorian Christian Socialists tended to be more interested in changing the way people lived their lives than in policy.

Yet if the aims of the Victorian Christian Socialists were diverse, former leader Andrew Bradstock explains that the founding of CotL (in his time, the Christian Socialist Movement or CSM) was rooted in clear dogma. In 1960:

> A new constitution committed CSM members to pray, give and work for Christian unity, international reconciliation, redistribution of wealth, a classless society, world peace with nuclear and general disarmament and 'the common ownership and democratic control of the productive resources of the earth'. Support of these positions placed the movement to the left of mainstream Labour Party thinking, and affiliation to the Party, though discussed, was rejected in favour of 'independence'.
>
> (Bradstock 2013)

These principles rooted CSM less in Victorian Christian Socialism than in the statist thinking of Tawney, Temple and Beveridge, in particular championing the welfare state. In 1988, the CSM became an affiliate of the Labour Party, which was later consolidated by the taking up of desk space in Labour Party headquarters. Alongside this association with conventional politics came a dilution of CSM's rigid dogma:

> The movement also sought to broaden its base, moving from being (as one of its documents put it) 'an association of people who accept the fairly precise description of Christian Socialism set out in its statement of aims' to a 'forum for the Christian left'. The new emphasis was to be more on engaging in debate and 'helping Labour to regain the ethical ground' rather than promoting individual policies.
>
> (Bradstock 2013)

In the 1990s and 2000s the party slowly increased its membership from about 500 to about 2,000, and the number of MPs affiliated with the movement from a handful to 44, or a tenth of the Parliamentary Labour Party. Yet the broadening of its base to a loosely defined forum does not seem to have helped its influence. The CSM 'vigorously opposed' the invasion of Iraq in 2003, but although a CSM MP tabled an amendment that the case for war had not been made, only eight CSM MPs voted for the amendment (Bradstock 2013). The result was that some CSM members suggested disaffiliating, while a number resigned altogether.

In 2006, CSM sought to reaffirm its values for a 21st-century context. The result was the affirmation of the following values:

- We believe that Christian teaching should be reflected in laws and institutions and that the Kingdom of God finds its political expression in democratic socialist policies.
- We believe that all people are created in the image of God. We all have equal worth and deserve equal opportunities to fulfil our God-given potential whilst exercising personal responsibility.

- We believe in personal freedom, exercised in community with others and embracing civil, social and economic freedom.
- We believe in social justice and that the institutional causes of poverty in, and between, rich and poor countries should be abolished.
- We believe all people are called to common stewardship of the Earth, including its natural resources.

(CSM 2006)

In 2013, after a long process of debate, the CSM changed its name to Christians on the Left (CotL), reflecting the broadening of its base.

This short context provides a background for understanding the beliefs and practices of CotL. Starting out as an organisation with a clear aim to bring the means of production into the control of labourers, the organisation has now become an open forum for Christians with a vaguely left-wing agenda. The process has enabled the organisation to increase its following, and to be given office space within Labour Party headquarters, though has perhaps made its aims harder to define, and its influence on particular MPs and members less predictable.

In choosing to work with HCVS, I drew on Lee's (2015: 19) distinction between nonreligious action, shaped in deliberate contradistinction to religion, and secular action, oriented towards issues in which 'religion is no more than a secondary concern'. By exploring HCVS, which I designate as secular, I hoped to understand how those who do not reflect on religion seek to form a collective search for solidarity in a space of radical belief and practice diversity.

Rochester has explained that Councils for Voluntary Service (CVSs) originated out of the pioneering work of Thomas Hancock Nunn, a Christian social reformer. Hancock's aim was to establish a 'broadly based body that would combine the resources of "all the churches, all the municipal bodies and all the voluntary associations in a given local government area"' (Rochester 2012: 103). CVSs thus spring from the period of Christian associationism lauded by Prochaska (2006), and discussed in more detail in chapter 3. From their outset CVSs can be regarded as combining the resources of multiple institutions, without prioritising any one in particular. By 1945, Bourdillon suggests, the role was more clearly defined, and additionally had a distinct ideological agenda:

> to survey the social needs of the area as a whole, and, where it perceives a gap, to initiate action. Only if no other body can suitably meet the new need should the Council itself take direct action, and where it does so it will be on the understanding that the new activity is to be floated off as an independent organization, or passed over to some other body at the earliest possible moment.
>
> (Bourdillon in Rochester 2012: 103)

CVSs would act directly where necessary, but prioritised the grassroots action of organisations established in the community, since these encouraged participation amongst ordinary people.

In the decades following the war, however, Prochaska suggests social policy was characterised by secular ideals, wherein redistribution and material equality took priority over 'personal service or participatory citizenship' (2006: 152). Prochaska observes a 'tendency of post-war prime ministers, sometimes consciously, sometimes not, to undermine the independence of voluntary institutions' (2006: 163). This ideology was imbibed by the wider public, for whom 'the payment of taxes had become the primary civic duty' and who, when they do volunteer, do so for reasons of 'altruism, filling spare time, or the need for a more imposing CV' (Prochaska 2006: 150, 160). This criticism can be extended to policy discussions relevant to CVSs. Wolfenden, a path-defining report for CVSs in the post-war period, was said to have 'little to contribute to the debates about participation or the alienation of so many citizens from the power structures which control them' (Rowe 1978: 491). As a result, CVSs have often risked appearing as the 'Council's poodle' (Zammer in Rochester 2012: 108). Moreover, when they have managed to distance themselves from the state, CVSs often fall into a market logic, which emphasises the CVS' 'role as a provider of services and reduces its relationship with its members to that of seller and customer' (Rochester 2012: 109).

Without himself showing a distinct research interest in cultivating a spirit of association, Rochester has called for:

> recovering some of the original values underlying the work of CVSs and replacing the culture of the market with traditional voluntary sector behaviours . . . Return to the roots . . . would involve a greater emphasis on voluntary effort rather than the employment of paid staff . . . The central thrust of its work would be to facilitate mutual aid and shared learning across the local voluntary and community sector.
>
> (2012: 109)

Unfortunately, there is a neglect of the role of this elusive spirit of association in Rochester's account. In the absence of this spirit, I will make clear, the tendency to drift between the state and the market seems inevitable, unless the organisation itself can frame an imagined community with an associated appeal for volunteers.

I became interested in the Department for Communities and Local Government–funded (DCLG) Faith-based Regeneration Network (FbRN) because, after a long period of secularisation in policy making, it represented a renewed interest in the role of religion in the public sphere. FbRN seemed an interesting case study since it appeared to offer a measured (though unwitting) incorporation of postliberal theory in a diverse landscape: it recognised the important role of religion in the public sphere, but saw that simply reviving the old religious landscape was neither practical nor desirable. Instead, FbRN followed the multi-faith paradigm, seeking to include all faiths and none in developing a socially active society.

Yet the reality is somewhat more complicated. Dinham explains that the multi-faith paradigm emerges out of a dual context: on the one hand, a neoliberal context in which faith groups are seen as 'repositories of resources – staff, buildings, volunteers, networks, money – which could be deployed to the social good'; on the other, in a post–9/11 and 7/7 context, as potential sources of cohesion or division, depending on how they are engaged (Dinham 2012: 577).

While it is important to keep these influences in mind, *Face to Face, Side by Side: A framework for partnership in our multi-faith society*, the founding document associated with the multi-faith paradigm, demonstrates an awareness of the potential of faith to revive a shared spirit of association, whilst recognising that religion has significantly changed since we last paid attention to its role. Faith groups are seen as providing 'leadership in organising their communities to be active' by 'linking the development of citizenship to the beliefs and teachings of faith traditions' (DCLG 2008: 2014). Alongside this, the document suggests that 'English society is now more diverse than ever before' and acknowledges 'diverse stories about the different role of religion and belief in individuals' everyday lives' (ibid 2008: 2013).

Following *Face to Face, Side by Side*, DCLG provided funding to regional development agencies to develop multi-faith networks, as well as to FbRN, which regarded itself as intermediary infrastructure organisation for numerous other bodies.

I was interested to work with London Citizens (LC) because without being read in postliberal political theology, and without any particular religious creed, they nonetheless seemed to fit with the postliberal ideals of developing a shared spirit of association outside of the state, and working creatively against both government and big business, within the marketplace. I knew from the beginning that working with LC would present interesting tensions between the postliberal critique and the lived experience of activists. This tension is made obvious by a reading of the organisation's history.

In the 1930s, Saul Alinsky, a student at the University of Chicago, became angered by the poverty of certain districts surrounding the university. He became instrumental in organising the multiple conflicting groups into a community organisation, collectively struggling against the institutions that formed the structural basis of their oppression. The organisations he established were broad-based and dues-based. Being broad-based means that they were made up of a combination of religious and secular community leaders, while being dues-based means that all funding for the organisations comes from members themselves. It is believed that being broad-based recognises the multiplicity of interests in a given community, and allows for maximum relational power, that is, power defined by the number of people one can involve in a campaign. Being dues-based helps to guarantee independence, as well as gives each dues-paying member both a stake and an interest, which together combine to provide an impetus for action.

LC is similarly broad-based and dues-based, aiming in particular to work with any organisation in a geographical community that has 'relational power', that is, the ability to bring large numbers of people to actions. By working with any organisation with relational power in the community, from churches and mosques to schools and trade unions, community organisations can be seen as very early adopters of a postsecular orientation to the world. From this perspective, LC provides a good case study for critically exploring the notion of the postsecular, as will be discussed in chapter 2. This orientation was carried over to the UK in 1996 when LC was formed. Today, LC is often criticised for its excessive favouring of faith groups. Secular organisations feel themselves to be left out.

Since 1996, London Citizens has worked to reweave the fabric of civil society. As one of my participants puts it:

> if you want to look at society in three sectors, or three cultures, private, public and civil society, it's the civil society which is under-organised, less powerful, missed out in terms of big decisions, so our primary purpose is to organise in the civil society sector, especially in areas that are disengaged and disadvantaged from political and economic success, and to allow that sector to have greater political influence as the other sectors.

Ostensibly LC's aim is coextensive with that of rebuilding a shared spirit of association. Yet LC is very adept at working 'with the world as it is'. The employees and volunteers are trained to understand that without power, they cannot act, and to see themselves, in the absence of positional or financial power, as building relational power. Campaigns are curated by dedicated organisers, but the specific agendas are defined by the diverse groups organisers bring together.

In 2010, however, London Citizens bid for a large state contract to roll out community organising across the country, suggesting that its independence from the state is negotiable. Similarly, London Citizens perceives itself as distinct from the market, although it often takes grants from big business.

I spent three to six months with each organisation between late 2011 and early 2014. I worked as a participant observer, meaning that I was treated with the same obligations as a volunteer. I combined field notes with formal interviews with leaders, employees and volunteers and informal discussions with single-issue participants and affected members of the public. All names of participants are pseudonymised, and stories excessively betraying their identity omitted, in order to maintain their privacy.

Chapter summary and key themes

The primary aim of this book is to place the postliberal analysis of the contemporary political context into dialogue with the lived realities of ordinary people in this context.

Chapter 1 introduces postliberalism from its origins to its key ideas. It divides these key ideas into an analysis of the contemporary religious, political and economic contexts. Crucially, it complicates the theoretical picture, explaining how postliberals regard solidarity as rooted not merely in a general concept of shared beliefs and practices but in a particular idea of transcendence with strong implications for practice. In particular, a shared sense of transcendence enables us to imaginatively transcend our everyday circumstances, and develop a sense of narrative or journey from humans as they are to humans as they could be. The central argument of chapter 1 is that while the postliberal analysis of the contemporary political context is indispensable, and that while the focus on transcendence itself may be incorporated into liberal understandings of the world, still the postliberal response struggles to reconcile with the reality of radical diversity of belief and practice. Their response is either to revalorise solidarity rooted in Christian theology, or else to rely on the same belief-independent rationality they critique. What is required by way of an alternative, I suggest, is a thorough examination of how people develop solidarity in contexts of radical diversity of belief and practice.

Chapter 2 outlines this alternative. It suggests that neither the postliberal revalorisation of a notion of transcendence rooted in Christian theology nor the liberal reification of belief-independent rationality places adequate faith in ordinary people to navigate difference in developing solidarity. It finds support in sociological and anthropological theory for the centrality of transcendence in the development of solidarity. But it suggests that to root transcendence in Christian theology is to reproduce a religious/secular, mythic/rational binary, which posits religion as mythic and secularity as purely rational. Instead, I draw on ethnographic data to develop the concept of 'myth', which intends the stories people tell of great characters and events that inspire them to live in solidarity with one another. While transcendence provides an imagined realm that calls on people to act differently, myth is the manner through which transcendent ideals are articulated, gain substance, and through which people become convinced that these ideals can be lived out in the less than ideal world they see around them. The concept of myth cuts through a religious/secular, mythic/rational binary, allowing me to reveal sources of solidarity amongst religious and secular actors alike. Christianity is one such myth but there are plenty of secular alternatives. I suggest that the rationality of myth is found less in its discursive content than in the performances it produces. It is thus not on their content but on the performances they inspire that myths should be judged. Moreover, challenging liberal theory, myth is the lens through which people recognise the other. Rather than searching for solidarity rooted in shared beliefs and practices then, in spaces of radical diversity of belief and practice, it might be better to imagine solidarity as rooted in the *sharing* of myths and associated practices. I further stress that adopting this framework of transcendent ideals reified through myth allows secular actors themselves to cut through a religious/secular, mythic/rational binary, and develop a level of reflexivity about the ideals they harbour, the myths through which these ideals are articulated, and the implications for performance.

Chapter 3 incorporates these theoretical innovations into an analysis of the state. It suggests that the religious/secular, mythic/rational binary is core to how the state is imagined by social theorists, such that even as they recognise the fecundity of transcendence in developing solidarity, they cannot conceive of how to reconcile this recognition with the reality of radical diversity of belief and practice. The result is that the state and its mechanisms become increasingly rationalised, and thus increasingly unable to inspire a sense of solidarity. By way of an alternative, I suggest that the state need not be conceived as a purely rational mechanism. I demonstrate how people operating within the state are able to transform how they conceive of themselves: less as devising policy that is delivered to ordinary people than as empowering ordinary people to develop policy for themselves. I then suggest that rather than regarding themselves as divining those myths that resonate with people, or else as constructors of new myths, policy makers should regard themselves as curators of myth-sharing amongst ordinary people.

Chapter 4 incorporates theory from chapters 2 and 3 into an analysis of capitalism. It suggests that both theory seeking to support and theory seeking to challenge capitalism reifies the religious/secular, mythic/rational binary. Theory seeking to support capitalism often fails to recognise what Lambek (2010a) has called the 'contract behind contracts', that is, the underlying myths that sustain capitalist negotiation. And the chapter stresses that by failing to recognise these myths, those seeking to challenge capitalism tend to reproduce the assumption that capitalism is natural. Yet it also demonstrates that in comparison to theories of the state, theories of capitalism have demonstrated a far more nuanced awareness of the underlying myths that sustain capitalism by resonating with ordinary people. This is perhaps because, in comparison to theories of the state, which have been stultified by the assumption that the latter must be confined to synthetically constructing ideals which must be imputed into people (an assumption that chapter 3 seeks to challenge), evolving to appeal to people on a mass basis is seen as capitalism's *modus operandi*. I develop theories of the relationship between myth, solidarity and capitalism by drawing theoretical comparisons between transcendence and timelessness. I suggest that the eschewal of timelessness in favour of rationalised time is core to the capitalist myth, a myth epitomised in the dictum 'time is money'. I argue that this myth becomes embodied in the daily lives of people living in capitalist societies, such that they begin to perceive their relationship to others, and even their own receding leisure time as instrumentally divided into pockets of capitalist time. By creating a clash between timelessness and capitalist time, I am able to suggest that reimagining timelessness may be core to redeveloping a shared sense of transcendence between people of all religions and none. And by suggesting that capitalist time becomes embodied, I am able to stress that the body becomes a locus for resisting capitalism through performances of shirking capitalist time.

In chapter 5, I return to normative arguments, only this time assisted by a careful study of lived realities, and occasionally offering new ethnographic insights where doing so is deemed useful. If the reader regards a conclusion as the culmination of a book's explorations and arguments, its *telos*, its purpose, where it has been heading, they will find it here. Alongside general suggestions for ethics, politics and economics, I develop a specific policy suggestion, namely, the development of solidarity centres that will act both as exemplars and as linchpins tying my many general suggestions together. Solidarity centres will develop a shared sense of transcendence in local communities by providing safe and inclusive spaces for the sharing of myths. They will be core-funded by the state, but otherwise funded by institutions tied to the community, with payment acting as a stake the binds multifarious institutions together in a reciprocal search for solidarity. Businesses will be treated as any other institution, requiring both payment and active involvement to become members. It is envisaged that tying businesses into solidarity centres will ensure that businesses will place solidarity at the core of their practice, rather than treating the payment of tax as their sole public duty. And it is envisaged that placing solidarity at the core of their practice will provide businesses with much desired goodwill amongst the communities they support.

Finally, I conclude by outlining key theoretical contributions, as well as an awareness of what is missing in terms of research, both in numerous academic domains, and in this book. I call for further research in numerous fields, from history, to sociology, to anthropology, and particularly point to the next steps in my own journey.

To reiterate, this book is in no way treated as the final say on the ideas I explore. Rather it is treated as the beginning of a new way of undertaking research that draws normativity and social science, multiple disciplines and sectors, academics, politicians, policy makers and the wider public together in a collective search for solidarity.

Notes

1 This vitriol took a particularly ugly form in the UK recently, when first an uninspiring campaign focusing primarily on economics was offered for remaining part of the EU, and then later, when Brexit became inevitable, the suggestion abounded that people without a university degree should be barred from voting.
2 To those that would argue democracy is the dominant force in the West, I proffer the example of the EU's installation of Mario Monti as the prime minister of Italy as the condition of the European Bank's support for Italy's flailing economy in 2011, or the Spanish government's violent suppression of the Catalan independence referendum in 2017. Sadly, one need no longer speak of hypocritical foreign policy such as the refusal to recognize the democratic election of Hamas in Gaza. Our ideals are already being betrayed far closer to home and all of us who look on quietly as it happens are complicit.
3 It may also be worth noting here that I distinguish plurality, a state of belief and practice diversity, from pluralism: a political ideology that champions plurality. I leave out a comprehensive exploration of pluralism here, since I do not consider it to carry the same substantive content or influence as liberalism.

1 Postliberalism

Revalorising a lost world

Postliberalism, I have been saying, is about rediscovering a collective search for solidarity rooted in shared beliefs and practices, and revalorising this search to the centre of politics and economics. According to postliberals, liberal social theory assumes that ordinary people are incapable of achieving such solidarity without descending into violence. Thus for liberal social theory, belief-independent rationality is the only possible basis of politics and economics. And since the only belief-independent aspects undeniably common to all people are security and wealth, so improvements in security and wealth become the only means of legitimising political and economic decisions. Postliberalism questions both of these premises. First, it stresses that people are naturally generous and creative, and as such can overlook differences to collectively explore solidarity rooted in shared beliefs and practices. Second, and fundamentally, it stresses that solidarity cannot be rooted in belief-independent rationality alone, since this is to ignore what motivates people to live in solidarity with one another.

It is worth noting here that others (MacIntyre 1981/2007), including myself at other times (Stacey 2017b) have defined postliberalism as about rediscovering a collective search for the good life. I have come to find this designation unhelpful, since it tends to lead to abstract discussions about what the good life consists of, which ultimately anyway turns out to be one lived in solidarity with others. Moreover, focusing on the good life has at times (see in particular Skidelsky and Skidelsky 2012) led to a belief-independent and individual-centred construction of what the good life consists of, only after which can we turn to discuss how to ensure that all have the right to partake in this good life. This line of enquiry, I suggest, risks reproducing the same fault postliberals attribute to liberal social theory generally, namely that the good life must be rationally constructed by a university-educated elite, and subsequently bestowed upon grateful subjects. Instead, by focusing on a collective search for solidarity rooted in shared beliefs and practices, I seek to stress the rationally elusive and, because of this, fundamentally inclusive and political nature of this search. Solidarity denotes a state in which people are bound together in the mutual desire to uphold one another's dignity without expecting something immediately in return.

It is the cultivation of this mutual desire that I am interested in rediscovering and valorising to the centre of political and economic decision-making; without such a desire, any discussion of what the good life consists of remains purely abstract.

Of course, if the undermining of a collective search for solidarity rooted in shared beliefs and practices were a problem in liberal social theory alone, this would remain an ivory tower debate, and this book would be unnecessary. Yet the key point is that liberalism has risen to a status of hegemony. This means that liberal social theory has been the dominant paradigm shaping the thinking of university-educated politicians, policy makers and practitioners in the North Atlantic West for at least the last two centuries. For postliberals, the result is that whether or not you have read liberal social theory, if you are living in the Anglo-Saxon West, and indeed increasingly elsewhere where the latter's ideologies and practices have spread, you have probably imbibed liberal ideas: primarily, the idea that a collective search for solidarity rooted in shared beliefs and practices is paradoxical and dangerous in a context of radical diversity of belief and practice. The problem here is that we simply cannot develop solidarity without shared beliefs and practices, thus to relinquish to liberal pessimism is to relinquish to living parallel lives, divided across boundaries of faith, race, nation or economic status, each of us making individual or group-based claims to various and conflicting rights that a detached state is ever harder pressed to accommodate.

This point becomes particularly clear in the context of the postliberal analysis of the rise of the state and capitalism. For postliberals, pessimism regarding the possibility of a collective search for solidarity is the key to understanding liberal theories of the state and capitalism. If people are incapable of this search, then a strong state, a 'visible hand' is required to enforce order through policy, law and policing, upholding each individual's right to her own private beliefs and practices, which are themselves only permissible insofar as they do not infringe on any other individual's beliefs and practices. Belief-independent rationality is upheld by an enlightened few on behalf of an increasingly disconnected, belief-oriented populace. Running in parallel to this visible hand is a complementary 'invisible hand' of the market that curates solidarity, defined merely as improvements in security and wealth spread as widely as possible, out of the otherwise self-interested behaviour of multifarious disconnected individuals.

Put simply, any theory is liberal that takes as its starting point the impossibility of a collective search for solidarity rooted in shared beliefs and practices. Thus rather than 'left-wing' and 'right-wing', statist and capitalist, it is better to speak of 'left liberalism' and 'right liberalism'. By stressing this 'unity of liberalism', postliberals are able to show that reactions against both the state and capitalism are ultimately reactions against the mistrust liberalism places in people. From this perspective, postliberal political theory is vital in understanding the contemporary political context both in the Anglo-Saxon West, and in settings where the latter's ideologies and practices have and continue to spread. It cuts across a left-right divide in politics, helping us to understand reactions against the state as varied as neoliberalism, community development and populism, and reactions against capitalism as varied as social democracy and the neo-anarchism of movements like Occupy. Each of these movements, in its own way, at least claims to challenge the dominance of the state or the market to return power and dignity to ordinary people.

The key problem with postliberalism, I will suggest, is that in order to make these claims, it returns to pre-liberal Christian theology. In so doing, it prioritises Christian beliefs and practices at the expense of other religious and nonreligious positions. Postliberals, I will suggest, as much as the liberal theorists they criticise, reify a religious/secular, mythic/rational binary that forecloses creative possibilities for developing new ideas of solidarity amongst people of all religions and none. *Even if* we accept that a pre-liberal Christian society came closer to realising a collective search for solidarity, the emergence of diversity within the Christian faith, of nonreligion and secularity, and the mass immigration of people of other religions requires a reimagining of how to collectively search for solidarity today. Once the mould has been lifted from the clay, it cannot be replaced without cutting off the new archipelagos that emerge. What is required instead is a creative exploration of how to develop a sense of solidarity that speaks to people of all religions and none. Postliberals themselves recognise the fundamental importance of developing new ideas to fit the current context. But they have not, heretofore, managed to systematically seek out possibilities for such ideas.

Instead, in their recognition that Christianity will not resonate with everybody, postliberals make creative leaps from their predominantly Christian critiques of liberalism to entirely secular policy recommendations that can supposedly appeal to anybody on the basis of their rational content. The problem here is that, as postliberals recognise, rationality alone is not enough, since shared beliefs and practices are at the heart of a collective search for solidarity (Milbank and Pabst 2016: 195). Drawing on, or else developing shared beliefs and practices will thus be fundamental to implementing policies that resonate with people. Neither the state, in the form of policy, law and policing, nor the market in the form of incentives, can entirely convince people to act in the name of solidarity. Only shared ideas that people firmly hold faith with can do this. Thus to leap from a once shared Christianity, now largely gone, to policies adhered to on the basis of rational argument, is to undermine postliberalism itself (see Stacey forthcoming 2018).

In order to explore these points, I begin by briefly introducing the theoretical origins of postliberalism in theology. I then introduce postliberal political theory, in particular distinguishing the latter from liberal political theory. It is here that the theoretical picture becomes more complicated. The shorthand I have been using to describe postliberalism as the attempt to revive a collective search for solidarity rooted in shared beliefs and practices will be set aside. Instead, I will speak of the call to revive solidarity rooted in a particular idea of transcendence with strong implications for practice. I suggest that postliberal political theory may seem antithetical to liberalism, since its *raison d'être* is to revalorise a notion of transcendence that liberal political theory is constructed with the deliberate aim of replacing. Yet I also stress that liberal ideals, particularly that of plurality, are themselves rooted in particular ideas of transcendence, and thus suggest that a postliberal political theory may be considered a means of cultivating ideas of solidarity rooted in liberality, or plurality, without liberalism. In this sense, postliberalism may be conceived as a project of saving liberalism from itself. To make this distinction clear, it is again worth noting that when I refer to liberalism, I intend the political theory and not the notion of plurality.

I then explore the implications of a postliberal politics for understandings of the role of the state and capitalism. Each of these three explorations then becomes the basis for the next three chapters, the empirical core of this book, on religion, the state and capitalism respectively.

Origins

Although its roots can be traced into much earlier theological writings, postliberal theology first emerged through the work of Hans Willhelm Frei, George Lindbeck and Stanley Hauerwas at Yale Divinity School in the early 1980s. These scholars critiqued the colonising of theology by a liberal ideology rooted in the Enlightenment, which insisted on the possibility of a belief-independent rationality based on logic and empirical evidence, and the relegation of anything that could not be so evidenced to a matter of individual preference (Hunsinger 2003: 51; Michener 2013: 2). With the spread of this ideology into theology, the latter had largely fallen into two camps: what Hunsinger, in his definitive history, characterises as the evangelical and the liberal – although proponents of each might beg to differ at this characterisation (Hunsinger 2003: 44). The broad use of the term evangelical intends those that take a literalist approach to theology, often justifying 'faith commitments and propositions using the methods and suppositions of the rational and empirical' (Michener 2013: 2). The term liberal intends those that seek to identify a universal religious experience grounded in psychological or sociological processes, of which Christianity is just one manifestation. From this perspective, scripture is to be read metaphorically. Against both of these positions, postliberal theologians cast Christianity as an internally coherent narrative or set of narratives that cannot be interpreted but only undermined by methods grounded in different ontologies. The Christian narrative is unique, and the interpretation of this narrative must be situated in terms of the needs and struggles of a particular community as it evolves through time, providing a basis for holding one another to account and undertaking shared action (Hauerwas 1984).

Given its focus on internally coherent narrative and community-based interpretation, much of postliberal thought is aimed at changing either theological thinking generally, or else particular churches (Hauerwas 1984). But a few thinkers within the postliberal school, most notably Charles Taylor, Alisdair MacIntyre and John Milbank, aim to speak beyond theology and the church to society as a whole. These authors critique the dominance of supposedly belief-independent rational discourses of empiricism and individualism in secular societies, and press instead for a revalorisation of narrative generally, and of a Christian narrative in particular, which is seen as key to social solidarity.

In the writings of Taylor, MacIntyre and Milbank, postliberal thinking thus takes an explicitly political turn. Liberalism is regarded not as merely undermining Christianity, but as undermining human nature. These thinkers cast a collective search for solidarity rooted in shared beliefs and practices as the highest end of humanity. And they suggest that an unfounded pessimism as to the possibility of such solidarity is foundational to the rise of pretensions to a belief-independent rationality, which becomes the sole basis of politics.

In the following section, I offer a reading of postliberal political theory in contradistinction to liberal political theory. This primarily revolves around ontology and transcendence, and as such forms the basis of my exploration of postliberalism in relation to the sociology and anthropology of religion in chapter 2. In distinguishing postliberal and liberal political theories, I will simultaneously demonstrate the importance of the postliberal analysis in diagnosing the shortcomings of liberal political theory, and the shortcomings of postliberal solutions themselves. By pointing to these latter shortcomings in particular, I demonstrate the importance of this book. The following subsections then trace this argument into statism and capitalism. Although other political thinkers have adopted the term 'postliberal' (see Turnbull forthcoming 2018), Taylor, MacIntyre and Milbank become the primary focus of this chapter because their work has proved the most influential, both amongst academics and in the world of politics, policy and professional practice.

Postliberalism and transcendence

The story begins with the European Wars of Religion. Up until this time, both politics and ethics were, supposedly, conceived of as a collective search for solidarity rooted in shared beliefs and practices, where solidarity was imagined as a space of love and peace beyond human endeavour that could be approached but not achieved. But in the face of ongoing violence during the European Wars of Religion, a new pessimism as to the possibility of a collective search for solidarity emerges (Michea 2009: 14; Milbank and Pabst 2016: 100; Taylor 2007: 159).

Michea (2009: 15) explains the point very simply:

> [A]ccording to the dominant interpretation of the time . . . the two
> main causes of the madness of war were, on the one hand, the desire

for Glory on the part of the great, and, on the other, the pretensions of people to know the Truth about Goodness (the cause of all civil wars), so that they could set themselves up as competent to judge the salvation of others.

The search for a unitary idea of solidarity is merely a smokescreen for the search for glory or power, or else a deluded pretension to know the truth about goodness. It thus became popular to think that not only is there no unitary idea of solidarity that is verifiable in terms of a belief-independent rationality, but even if there were, people would not be capable of agreeing on this idea without descending into violence. In this situation, any attempt to develop a collective search for solidarity can only ever be subjective and violent, involving one individual or community imposing its views on another. Instead, all that can be hoped for is the relative safety and prosperity required for each individual to pursue her own security and wealth.

As a result, Michea laments, 'Western modernity thus appears as the first civilization in history that has undertaken to make self-preservation the first (or even the only) concern of the rational individual' (Michea 2009: 14). For the first time, the very possibility of a collective search for solidarity is called into question. As a result, the focus shifts from solidarity to order. Thinkers at the time sought

> a firm underpinning for an agreed public order. [This philosophy] was born in the midst of bitter and violent inter-confessional strife. One of the most important things it was meant to offer was a basis for rational agreement on the foundations of political life, beyond and in spite of confessional differences.
>
> (Taylor 2007: 127)

Thus the early development of a belief-independent rationality is an inherently political project, constructed in order to replace ideas of solidarity rooted in mere beliefs. Others have simply called this idea 'secularism'. I avoid doing so for three reasons: first, secularism is less precise than the notion of legitimising politics on the basis of a belief-independent rationality. Second, I am identifying the roots of secularism. Only by addressing liberalism, I suggest, can we seek to uncover the problems with secularism. Third, and because of this, focusing on secularism can result in a tendency to think that the political consequences of secularism can be addressed by merely reawakening to the continued presence of religion in the public sphere – what has been called postsecularism – without ever addressing the belief-independent rationality that forms the core of liberalism. This latter point in particular will be further developed in chapter 2.

This epochal shift from rooting politics in unitary ideas of solidarity to rooting politics in self-preservation and order has two consequences, the first ontological, the second political. Here, I seek to explicate the ontological consequence by differentiating between the postliberal understanding of politics as a collective search for solidarity rooted in shared beliefs and practices and liberal political theory's treatment of politics as a means of managing the divergent pursuits of multifarious individuals. This paves the way for the next section, which explains how this latter approach tends to undermine the very principles it is developed to promote, namely, by empowering bureaucratic elites at the expense of ordinary people.

Optimism versus pessimism concerning human nature

The most obvious distinction to make between postliberal and liberal political theory is the attitude towards human nature. John Milbank explains that whereas postliberal political theory is rooted in an optimistic ontology of goodness or peace, liberal political theory is based on an ontology of evil or violence (Milbank 1990/2006: 279–280). What this means is that postliberals hold people to be fundamentally good and therefore capable of achieving solidarity without descending into violence. There is an element of trust in people. Liberal political theory on the other hand, is based on the notion that, left to their own devices, people would descend into violence. It follows that people must be restrained and manipulated so as to bring the best out of them (Milbank 2013). Exemplifying this distinction, Milbank states that 'true society implies consensus, agreement in desire and harmony amongst its members' (1990/2006: 406). Thus 'the political is necessarily imperfectly social, because it contains elements of compulsion and of mere compromise' (ibid.). Milbank radically grounds this ideal of true society in the church, continuing: '[true society] is exactly . . . what the Church begins to provide, and that in which salvation, the restoration of being, consists' (ibid).

Transcendence versus immanence

This focus on salvation speaks to the second ontological rupture facilitated by the emergence of liberal political theory, namely, the shift from transcendence to immanence, that is from politics as anchored in and striving towards an imagined realm beyond anything purely material, to politics as anchored in and striving towards purely material needs. Thus, drawing on Taylor, it can be suggested that whereas for postliberal political theory 'that which makes [a] group of people as they continue over time a common agent . . . is something which transcends the realm of those common actions this agency engages in', for liberal political theory, 'the constituting factor [of common agency] is nothing other than such common action – whether the founding acts have already occurred in the past, or are now coming about is immaterial' (Taylor 2007: 194). From this perspective, postliberal political theory is just any theory that locates the constituting factor of common agency as prior to and as the reason for common action. In the terms I have been using, postliberal political theory is just any theory that roots solidarity in a notion of transcendence. Put in this way, as the next chapter will illustrate in more detail, postliberal political theory could potentially include a whole range of notions, from the apparently religious to the apparently secular: the Platonic notion of *eidos*, the Aristotelian notion of *telos*, or purpose; the Christian notion of *eschaton*, or the day of judgement; the broadly religious notion of millenarianism (Cohn 1957/1993; Worsley 1987); the first Christian and later socialist idea of utopia (Kumar 1991; Sargisson and Sargent 2004); the Hegelian idea of synthesis (Shanks 1991); Bloch's principle of hope (1954/1995); ideology (Eagleton 1991); or Durkheim's notion of the sacred and collective effervesence (Durkheim 1915/2008; Lynch 2012). It is from this perspective that postliberalism may be seen as opening up possibilities for saving liberalism from itself, a point I shall return to further down.

Liberal political theory, on the other hand, since it cannot conceive of agreement over a transcendent source of solidarity, places social contracts, agreements and common actions as the foundation of common agency. Examples of this might include things as big and abstract as obeying the law, paying tax, or contributing to the capitalist system, or something as local and tangible as joining in a protest or strike, or digging up a garden.

This differentiation strikes at the heart of what makes postliberalism simultaneously revolutionary and disquieting. In practice postliberalism is potentially dangerous. If something transcendent confers belonging to a group, then it may follow that demonstrating allegiance to this norm might become a prerequisite of citizenship, as was the case in the Middle Ages, when only Christians were considered full citizens (Southern 1970/1990: 16). It is exactly this sort of situation that liberalism arises to avoid. In contrast to this, liberal political theory holds that partaking in certain actions confers belonging. It does not matter whether I am a Christian, a Jew, a Muslim or whatever – so long as I abide by the law or pay tax.

But a shared idea of transcendence may also have its advantages. And this for two reasons: First, a shared idea of transcendence may enable us to envision policies that promote the good life but slow the development of security or wealth – a possibility that multiple authors suggest is currently unforeseeable, with wealth always trumping ethics in the formation of policy (Sandel 2012; Skidelsky and Skidelsky 2012; Milbank and Pabst 2016). Second, if something transcendent confers belonging, then failure to perform certain acts will not automatically exclude an individual or group. From this perspective, a shared idea of transcendence might offer remedies for the contemporary situation in the Anglo-Saxon West and indeed the wider world, where some politicians and newspapers suggest that the failure to contribute to the capitalist system removes certain individuals and groups of the right to receive benefits, or be treated with dignity – a point that will receive significant attention in chapter 4 (Skeggs 2011). From this perspective, having a shared idea of transcendence is actually more inclusive than neglecting transcendence altogether. Of course, the question of how to develop a shared idea of transcendence with the complex religious and nonreligious landscape facing us at present is problematic, but postliberals suggest that to neglect this question altogether is equally problematic. Exploring this question is thus the core focus of this book, and particularly of chapter 2.

Transcendence, ethics and narrative

The shift from transcendence to immanence has clear implications for how politics and ethics are conceived and performed. For MacIntyre, the point of having a shared idea of transcendence is that it enables us to transcend our everyday circumstances, be they political or economic structures of oppression or merely selfish desires, and thereby live out a more ethical life.

Whereas postliberal political theory is rooted in a tripartite model of 1) humans as they are, moving, via 2) politics and ethics, to 3) humans as they could be, liberal political theory is rooted in a bipartite model in which there is supposed to be a direct relationship between humans as they are naturally observed and their ethical and political potential (MacIntyre 1981/2007: 52, 54). MacIntyre's insights can be extended to suggest that whereas postliberal political theory casts politics as the practice of stewarding people towards better ways of living together, liberal political theory casts politics as a means of controlling unruly people.

It needs to be stressed that the transcendent is not merely a floating, abstract realm. MacIntyre adds that transcendence 'is not something to be achieved at some future point, but in the way our whole life is constructed' (ibid: 175). People are bound not merely by an imagined end point, an abstract and unachievable utopia towards which they are working, but also by the implications of that utopic vision on the way they live their lives now. Transcendence is thus radically immanent and embodied.

For MacIntyre, based on ideas of the good life, or as I prefer, solidarity, people develop certain virtues, such as fortitude, courage or kindness, which, through their practice, are in themselves realisations of solidarity (ibid: 149). In order to facilitate the development of such virtues, it is necessary to conceive of human life, both collectively and individually as a narrative, a journey, from humans as they are to humans as they could be. From this perspective, it is in the context of a journey, rather than on the basis of belief-independent moral rules, that political and ethical actions are judged. This journey is articulated with reference to the particular historical trajectory to which one belongs (ibid: 208).

Life itself, and thus politics and ethics too, is always conceived in narrative form, hence all ideas of solidarity must be told in terms of the narratives we tell: of our own lives, within a community, within a history (ibid: 216). But liberal political theory forecloses narrative in two ways: first, by truncating the political and ethical journey. There is no transcendence, and so there is no journey. Second, it does so by prioritising a tradition-independent rationality whereby isolated political and ethical actions are judged in terms of moral rules.

Transcendence within the liberal political order

Thus far I have been presenting the emergence of liberal political theory as representing a deep ontological rupture. From this point of view, post-liberalism seems antithetical to liberalism. Yet it is important here to stress two points that will be developed throughout the empirical sections of this book. First, whereas the difference between postliberal and liberal political theory appears ontological, the former rooted in transcendence, the latter in belief-independent rationality, it might be suggested that liberalism itself is rooted in a notion of transcendence. Liberalism constructs a realm of belief-independent rationality that, as it were, 'rises above' mere beliefs. This idea is what I will come to call the 'myth of the absence of myth'. Second, even if the difference between postliberal and liberal political theory is categorical, the difference between postliberal political theory and what might be called the lived political theory or political imaginary of people living under liberal hegemony is reflexive: The latter, as the following chapters will make abundantly clear, have strong ideas of transcendence that impinge on their understandings of and desire for solidarity – it is just that the dominant political imaginaries and structures fail to harness these ideas.

Still, and fundamentally, postliberals must not take from these points that their political theory can be unproblematically inserted into settings characterised by radical diversity of belief and practice. Postliberals, I suggest, tend to offer either too Christian an approach to resonate with the majority of people in the Anglo-Saxon West, let alone the rest of the world, or else end up slipping into the same belief-independent rationality for which they castigate liberalism. This approach not only undermines their aim, but neglects the multifarious ways in which people living in liberal settings draw on transcendence, as well as navigating very different ideas of transcendence, to develop solidarity. What is required instead is an approach that creatively engages with the question of what ideas of transcendence, and what kinds of processes for formulating such ideas, might inspire a collective search for solidarity in a context of religious and nonreligious plurality – the core focus of this book, and particularly of chapter 2.

Milbank, for instance, takes exception with the ontological premise of liberalism, which seems to suggest 'an irreducible religious pluralism stretching into the long-term future' (2013: 81). Conversely, he thinks it conceivable that

> [i]f Christian catholicity collapsed because of an entirely contingent deconvivialisation of its character in the Latin West (the Illich thesis), then how can one be sure a recovery of conviviality does not have the power to restore a lost universalism of Christian belief and practice?
>
> (ibid: 81)

This reading suggests that a Christian alternative to liberalism can be revived – the mould can be replaced. But here Milbank risks suggesting that plurality of belief is a reaction to hegemony, rather than a fact of life. Here Milbank potentially undermines his own ontology of peace, suggesting that a collective search for solidarity requires already agreed upon beliefs as a prerequisite.

Yet it should be stressed that for Milbank, revelation, or what those unfamiliar with Christian theology might prefer to call irrational commitments or creativity or inspiration, always underscores rational argument, which is merely the means by which such commitments are made intelligible and applicable. What this means is that although Milbank asserts Christianity provides the best narrative, he by no means thinks there is a rational standard by which to irrefutably justify this decision. Indeed, he does not even think we can choose which narrative we adopt; instead, there is only conversion. Thus for Milbank, to speak from outside of the Christian narrative would undermine his critique of the pretension to a tradition-independent rationality.

This specifically does not mean that others cannot speak from alternative traditions. Instead, what Milbank's position stands against is a rationalist position of the likes of Rawls (1971/1999, 1987) or Habermas (see Stacey 2017a). Although at different levels within the public sphere, Rawls and Habermas both require of people the ability to distinguish between commitments, and to make arguments on purely rational grounds, that is, to adopt arguments that are conceivably acceptable to anyone. Such arguments must be framed in a 'secular language' (Habermas 2010: 17, 2011: 25). But this point implies two things: first, secular argument is not itself rooted in some irrational commitments – a point that has already been brought into question; second, that it is plausible for people to leave their transcendent ideals to one side – a position that will be critically scrutinised further in chapter 2.

Notwithstanding the difficulty of a project that seeks to reconcile transcendence with plurality, postliberals already offer some possibilities. Vanheeswijck (2014: 5) stresses that for Taylor, the correct approach is "to be aware that [our deep commitments] always remain contestable and liable to revision . . . In other words, Taylor rejects any form of 'strong ontology' in favour of what Stephen K. White defines as 'weak ontology'" (ibid: 5). This idea of weak ontology is important because, if we can be aware of our own commitments being just one option among many, there is no need to choose one transcendence over another, or to stand outside of transcendences. Instead, we simply seek, through pragmatic discussion, a Rawlsian (1987) overlapping consensus of ideals, the justification of which depends on different arguments for different people:

A Christian or Muslim, for example, may justify fundamental rights by invoking the idea that every human being is a child of God, a Kantian rationalist that each individual is a rational being, a utilitarian that everyone is entitled to the highest form of happiness, etc.

(Vanheeswijck 2014: 3–4)

For Taylor, the weak ontology, or as postliberals might prefer to put it, the virtue of magnanimity required for one to accept that only those commitments that fit within the overlapping consensus are legitimate, is itself dependent on living within what Taylor calls the modern moral order (Taylor 2011: 46). In this order, transcendent legitimacy is replaced by the idea of society 'as existing for the protection and mutual benefit of its (equal) members' (Taylor 2011: 46). Here Taylor seems to go against his earlier distinction between postliberal and liberal political theories, suggesting that for moderns there are *ideas* of liberty, equality and fraternity that confer common agency: 'democratic societies are organised not necessarily around a "civil religion," . . . but certainly around a strong philosophy of civility' (Taylor 2011: 46).

But perhaps Taylor is not going against himself. Instead, it can be suggested that Taylor sees the current difference between postliberal and liberal political theory as one whereby the former uses transcendent notions to underpin politics, whereas the latter has no such deeper grounding. But, as a supporter of liberality rather than liberalism, that is, of openness to other positions, he is offering a way for liberalism to learn from postliberalism without undermining, and indeed actually bolstering, its core ideals. It is not that liberal political theory is *inherently* incapable of developing a deeper grounding, just that it has tended to neglect such a grounding.

The problem here, as acknowledged by Milbank (2013: 81), is that Taylor seems to reproduce the liberal assumption of irreducible plurality. The only possible basis of collectivity is agreeing to disagree.

MacIntyre offers an alternative. For MacIntyre, when seeking to engage with another tradition, one must learn it well enough to translate it; that is, like the anthropologist, one must

> [c]ome to understand what it is to think in the terms prescribed by that particular rival tradition, to learn how to think as if one were a convinced adherent of that rival tradition. To do this requires the exercise of a capacity for philosophical imagination that is often lacking.
>
> (1981/2007: xiii)

Whereas Taylor suggests that one need not understand another tradition in order to achieve agreement, but rather have enough magnanimity to discover an overlapping consensus justified differently by different traditions, MacIntyre indicates the reality will be more challenging than this, requiring complex debate and perhaps a component of multilingualism. Like Taylor, this implies that a kind of magnanimity is required to recognise that another tradition is worth engaging with.

But like Milbank, MacIntyre seems to think it is possible, even desirable, for one tradition to win. As MacIntyre puts it himself:

> I see no value in community as such – many types of community are nastily oppressive ... the best type of human life, that in which the tradition of the virtues is most adequately embodied, is lived by those engaged in constructing and sustaining forms of community directed towards the achievement of those common goods without which the ultimate human good cannot be achieved.
>
> (1981/2007: xiv)

Now, this becomes complicated when we scrutinise the means by which one tradition may win over another. MacIntyre explains that

> [w]hen the adherents of a tradition are able through such acts of imagination and questioning to interrogate some particular rival tradition, it is always possible that they may be able to conclude, indeed that they may be compelled to conclude, that it is only from the standpoint of their own tradition that the difficulties of that rival tradition can be adequately understood and overcome. It is only if the central theses of their own tradition are true and its arguments sound, that this rival tradition can be expected to encounter just those difficulties that it has encountered and that its lack of conceptual, normative, and other resources to deal with these difficulties can be explained. So it is possible for one such tradition to defeat another in respect of the adequacy of its claims to truth and to rational justification, even though there are no neutral standards available by appeal to which *any* rational agent whatsoever could determine which tradition is superior to which.
>
> (1981/2007: xiii)

So we recognise, by anthropologically entering another tradition, that its resources are not apt to respond to particular ethical or political problems. And this recognition is pragmatic. We see the failures of one tradition against the successes of another, rather than judging each against some neutral standards.

But Milbank nonetheless takes issue with MacIntyre for fundamentally suggesting that 'tradition-governed inquiry in general is rational' (Milbank 1990/2006: 262). Inherent to MacIntyre's description of how traditions learn from and win over one another is a dialectical notion of progress. Conversely, for Milbank, 'the only possible response to nihilism is to affirm one's allegiance to a particular tradition, and derive an ontology from the implicit assumptions of its narrative forms' (ibid: 262).

The ongoing conflict between these thinkers suggest that postliberalism will struggle to reconcile its call for transcendence with the fact of plurality. Indeed it may be that we must follow MacIntyre's advice and be compelled to conclude that it is only from the standpoint of an alternative tradition that this issue can be resolved. A fundamental component of the postliberal project is reviving a Christian tradition that no longer resonates with most people. And yet the step from this tradition to a genuinely collective search for solidarity seems always to capitulate to liberal assumptions of irreducible plurality or the reification of rationality as the standard by which to mediate between rival ideas of the good.

This idea of either holding on too firmly to Christianity, or else capitulating to liberalism, is further evidenced by the tendency amongst postliberals to drop Christian arguments in favour of instrumental arguments in formulating policy (see Stacey forthcoming 2018). As will be made clear in the following sections, this deficiency is particularly evident in a recent policy-focused tract from Milbank and Pabst (2016).

This section drew on postliberal literature to suggest that the fundamental distinction between postliberal and liberal political theories is the attitude towards the possibility of a collective search for solidarity. It suggested that by neglecting transcendent ideas, liberal political theory could not cast politics as a means of cultivating a collective search for solidarity. Instead, politics becomes a means of managing people as they are. Developing these points, I suggested that in reality transcendent ideas such as plurality may be central to people living under liberal hegemony. The fundamental distinction between postliberal and liberal political theories is ontological, but that between postliberal political theory and the political imaginary of people living in liberal settings is reflexive. The point may simply be that insights from postliberal political theory can be integrated into liberal settings. Yet I have also stressed that postliberals themselves render any such integration problematic. In the next section, I explore how postliberals regard pessimism as core to liberal theory regarding the state. And I suggest that cultivating reflexivity regarding transcendent ideas may provide a means of overcoming this pessimism.

Postliberalism and the state

In the previous section, I said that the European Wars of Religion are the primary cause of so much pessimism amongst liberal theorists as to the possibility of a collective search for solidarity (Michea 2009: 14; Milbank and Pabst 2016: 100; Taylor 2007: 159). I stressed that this pessimism resulted in two shifts, one ontological and one political. The previous section detailed the ontological shift. In the following I explain the political shift. In particular, I will suggest that liberal political theory, particularly as adopted by left liberals, has given rise to a contradictory politics that ends up undermining the liberal values it seeks to promote.

I focus on two components: First, I suggest that pessimism as to the possibility of a collective search for solidarity rooted in a shared notion of transcendence leads to a focus on individual emancipation secured by an absolute sovereign. The dominance of the state is then reinforced by social fragmentation. The darker side of this process is implicit support for the dismantling of intermediary institutions from the church to charities, from the family to local government; the more popular side is the creation of the welfare state. Yet for postliberals, both processes undermine solidarity. I then suggest that while at first this culture empowers the state, soon emancipatory momentum turns on the state itself. The very idea of representation is called into question. I then explore the postliberal alternative. I suggest that while the intention may be to revive solidarity at the grassroots, the outcome may be to collude with narratives of neoliberalism.

The death of transcendence as the birth of the state

According to Milbank, pessimism as to the possibility of a collective search for solidarity is at the heart of the liberal political project. Pessimism leads Hobbes, the forefather of liberal political theory, to stress that there can only ever be individual pursuit of security and wealth, underpinned by an absolute sovereign with a monopoly of violence:

> It is precisely the formal character of state power as guaranteeing personal security and non-interference in 'private' pursuits (selling, contracts, education, choice of abode) which demands that this power be otherwise unlimited and absolutely alone.
>
> (1990/2006: 14)

Yet the handing over of power to a sovereign is not legitimised on the basis of practicality alone. As explained in the previous section, the impossibility of a collective search for solidarity leads liberal political theorists to promote belief-independent rationality as a new grounding for politics. It soon followed that a state must be required to uphold this rationality, both intellectually, in terms of recruiting an educated governing class, and militarily in terms of policing (Taylor 2007: 127). The shift is thus very quick from legitimising politics on the basis of belief-independent rationality, to rooting it in a social contract between disparate individuals and a state with a monopoly of violence. Taylor suggests that this idea extends further under Rousseau, for whom the love of self must be harmonised with the love of society. This harmonisation has to be enforced by the state, and 'the egoist becomes identified as traitor' (Taylor 2007: 204). Thus the state arises as a way of imposing harmony.

The death of transcendence as the beginning of fragmentation

Simultaneously, postliberals assert, the loss of transcendence also facilitates social fragmentation, which in turn further legitmises the role of the state as harmoniser:

> The danger is not actual despotic control but fragmentation – that is, a people increasingly less capable of forming a common purpose and

carrying it out. Fragmentation arises when people come to see themselves more and more atomistically, otherwise put, as less and less bound to their fellow citizens in common projects and allegiances. They may indeed feel linked in common projects with some others, but these come more to be partial groupings rather than the whole society: for instance, a local community, an ethnic minority, the adherents of some religion or ideology, the promoters of some special interest.

(Taylor 1992: 112–113)

Taylor stresses that this same pessimistic attitude comes to influence individuals' understanding of their own ethical responsibility, as well as the legitimacy of criticizing others' behaviours, including selfish behaviours: 'everyone has the right to develop their own form of life, grounded on their own sense of what is really important or of value.' (Taylor 1992: 14). The result of this relativism may involve 'a shutting out, or even unawareness, of the greater issues or concerns that transcend the self' (Taylor 1992: 14).

As the prefix 'post', rather than 'anti' implies, postliberals are not mere critics of liberal values (see Milbank 2009; Milbank and Pabst 2016: 29). Regarding individualism, Taylor (1992: 2) stresses that

[we] live in a world where people have a right to choose for themselves their own pattern of life, to decide in conscience what convictions to espouse, to determine the shape of their lives in a whole host of ways that their ancestors couldn't control.

What postliberals want to balance is on the one hand the promise of modernity, that everyone has the right, if not the duty, to be true to themselves, and on the other hand, the political worry that people 'will prefer to stay at home and enjoy the satisfactions of private life, as long as the government of the day produces the means to these satisfactions and distributes them widely' (Taylor 1992: 9). Perhaps more strikingly, Milbank demonstrates that postliberalism in fact supports those liberal ideals that liberalism itself undermines. In his provocatively titled, 'Liberality versus Liberalism' (2009), Milbank explains that in the name of upholding individual rights, the state can actually undermine the autonomy of intermediary institutions we associate with a free life: the church, the school, the family.

Postliberals adopt a neo-Aristotelian stance; they criticise both statism and individualism for the same reason, namely, that they see political engagement as an end in itself – the highest end of humanity (Taylor 1992: 109–122; Milbank and Pabst 2016: 2–3).

It is thus a dual pessimism as to the possibility of discovering an objectively verifiable understanding of transcendence on the one hand, and of individuals agreeing on this understanding without descending into violence on the other hand, that sustains liberal political theory's focus on belief-independent rationality. And this same pincer movement against transcendence also impinges on political, social and individual self-understanding such that people can barely conceive of criticising the apparently selfish behaviour of their friends and family, let alone developing a political movement that valorises some behaviours at the expense of others.

The state as undermining solidarity

One of the key postliberal arguments is that the state does not merely arise in the context of the perceived absence of solidarity but also serves to undermine solidarity. Partly, this is because the state itself comes into being in the perceived absence of shared transcendent ideals and is thus in a sense coterminous with the instrumentality illustrated in the previous section. As Taylor puts it, 'once society no longer has a sacred structure, once social arrangements and modes of action are no longer grounded in the order of things or the will of God, they are in a sense up for grabs' (Taylor 1992: 5). The void left by the loss of transcendent ideals is filled by instrumental ideals of efficiency. As MacIntyre puts it, 'the goods of excellence' are replaced by 'the goods of efficiency'. Thus embodying these ideals, the state corrodes the ethical narratives of the industries and individuals it oversees:

> The danger posed by state and corporate institutions is that they will 'corrupt' practices by reducing them to the position of means to the end of accumulating power and wealth . . . So subordinated, individuals are denied opportunities to cooperatively pursue and sustain goods of excellence, subjected to institutionalized demoralization, and encouraged to believe that social interaction can comprise nothing other than a competitive struggle over zero-sum, external goods.
>
> (Knight 2005: 264)

For MacIntyre, this same instrumentality affects even and especially the welfare state, which he claims supports the interests 'not of workers, but of managers' (MacIntyre in Knight 2005: 267; see also Milbank and Pabst 2016: 52). In the contemporary world at least, MacIntyre cannot imagine a macro-politics capable of cultivating a collective search for solidarity:

> A crucial turning point in . . . earlier history occurred when men and women of good will turned aside from the task of shoring up the Roman imperium and ceased to identify the continuation of civility and moral community with the maintenance of that imperium. What they set themselves to achieve instead – often not recognizing fully what they were doing – was the construction of new forms of community within which the moral life could be sustained so that both morality and civility might survive the coming ages of barbarism and darkness. If my account of our moral condition is correct, we ought also to conclude that for some time now we too have reached that turning point. What matters at this

stage is the construction of local forms of community within which civility and the intellectual and moral life can be sustained through the new dark ages which are already upon us. And if the tradition of the virtues was able to survive the horrors of the last dark ages, we are not entirely without grounds for hope. This time however the barbarians are not waiting beyond the frontiers; they have already been governing us for quite some time. And it is our lack of consciousness of this that constitutes part of our predicament.

(MacIntyre 1981/2007: 263)

The kind of politics MacIntyre promotes is best reflected in communities of practice, which, in the modern world of state and market dominance, often become communities of resistance. Perhaps the best examples of such communities in the Anglo-Saxon West are labour movements.

Yet recent years have seen even these movements become incorporated into and undermined by the state. Here it is useful to draw on Glasman, who demonstrates how the liberal emphasis on the centrality of the state came to influence the thinking of the British Labour Party. If belief-independent rationality is the only basis of politics, very soon it appears that politics is the preserve of university-educated elites who are 'suited to the demands of the modern world, capable of understanding the big picture, developing technical, complex policies, managing change' (Glasman 2011: 22). In the late 19th century, the labour movement in Britain began as a neo-Aristotelian attempt to revive political engagement amongst the most disadvantaged in society. Political engagement was seen as an end in itself that could protect people from 'degradation, drunkenness and irresponsibility' (ibid). But in the 1930s, the British Labour Party, under the influence of Fabianism, rooted itself in the idea that

the state, guided by correct method and modern management, can achieve a more equal and free society, in which all can share in the prosperity of the nation through redistributive taxation, effective public sector administration and a progressive orientation.

(Glasman 2011: 26)

Socialism was thus no longer a way of life but became rather a bureaucratic technique. This shift was exasperated by the rise of the welfare state, especially following the Second World War. Glasman's analysis can also be seen in the way that political parties move from mass mobilisation based on a collective search for the good life to management by social-scientific experts who analyse the sentiments of voters and formulate policies on this basis (see Stacey 2017b: 123–125). This argument will be critically scrutinised in chapter 3.

Thus the pessimistic attitude towards the possibility of a collective search for solidarity empowers an absolute sovereign, which is then further legitimised by the fragmentation of society on the one hand, and the hegemony of social scientific expertise on the other. Even in purportedly democratic countries, indeed even amongst movements with fundamentally democratic origins, power is eventually placed in the hands of technocratic elites. One might draw from this idea that it is specifically liberalism, and not its betrayal as so many other researchers, politicians and journalists seem to suggest, that has facilitated the rise of reactionary post-political movements. Ironically, it might be suggested that these movements reveal the deep hold that liberalism has on political, social and personal self-understandings: in the face of disempowerment from the structures of conventional politics, people turn to what are perceived as benevolent dictators who promise to dismantle these structures.

From solidarity to emancipation

This shift towards elitism thus provides the first political consequence of liberalism. The second consequence is from a politics of solidarity to a politics of emancipation. With no shared transcendence to draw on, and excluded from meaningful democratic participation, people turn their attention to emancipating themselves, either as discrete identity groups or as individuals, from oppressive structures. Rather than cultivating a collective search for solidarity such as might challenge the overall structure of society, this new politics of emancipation seeks to either guarantee greater inclusion in an overall unjust system, an idea exemplified in 'social mobility', or else it seeks "to show that an overlooked 'exception' – of gender, sexuality, race, disability, religion or culture or inclination – does not and cannot conform to a shared norm" (Milbank and Pabst 2016: 27). Initially the focus on identity ends up reproducing the power of the state: in part because it is primarily intermediary institutions such as the church that seem to incarcerate people; in part because the state is identified as the target and thus as the locus of power; and in part because hunkering down in identity reproduces the impossibility of solidarity beyond differences in identity. But as the state shifts towards bureaucratic control, so the emancipatory momentum turns on the state. Hence the turn to the post-political is not merely a product of the individual incapacity to judge others, but also mistrust of any institution that seeks to promote some ways of living at the expense of others.

The postliberal state

Thus far the postliberal alternative might seem little more than to opt out of conventional politics. But Milbank and Pabst (2016: 41, 83) offer a different approach, which they call a mixed constitution, but what I prefer to call institutional democracy. This approach involves treating the state less as a unitary authority and more as a 'community of communities' that combines a democratic search for the good life with an insistence that institutions not oriented towards this search are of less value. For example, institutions from universities to trade unions will receive real power by being represented in parliament. Yet institutional democracy also means empowering voters with greater power than they can exercise through the ballot box alone (2016: 4367). Thus within these institutions, greater democratic control will be encouraged, entailing not only more freedom from the state, but also more collective models of ownership that empower lower-level members. This approach is designed to simultaneously allow that certain institutions contribute to the search for solidarity, even where we may not agree with all of their practices (ibid: 2024), and to ensure that individuals, empowered through their institution, feel more inclined to engage (ibid 1997). For these reasons, it is only those institutions that create spaces in which people can collectively search for solidarity that will be recognised and represented within the state (ibid: 2112; 4993). This approach ensures a collective search for solidarity both within an institution and between institutions within the state.

For postliberals, the alternative to liberal political theory is thus not to turn away from conventional politics altogether. Instead, the aim is to revive an optimistic attitude towards human nature such as can reinvigorate a collective search for solidarity rooted in a shared notion of transcendence within institutions that already exist. The point here is that without a collective search for solidarity, the power of the state can only ever be seen as arbitrary.

Yet as already stated in the previous section, this alternative is promoted using either Christian narratives, offered primarily to an academic elite, or else entirely secular rationalisations. Even in discussing institutional democracy, there are no standards of ensuring that solidarity is rooted in transcendence, but rather only discussion of how offers of greater power will facilitate more genuinely democratic behaviours. This implies that it is not transcendence but power that is at the heart of solidarity. As a result, postliberalism risks either imposing a narrative that has no resonance with ordinary people, or else undermining the postliberal project (see also Stacey forthcoming 2018). It is of fundamental importance to question whether, given this new power, institutions and individuals will have any narratives, any impetus from which to draw inspiration for a collective search for the good life.

A good example of this problem comes from the UK, where postliberals have an emerging impact on policy through various political channels, and most clearly through the Red Tory and Blue Labour movements. Red Tory, insofar as it is manifest in the works of think-tank ResPublica, has opted at times for Christian narratives, and at others for secular rationalisations.

One ResPublica paper in particular stresses the role of the Church of England in reinvigorating social activism (Noyes and Julian 2013). This response is particularly worrying, since it is questionable whether the church has either the ideological or the material resources to cultivate stronger communities. Not only do we now live in a world that is complexly Christian, secular and religiously plural, but also the church has little money and a dwindling register of support consisting primarily of old women (Day 2017). As Dinham (2014) puts it, it is questionable enough whether Christianity is really relevant for people today, 'even if the old ladies could live forever'.

Another trend has been to open up the state to provide opportunities for institutions and individuals to take greater control of their own communities. This is seen in ResPublica's support for the Sustainable Communities Act 2010, the Localism Act 2011 and the Social Value Act 2013, each of which seeks to hand powers to institutions, ensuring that they have the space for and the power to collectively search for solidarity. But the question arises, is it enough to simply provide space and power for a collective search for solidarity? What narratives are required to inspire people to collectively search for solidarity? ResPublica has itself questioned why there was not more enthusiasm for the Localism Act, and this disappointment is evidenced in articles such as 'The Localism Act: One Year On' (2013a) and subsequent research such as *Acting on Localism* (2013b).

In the face of a receding state, postliberals hope that individuals will rise to the challenge – be drawn out of their self-referential spheres and into their communities. The question is how. If this question goes unanswered, the risk is that postliberalism will be indistinguishable from neoliberalism, seeking to remove the safety net of the state to observe the human responses that emerge, or fail to emerge, in its wake.

Blue Labour may offer the beginnings of an alternative, focusing on empowering existing institutions and building new institutions that themselves aim to bring together various and often conflicting institutions, religious and nonreligious, businesses and poorly paid workers in a collective search for solidarity. It is by drawing on these ideas, and by ethnographically exploring such institutions, that I seek to offer an alternative in the remaining chapters of this book.

The postliberal criticism of the state is thus that it is drawn from and reinforces pessimism as to the possibility of a collective search for solidarity. It cultivates the idea of the state as a means of rationally arbitrating between disparate identity groups and individuals. This attitude results in an elitist politics that neglects the duty to engage ordinary people, and instead justifies itself on the basis of serving social-scientifically deciphered popular demand. The postliberal alternative is to turn the existing structures of power into organs for facilitating a collective search for solidarity. But where the motivation will come from to inspire this change, either from the institutions themselves or from the people, remains unclear. Postliberals themselves seem to opt either for Christian narratives that no longer resonate with the majority of people, or else the same kinds of secular rationalisations they blame for creating the current situation.

Postliberalism and capitalism

Postliberals treat the rise of the state and of capitalism as two sides of the same coin: left and right liberalism. Just as pessimism as to a collective search for solidarity leads left liberals to argue for a strong state to reconcile people to one another, so it encourages right liberals to argue that people can only be reconciled to one another through the market. Postliberals moreover stress that as with the state, capitalism undermines the very thing it is conceived to support, namely, the freedom of ordinary people.

I begin by offering the postliberal account of the rise of capitalism, and how this is deemed to undermine solidarity. I then explain why, for postliberals, social democracy has failed to offer an alternative. Finally, I offer the postliberal alternative. While a number of postliberal thinkers are deeply critical of capitalism (see Turnbull forthcoming 2018; Wood 2017), a comprehensive critique set alongside a postliberal alternative has only arrived recently in the work of Milbank and Pabst (2016), which thus becomes the key source of this section, and the key basis on which I critique the postliberal alternative.

Capitalism as alternative harmoniser

As with the rise of the state, Taylor treats capitalism as an inevitable consequence of the emergence of liberalism, since with the loss of the possibility of a shared notion of transcendence, some kind of mechanism is required for harmonising individual and collective interest. What is interesting about capitalism, however, is that whereas the state is an artificial mechanism for inculcating harmony, capitalism is based on the idea that 'harmony is . . . already there' (Taylor 2007: 130). According to this view 'human life is designed so as to produce mutual benefit' (ibid: 177; see also Milbank and Pabst 2016: 24). Taylor sees this view as exemplified in Adam Smith's notion of the hidden hand, illuminated in the much-quoted passage:

> It is not from the benevolence of the butcher, the brewer, or the baker that we expect our dinner but from their regard to their own interest. We address ourselves, not to their humanity but to their self-love, and never talk to them of our own necessities but of their advantages.
>
> (Smith 1776/1982)

Thus both the state and capitalism claim to be able to rationally coordinate disparate desires without needing any discussion as to the good life (Milbank and Pabst 2016: 132). But in reality, both positions depend upon an ontology of violence and self-interest. Instead, suggest Milbank and Pabst (2016: 137, 138–143), human behaviour is far more nuanced than this, usually demonstrating self-interest and sympathy simultaneously (see also Mauss 1954/2010). Milbank (2014) explains that

Adam Smith's economist contemporaries in Naples and Milan tried to revive the civil economy and they thought that when you bought meat from your butcher you *did* do so partly out of benevolence, because he was your friend and you needed his shop still to be there.

Yet while a natural human state may embody self-interest and sympathy simultaneously, Milbank and Pabst nonetheless stress that the hegemony of liberal capitalism has created a self-fulfilling prophecy. The capitalist focus on profit leads policy makers to project self-interest onto individuals such that, to some extent, we are all capitalists now (Milbank and Pabst 2016: 3, 13–14, 47, 54, 122). Using MacIntyre's vocabulary, it might be suggested that wealth creation becomes the shared transcendence, and economics becomes the means of cultivating the kinds of people for whom wealth-creation is a primary end. This shift, moreover, is not isolated within the economic sphere. If the first consequence of capitalism was to dis-embed the economic from the social, making economic actions entirely amoral, the second consequence was to re-embed the social in the economic, making the social realm itself amoral. Capitalism becomes a dominant component of our identity and is reproduced in our performances and relationships.

Capitalism as undermining solidarity

For postliberals, the key consequence of this shift is that a sense of solidarity is undermined. Regarding business practice, so long as people proceed in agreement with contract, that is, so long as they follow the letter of the law, anything is permissible (Milbank and Pabst 2016: 72; Taylor 1960: 11). Alongside a weakening of trade unions – themselves castigated for holding society to ransom – the result is that people have so little free time and money that they can no longer focus on creative pursuits – not least imagining a different economic arrangement (Milbank and Pabst 2016: 69, 72).

Regarding the social realm, two consequences of this change are worth noting. First, because capitalism makes wealth-creation a primary aim, more timeless qualities such as being a good mother, brother, lover or friend are distorted or neglected. It is worth noting that this position does not necessarily imply that people are cynically self-interested. Rather, if the only justification for public action is improvements in security and wealth, then to create wealth is to contribute to the public good. Moreover, to independently satisfy one's own security and wealth needs is to relieve the burden on society. Self-responsibility is a moral good under capitalism. Second, and feeding into this, people are pacified in their desire to revolt by the illusion of choice and by mass entertainment (Milbank and Pabst 2016: 112, 119–120). The illusion of choice is particularly threatening, since it locks people into a serf-like relationship with capitalism, always requiring more money in order to buy more goods that they do not need, and thus having ever less time to focus on family and friendship. This situation is supposedly exasperated by the creation of cheap credit, which encourages people to act as consumers, seemingly serving their own needs, but in reality serving large businesses which have themselves invented these needs in the first place (Milbank and Pabst 2016: 94).

Capitulating to capitalism

Postliberals suggest that social democracy has failed to challenge these changes. This is because social democrats share roots in liberal pessimism as to the possibility of shared transcendence. Social democrats accept that the only possible justification for public action is material improvement spread as widely as possible. Eventually this means they must accept capitalism, which is the best means of delivering this end (Milbank and Pabst 2016: 130; see also Stacey 2012). Thus instead of challenging capitalism, social democrats seek to tame the beast through redistribution, as exemplified in Keynsian economics.

Postliberals' concern with redistribution is fourfold: First, it means accepting, indeed encouraging for the purposes of tax intake, an amoral market onto which morality is added *ex post facto*. Instead, postliberals seek to direct all economic activity towards the cultivation of solidarity. Second, postliberals are concerned with what redistribution implies about the possibility of a collective search for solidarity. Redistribution is a compromise that historically came alongside a reduction in the powers of unions to agitate for better pay and working conditions. It thus implies a lack of faith in ordinary people to achieve consensus. Third, redistribution also directly supports capitalism by assuaging workers' desire to revolt (Milbank and Pabst 2016: 54). The social democratic focus on redistribution thus comes at the expense of empowering workers. With no power, there is little impetus for people to become engaged. Instead, they become reliant on the state to solve issues of injustice. Finally, postliberals challenge redistribution on the grounds that it favours equality over solidarity. If capitalism rewards people for selfish behaviour, social democracy seems to support people irrespective of behaviour. Redistribution is itself amoral. Instead, postliberals seek to give the highest rewards to those that perform the most vital social roles (Milbank and Pabst 2016: 74). Drawing on Brennan and Pettit (2004), Milbank and Pabst (2016: 75) suggest that there is already evidence that people favour this system, 'witnessed in a growing desire on the part of many people to combine the pursuit of material well-being with honourable social service'. Chapter 4 will offer further evidence for this claim.

A postliberal market

The postliberal alternative is to place a collective search for solidarity at the centre of the economy (Milbank and Pabst 2016: 112). Sanction alone, they suggest, cannot persuade people to act in the interests of solidarity.

Rather, a new ethos is required (Milbank and Pabst 2016: 112–113). Moreover, without a comprehensive understanding of where people are aiming, it is impossible to define the roles required to get there, or the just allocation of rewards for certain types of work (Milbank and Pabst 2016: 69, 70, 73, 148).

The primary change postliberals envisage is a focus on common ownership. For Taylor

> [t]he only way that we can really get our priorities right is to do away with the dominating influence of the profit system, and to put in its place a system primarily based on common ownership . . . Certainly it is true that, given common ownership (*not* state monopoly), we shall have to experiment with different forms of control, so as to draw upon the social responsibilities of people . . . We do not want to replace capitalism by yet another form of paternal bureaucracy. . . . But before us stand the inhuman priorities of capitalism: the *only* political question is how we can understand and change them in order to achieve an enlargement of freedom and responsibility, and a greater control by people over the society in which they live.
>
> (1960: 11)

For Milbank and Pabst (2016: 145), Taylor's vision is encapsulated in mutualism, whereby all workers within a company receive a share in profits. It might be suggested that mutualism reflects an attempt to reverse Marx's alienation effect in a way that replacing capitalism with state ownership failed to, namely, by turning all workers into stakeholders and thus part-owners of their own labour.

It might moreover be suggested that worker empowerment is equally the solution to the entrapment of individuals within the capitalist system. Giving workers power incentivises them to pressure for better working conditions and wages. Not only will higher wages themselves free up time and energy for more creative pursuits, but also the process of engagement itself is a distraction from the apparent needs that businesses invent.

Unfortunately, very little work has been offered to explain exactly where the new ethos that might engender these changes will come from, and how it will be developed in a context of all religions and none. Once again, the recommendations offered by postliberals tend to focus on either Christian narratives or secular rationalisations, and primarily the latter.

Milbank and Pabst (2016: 142) give credit to Catholic Social Thought, suggesting that 'we need to learn from traditions that always stood outside the totalising logic of modern politics and economics'. But their primary focus is nonetheless on secular rationalisations. They stress that cultivating a new ethos makes good economic sense, since doing so will cultivate trust within organisations (Milbank and Pabst 2016: 120–121). They say that higher wages results in less staff turnover and higher motivation (Milbank and Pabst 2016: 160). It should be noted that they finish their discussion of an alternative to capitalism by emphasising that although restoring ethics to economic activity makes good economic sense, if restoring ethics is not done for ethical reasons, it will not be done properly. But again, there is no discussion of where the new ethos will come from or how it will be cultivated – unless, that is, it is to come from Catholic Social Thought, which, I suggest, would have difficulty resonating with those that are not Christian.

This shortcoming is carried over into the work of postliberal think-tanks. ResPublica, for instance, has particularly promoted mutualism, and has sought to encourage demand for these ideas by offering tax incentives (Noyes and Julian 2013). A new ethos is sidestepped and again incentives appealing to self-interest are prioritised. Thus in its very strategy, ResPublica seems to undermine the postliberal focus on ethics. Yet there does appear to be evidence of groups working within a context that postliberals would recognise who better engage with a diverse religious and nonreligious landscape to offer creative responses to capitalism. Exploring these engagements will be the focus of chapter 4.

As with the state, the postliberal criticism of capitalism is that, grounded as it is in a pessimism as to the possibility of a collective search for solidarity, it undermines the very thing it is designed to enable: individual freedom. By undermining the impetus for solidarity, amongst businesses and workers alike, capitalism creates an atmosphere of mutual mistrust, whereby the only place to turn is the state. Treating capitalism as inevitable, social democrats reinforce this position, rendering the state, rather than ordinary people themselves, as the champion of social justice. Meanwhile, since capitalism functions on the basis of invented needs satisfied by cheap consumer credit, people are driven ever further into material and psychological bondage. Yet while the postliberal alternative of mutualism seems to offer real possibilities of change amongst businesses and workers alike, this alternative relies on a new ethos that seems to repeatedly elude postliberal theorists. Instead, postliberals seem to fall back on either an old ethos, namely, Christianity, or the current ethos of financial incentive.

A postliberal future?

Postliberalism provides an appealing dream in which people are fundamentally good, despite their many faults, and are capable of collectively exploring and working towards solidarity. These people do not need to be manipulated by legislation from the state, or by self-interest. Indeed, such interventions actually tend to undermine the idea of solidarity. Instead, grounded in the insights of ancient philosophy and theology, people can work together. This dream seems especially appealing given the alternative that has been painted of disparate and selfish individuals cooperating only because they are bound by a social contract, which is reinforced by state legislation and market incentive. As soon as the social contract breaks down, so will the collective search for solidarity.

Now is just such a time. The postliberal critique fits neatly with populist critiques of liberal elites found in campaigns from reactionary politicians across the globe. Postliberalism moreover legitimises these critiques, since it stresses that liberalism itself promotes a belief-independent rationality, safeguarded by a university-educated elite that seeks to control, rather than engage, ordinary people. But specifically because it justifies the complaint, postliberalism undermines the retrenching in themes of faith, race, nation, gender or economic status. It is not necessary to revolt and reject liberal values as such. Indeed, doing so may merely justify a benevolent dictatorship that further alienates ordinary people from the political process. Instead, we need to carefully rethink how to cultivate a collective search for solidarity, and place this search at the centre of political and economic activity.

Yet while the postliberal critique might seem convincing, the postliberal alternative appears to be lacking in imaginative content that can speak to people in a complexly religious and nonreligious landscape. It must be stressed that my critique of the postliberal alternative is not grounded in a mere fixation on liberal values of plurality. Rather, inspired as I am by the postliberal focus on rediscovering a collective search for solidarity, and intrigued as I am by its rootedness in a sense of transcendence, I am eager to find ways of making this focus relevant in the contemporary world. Revalorising Christianity will not do. Given political support, the result would be a new hegemony that forces people to instrumentally endorse Christian institutions, discourses and practices on the basis that doing so will be to their advantage – a position that can only undermine the postliberal focus on an authentic and democratic search for solidarity. Of particular note here is the way that certain political leaders in the Anglo-Saxon West in recent years have drawn on Christian narratives to fuel sentiments of division. As is more likely in the current secular climate, given no political support, the result of revalorising Christianity would be that postliberalism could only ever speak to an always decreasing minority – and perhaps adding fuel to the fire of anti-liberals rather than persuading liberals.

Yet simply dropping Christianity in favour of secular rationalisations is to entirely undermine the liberal project, since it capitulates to the notion that ideas of transcendence must be entirely dropped in order to speak in a belief-independent, secular language.

By way of an alternative the next chapter draws on my ethnography to suggest that the postliberal oscillation between Christianity and secular rationality leads to a reproduction of what I call the religious/secular, mythic/rational binary. We either frame our arguments in terms of our own myths to the exclusion of all others, or else we speak in a secular language, shorn of all myths. I begin to adopt the term myth to speak of how all people, religious and secular alike, draw on stories of exemplary characters and events in order to render solidarity tangible within the world as it is. Myth allows me to stress that secular actors may have myths of their own that do not fall into reified religious categories. This paves the way for engaging with theories of the state (chapter 3) and capitalism (chapter 4) to finally offer a postliberal-inspired alternative that might better resonate with the contemporary world (chapter 5).

2 Myth and solidarity in pluralist settings

At the heart of postliberal theory is the search for a unifying concept of transcendence through which solidarity is made possible. At the heart of liberal theory is the exclusion of such concepts from the public sphere to facilitate fair and reasoned judgement regarding solidarity. At the heart of both is mistrust in the human capacity to creatively engage with different and conflicting notions of transcendence in the search for solidarity. This chapter seeks an alternative: from solidarity rooted in a shared concept of transcendence, to solidarity rooted in the sharing of ideals through the sharing of myths.

Chapter 1 explained that postliberals regard solidarity as rooted in the concept of transcendence, which is primarily realised in narratives of how humans could be rather than rational arguments concerning how humans are, and thus enable people to envisage themselves as partaking in a shared ethical journey from mere animal or rational-calculator to ethical being. Without such narratives, the notion of a transcendent realm and a concomitant shared journey towards that realm is replaced by a social contract, whereby each individual is provided with the security to pursue her own beliefs and practices. Any notion of transcendence can only be found in voluntary communities that are recognised as having a legitimate space in the public sphere only insofar as they do not impinge on the social contract – that is, so long as they remain voluntary and respect individual liberty.

I slowly develop a complex conversation between postliberal theory and lived realities by: placing postliberal theory into dialogue with sociological and anthropological theories of religion; placing both of these into dialogue with the recent history of religious change in the Anglo-Saxon West generally and the UK in particular; and, finally, exploring original ethnographic research to demonstrate how civic activists in the UK develop solidarity amidst plurality.

Because postliberal theory is normative rather than simply empirical, the aim of creating a conversation between this theory and reality is not to credit or discredit the former. Rather, the idea is to ask whether the theory has resonance in terms of what can be observed about lived realities. Where crediting or discrediting comes in, however, is when those normative accounts rely on assumptions about the connection between transcendence and solidarity that can be empirically explored. Hence I focus on two claims: that the possibility of shared transcendence has been undermined by secularisation, and whether and how this claim can be reconciled with the fact of religious and secular plurality. In speaking of secular people, rather than intending those that believe there should be a distinction between public reason and private belief, I draw on Lee's (2015: 19) distinction between nonreligious people, whose identity is formed in deliberate contradistinction to religion, and secular people, for whom 'religion is no more than a secondary concern'.

Chapter 1 suggested that the postliberal focus on transcendence and narrative is heavily inflected with a Christian understanding of these terms. The consequence is to assume that as Christianity declines, so too do transcendence, narrative and with them solidarity. My exploration of sociological and anthropological literature will demonstrate that a simplistic subtraction story from Christendom to the hegemony of a liberal political theory that excludes transcendence is insufficient for understanding religious change in the Anglo-Saxon West. I will suggest that in adopting this position, like the liberal theory it critiques, postliberal theory reproduces a religious/secular, mythic/rational binary, and, in so doing, encourages the facilitation of a false dichotomy between transcendence and plurality. I will draw on sociological and anthropological theories of transcendentally anchored solidarity as realised in the notion of the secular itself, in the nation, in the economy, in law, and in communicative action. While each of these theories falls short of viably replacing a deeper grounding for solidarity, what they have managed to do is to demonstrate an awareness of what is missing from a purely secular public sphere whilst fully engaging with plurality. A shared transcendence of some kind, theory suggests, is always implicit in the way that we form communities, irrespective of whether that sense of transcendence is explicitly promulgated or consciously recognised. Just as in Christendom people were granted or denied full citizenship on the basis of their religion, today people are granted or denied dignity on the basis of their contribution to other notions of transcendence, be they secular, nationalist, economic, legal, communicative or otherwise. It is moreover arguable that for all their faults, both Christendom and the Soviet Union provided alternatives on the horizon, harbingers that another way of living was possible. As what F. Scott Fitzgerald might have called the 'count of enchanted alternatives' evaporates from the horizon, so people cling at more obvious sources of solidarity such as race and nation. The question is thus not whether transcendence should play a role in cultivating solidarity – it does. Rather, the question is what kind of transcendence and associated practices we want to cultivate, how they should be cultivated, and who should be cultivating them.

I then explore the implications of these theoretical developments in terms of religious change in the Anglo-Saxon West generally and the UK in particular. Using the broad geographical construct of the Anglo-Saxon West may seem sweeping. Yet while the Christian legacy meets secularity and religious plurality in different manners and at different speeds depending on the region in question, the similarity lies in the fact that defining this encounter is core to understanding solidarity in the contemporary landscape. In each case, conceptually significant yet historically overlapping and intertwining paradigms can be observed: Christian, secular, religiously plural and postsecular. In each case, a Christian legacy remains and directly feeds into questions of solidarity, even where these are treated as secular questions (Williams 1999). In each case the construction of a purely secular sphere leads to a questioning as to whether something is missing in terms of solidarity (Bellah et al. 1991; Habermas 2006; Taylor 2007). And in each case, the turn from an exclusionary secular public discourse towards a recognition of religious plurality risks oscillating between a revalorisation of Christianity and renewed secularity that further disenfranchises both religion generally and some religions in particular. A shared Christianity is certainly waning, yet while the secular has failed to offer an alternative, a subconscious secularity still dominates in the public sphere (Dinham 2014). The result is that religious and ideational plurality are treated as a problem (Beaman 2014). With no metanarrative for grappling with religious change, people potentially retrench themselves in old ideas of belonging that no longer fit with the contemporary landscape and thus are necessarily exclusionary. Yet new possibilities of postsecular awareness do appear to be on the rise, with institutions and individuals able to recognise the public worth of very different religious and secular perspectives. Still, how to capture this awakening in a new understanding of solidarity in religiously plural settings remains to be seen.

To explore this idea further, I turn to ethnographic findings. In support of the postliberal view, I will demonstrate that transcendence is a key source of solidarity. Imagining another world, in the future yet never quite to come, ignites people to live in solidarity with one another. Yet I develop postliberal theory by introducing the concept of myth. I use the term myth to imply the stories people tell of great, almost impossible events and lives that make their transcendental ideals more tangible, the possibility of carrying them out in the world as it is more practical. I have already pointed to the tendency amongst postliberals to frame both transcendence and narrative according to Christian preconceptions. I have also pointed to the embodiment of a zero-sum game that assumes either Christianity or secularity, and predominantly the latter when speaking to the political and policy world. This binary attitude seems encapsulated in the term 'narrative' in particular, which, shorn of its Christian content might easily be read merely as any story, rather than a particular kind of story that elucidates a transcendent ideal and thus is key to a person's whole way of being. By using the term myth, I aim to awaken both religious and secular readers to the transcendental ideals found in the stories of secular people, as well as the ways in which these stories tend to give certain events and characters an extraordinary, indeed almost religious quality. Although numerous frameworks have been developed for discussing transcendence in a manner amenable to religious and secular actors alike, allowing us to find parity between, for instance, the forbidding of depicting the prophet Muhammad amongst some Muslims and the fundamental status of free speech amongst some liberals, I find that few of these frameworks provide a discourse for understanding the stories of events and characters that bring these ideals to life and ignite public imagination and support.

Just as it challenges the hegemony of Christianity, my use of myth is also a deliberate attempt to stir controversy amidst the dominance of secular rationality. Since the enlightenment, myths have become synonymous with lies or misunderstandings. Yet as Midgley is aware: 'myths are not lies . . . they are imaginative patterns, networks of powerful symbols that suggest particular ways of interpreting the world' (Midgley 2003: 1; see also Ward 2014: 161–186).

Myths, I will suggest, are not only a key source of solidarity generally, but also of respect for plurality in particular. Myths act as the framework through which the other is recognised – as having a myth, or a 'faith' as my participants so often put it, of their own. This is not, of course, to say that all myth is good, but rather that myth of some sort is always impinging upon, hermeneutically feeding into if not determinative of, transcendental ideals. This point speaks particularly to the public fear of myth as wantonly deployed by reactionary politicians. Given the ubiquity of myth, the appropriate response to myths of division is not rationality, but myths of solidarity.

The wide use of myth amongst my participants, from Christians to Muslims to atheists also challenges the postliberal position in another way. Far from adopting calculating moral positions, actors adopt myths with implicit ideas of moral responsibility. Most importantly, this includes secular people raised in what Bellah et al. (1991) describe as instrumental institutions. Somehow the mythic is resilient not only to religious change, but also to institutional pressure. This chapter will thus suggest that postliberalism will have to better engage with the realities of people living in a postsecular landscape if it is to have resonance.

Liberalism is challenged on similar grounds. The liberal discourse suggests that in order to meet the demands of a secular society, religious actors need to reach a level of rational reflexivity whereby they can look upon their transcendental ideals as mere beliefs that can be challenged by secular reason. Yet secular rationality is not the means by which either religious or secular actors engage with plurality. Rather, it is through their own myths that people are able to recognise different religious and secular others. These myths draw on alternative ontologies and epistemologies that are not secular, or irrational. In order to explain this point, it is important to distinguish between discursive and performative rationality. I will stress that the rationality of myths is not found in their discursive content, which may be rational or irrational, but in the performances they inspire. This leads me to call for myths to be judged on the basis of the performances they inspire, and in particular, on the basis of whether or not they inspire performances of solidarity. This analysis further enables me to make a third claim, alongside the predominance of myth, and the importance of understanding myth as performance: while achieving a level of reflexivity is fundamental to mutual respect in spaces of radical diversity of belief and practice, reflexivity is not a matter of standing outside of one's transcendental ideals and judging them on the basis of secular reason. Instead, given the ubiquity of these ideals, of the myths through which they articulated, and the performances thus inspired, reflexivity is a matter of gaining an understanding of how these processes interconnect: how one's ideals are articulated in myths, and how one's myths shape one's performance. Without this awareness, people are not only liable to disillusionment, but also become susceptible to adopting myths and performances from elsewhere that potentially undermine their ideals.

Thus far it might seem that the natural conclusion of these arguments is the construction of a new metanarrative, a new idea of transcendence with associated myths to act as a source of solidarity across religious and nonreligious differences. This is not what I conclude. Instead what I suggest is that since myth is the source of the ethical imagination, and therefore of engagement with plurality, myths need to be offered ways to flourish in inclusive ways and settings. Elsewhere (Stacey 2017a), I have called this idea performative postsecularism. With the greater space for ethnographic insight available to me here, I am able to flesh this idea out, especially remarking on the difficulties of performing postsecularism in the absence of reflexivity. I offer a fuller description of the content of performative postsecularism towards the end of the ethnography. Performative postsecularism then becomes key to the response offered to the current political climate offered throughout the book.

Social theory: (post)religious sources of solidarity

I have explained that postliberals regard transcendence as core to solidarity. And I have explained the insufficiency of a simplistic subtraction story from Christendom to the contemporary context in the Anglo-Saxon West. In this section, I complicate this picture. Ostensibly supporting the postliberal narrative, I will demonstrate how the loss of shared transcendence was a subject of great concern in the founding works of sociology and anthropology. Indeed, I will go as far as to suggest that seeking to understand what would take the place of Christianity in what was perceived as a radically altering religious world provided the *raison d'être* of these emerging disciplines. Yet I will also show that this anxiety proved productive. The most influential scholars in the disciplines of sociology and anthropology can be counted amongst those that have observed alternative sources of solidarity emerging in the secular itself, in the nation, the economy, law and communicative action: Comte, Tonnies, Durkheim, Turner, Bellah, Anderson and Habermas. Far from failing to appreciate what has been lost with the demise of a shared

Christianity, as postliberals may suggest, these scholars manage to show a deep appreciation for the connection between transcendence and solidarity while paying attention to the realities of life in an always altering social context. As a result, they are able to offer new ways of imagining solidarity. Still, I will suggest that the majority of these theorists themselves reproduce a religious/secular, mythic/rational binary, which acts as a prism through which their authentic recognition of what has been lost from a purely secular idea of society cannot pass.

I then turn to two sets of theory that begin to push through this binary. First, I explore empirical explorations of postsecular rapprochement between religious and secular social actors. This literature offers key insights into how religious and secular actors may develop crossover narratives that facilitate shared action. Second, I explore recent developments in the sociology and anthropology of ethics. This literature offers ways of understanding what is missing from a purely secular idea of the public sphere without treating religion as special.

The demise of Christendom as the backdrop of sociology and anthropology

It is useful to imagine the founding of sociology and anthropology as split across a spectrum on the question of the relationship between transcendence and solidarity in the new world emerging after the enlightenment. On one side of this spectrum sits Comte, who far from endorsing the postliberal view appeared triumphant about the possibility of a secular worldview, safeguarded by high priests of empirical evidence, and around which rituals of solidarity would be constructed. On the other side of the spectrum sits Tonnies, for whom the loss of a shared sense of transcendence would result in a qualitatively weaker solidarity, in which the only rituals binding people together would be those of market exchange. Between these two poles, a tension emerges that produces the creative insights of Durkheim, Turner, Bellah, Anderson and Habermas.

Comte is widely regarded as the grandfather of social science. As the bulwark that was Christendom declined around him, Comte's primary concern was in explicating a secular, scientific alternative – what Wernick (2001) has called socio-theology. According to Comte, society has moved through three conditions or stages: from a theological stage, to a metaphysical stage and, in his time, and partly ushered by his own undertakings, a positivist, or scientific stage (Comte 1844/1988: 1). In this new positivist era, theology would be replaced by science as the cornerstone of political considerations: from economics to social policy. Theology would also be replaced by science at the social and individual levels, with priests being replaced by social scientists as the chaperones of the good life (Wernick 2001: 5). While Comte's position itself reproduces the religious/secular, mythic/rational binary, his theory provides a useful place to start thinking about what a post-Christian approach to imagining solidarity might look like at the level of society.

Tonnies offered a much bleaker picture of societal change. Tonnies distinguished two types of social arrangement, *Gemeinschaft* and *Gesellschaft*. *Gemeinschaft* loosely translates to community, that is, 'small-scale, kinship and neighbourhood-based' social arrangements, and *Gesellschaft* to civil society, or 'large-scale, competitive, market "societies"' (Harris 2001: i). Tonnies believed that community was organic, characterised by instinctive bonds, whereas civil society was mechanical, characterised by contract and rational calculation. Notwithstanding exceptions to the rule, he associated the former with children, women and rural settings, and the latter with adults, men in particular, and urban settings. It was therefore the case, in Tonnies opinion, that community had slowly declined with the rise of modernity, especially with the rise of capitalism, and was somewhat difficult to stop, as towns grew ever larger in population.

Brint (2001: 9) suggests that Tonnies is too dogmatic in his articulation of community:

> Tonnies' tendency was to see community relations . . . as thoroughly noninstrumental in character. These assumptions seem unrealistic and unhelpful in an age of mass transportation and communication, geographic and social mobility, and cross-cutting social worlds.

It is possible to amend Brint's critique: the problem is not over-idealising community, but rather failing to see opportunities for its flourishing in modernity. The problem is that Tonnies fixes his idea too much in specific settings, the Greek polis, medieval Christendom and its city-states and rural communies, suggesting that as we move into more complex, urban societies, a sense of solidarity cannot be maintained. Essentially, Tonnies seems atavistic. Aldous et al. (1972) have shown that this is the basis of the critique offered by Durkheim.

Brint (2001) also offers a further criticism. Having suggested Tonnies is too idealistic, Brint later implies that Tonnies own attempts to realise community in the modern context, by organising labour, would themselves have failed to meet his theoretical standards, since organised labour is ultimately based on the self-interest of multifarious individuals. Tonnies was apparently too idealistic in theory, and not idealistic enough in practice. For those seeking such idealism, this latter criticism seems problematic. The subtraction story of a shift from transcendence to social contracts is thus too simplistic.

The search for a secular transcendence

Between the poles of Comte and Tonnies, in the liminal space of ambivalence towards religion, some of the most creative sociological and anthropological insights have emerged. Like Tonnies, Durkheim stressed that religion provided a central cohesive function in society, but nonetheless felt that this function would be replaced. Durkheim distinguishes between the religious and the sacred. He suggests that religion is 'a set of rituals and practices with respect to sacred things', where 'sacred things' are non-negotiable categories opposed to the profane (Durkheim 1915/2008: 37). By making this distinction, Durkheim paves the way to the idea that while religion may decline, sacred forms will nonetheless survive to provide a social glue. The sacred is inextricably bound up with the social for Durkheim. He identifies a process known as collective effervescence, whereby one's presence in a crowd lifts one out of oneself, subsuming one's identity into that of the crowd. Mellor and Shilling (1997: 53) have said of collective effervescence that it 'is the very essence of the sacred and of society itself' such that 'society would die along with the sacred' and 'individuals would succumb to an egoistic absorption, if this effervescent sociality was not experienced'.

Durkheim's key example of the sacred in contemporary society is the cult of the individual. As society progresses, and as the foundation for solidarity shifts from homogeneity to interdependence, so the individual 'becomes sacrosanct' (Chriss 1993: 6). As Durkheim (1902/1984: 336) explains:

> Since human personality is the only thing that appeals unanimously to all hearts, since its enhancement is the only aim that can be collectively pursued, it inevitably acquires exceptional value in the eyes of all. It thus rises far above all human aims, assuming a religious nature.

One should note here Durkheim's absolute commitment to the ontological status of the sacred, and to its foundation in the social: as religious homogeneity declines, as people lose a shared sense of transcendence, it is inevitable that the only aspects of commonality remaining to them will achieve a sacred status.

Chriss (1993: 7) stresses that the cult of the individual does not imply egoism but rather is the basis of moral responsibility. Support for this assertion might be found in those moments in which the cult produces collective effervescence, namely, when it is challenged. For Durkheim, this moment was the Dreyfus affair. When Captain Dreyfus was falsely accused of passing military secrets to the Germans, there were mass protests in Paris. Durkheim felt these protests exemplified the sacralisation of the rights of the individual. What Durkheim fails to note here is the ways in which transcendence, or the sacred as he prefers, is reified through particular events, characters and stories. For Durkheim, the response to the Dreyfus affair is a consequence of an abstract sacred ideal. But it may also be a vehicle through which the sacred is made real: indeed it is possible that the sacred status of the individual might not exist at all apart from particular people, events and the stories through which they are remembered. The reality of the sacred is that it is always in the process of being socially constructed through the stories we tell. Thus amidst so much division, the nature of the most pressing political project of our time might be described as socially constructing the sacred across difference – religious, ideological, racial, gendered, sexual and economic.

Olaveson has suggested that a similar idea to collective effervescence finds expression in Victor Turner's notion of communitas (Olaveson 2001). Referencing Turner, Olaveson (2001: 104) has summarised communitas as

> "human beings stripped of status role characteristics – people 'just as they are,' getting through to each other . . .". The experience of communitas is also usually a "deep" or intense one, and belongs in the intuitive or emotional realm, as opposed to the rational one.

Collective effervescence and communitas are the means by which the individual becomes emotionally connected with and dissolved into the group.

Yet by designating communitas as 'human beings stripped of status role', Olaveson suggests that Turner is offering a complicated picture of communitas, whereby rather than simplistically supporting structural elements, communitas is taken as simultaneously reinforcing and challenging structure, providing the emotional energy that underscores solidarity, but also being rooted in anti-structural sentiments. The result is that while organisations can seek to harness communitas, they do so at the risk of undermining hierarchy (Olaveson 2001: 104). Olaveson further stresses that Turner's communitas is at its strongest when it is spontaneous, thus the very attempt to harness or construct communitas can only ever produce a diluted equivalent (2001: 105). Yet without ignoring this focus on spontaneity, it is equally important not to reify solidarity as an impulse related to structural or even biological arrangements alone, or to the exclusion of cultural influence. As both Alexander (2003) and Lynch (2015) have shown, failure to reflect on the influence of culture can lead to the justification of otherwise unconscionable opinions and actions. We might add that it also leads to lost potential to generate social engagement.

John Milbank offers a slightly different criticism. He suggests that such theory tends to reduce the religious to the social. What is held sacred is no longer of any particular importance – only that it strengthens social bonds. The reduction of the sacred to the social is ethically precarious, since it does not matter what ideas are used to promote solidarity; these might be anything from the idea of a master race, to the principle of equality, to the notion of self-responsibility. Milbank also finds Durkheim's focus on the individual to be uniquely problematic: in this case the good 'is no more than the universal abstraction of all the individual particular wills, who merely will their own freedom of life and property' (1990/2006: 163). One might suggest that a community cannot be authentic if it suppresses self-autonomous expression, yet Milbank would suggest that he is not against self-autonomy – just against it as the sole aim of society.

Milbank's position is supported by research from Bellah et al. (1985, 1991), for whom ideals of a good society have been supplanted by the instrumental logic of success in a capitalist economy. For Bellah et al., it has become almost impossible to envisage institutions as settings for realising solidarity, since institutions must always be subservient to the demands of capitalism. Sennett (1998) too seems to support this position, demonstrating how modern institutions in a capitalist economy create a disconnect between the virtues one wishes to teach one's children and the virtues one must cultivate to be successful. This position will receive further scrutiny in chapter 4, in which I explore the personal and social consequences of capitalism.

Notwithstanding the normatively precarious way in which it is made manifest, Durkheim's reading of the sacred would seem to lend support to the postliberal call for transcendence. The importance of sacred ideas in providing social glue and enabling collective action has remained a key theme in social theory long after Durkheim, being explored in numerous ways.

One such idea comes from Anderson's notion of imagined communities. For Anderson, imagined communities can be constructed around the idea of nation, which creates a sense of solidarity between people even if they never meet in person: 'in the minds of each lives the image of their communion' (Anderson 1983: 6). Mayo (2000: 39) has discussed how this same idea can develop around race.

Both nation and race have proved particularly powerful themes for developing imagined communities. Yet they have also proved the most divisive themes of the 21st century. Thus seeking to reimagine the connection between transcendence and solidarity by moving from religion to nation or race is simply to redraw boundaries, rather than to engage with plurality. Because of this, however, what Anderson and Mayo do provide is a framework for understanding the fundamental role of transcendence in developing solidarity, and a warning against what happens when transcendence is left unattended: it becomes, as Taylor puts it 'up for grabs' (see chapter 1) or else can latch onto divisive categories. People seem to need an imagined future which provides them with a sense of belonging. Any version of secularity that ignores this need is risky.

Inklings of a postsecular transcendence

In this context, the work of Habermas in exploring the replacement of religion by communicative action may be helpful. Habermas explains that in contemporary society

> The aura of rapture and terror that emanates from the sacred, the spellbinding power of the holy, is sublimated into the binding/bonding force of criticisable validity claims and at the same time turned into an everyday occurrence.
>
> (1985: 77)

It is thus not any particular idea but the deliberative process itself that becomes sacred. This position might be considered particularly useful in the context of plurality, since no particular idea receives legitimacy withc offering criticisable validity claims.

In his later work, Habermas envisages communicative action as including religious and secular actors alike. Observing a 'postsecular' shift in society, whereby the continued presence and contribution of religion is recognised, Habermas (2008, 2006) suggests that liberal democracies need to reconnect with religious wisdom in order to rediscover deeper ideas of what politics is for. Yet the concept of the postsecular as used by Habermas and his followers is problematic. Habermas' earlier work has widely been interpreted as advocating an exclusionary idea of the public sphere that casts religion as irrational and potentially subversive (Mendieta 2002: 11). Although this reading is somewhat narrow given Habermas' deep reflection on Durkheim regarding the role of religion in underscoring public morality, still he claims that in a secularised society 'only a universalistic morality can retain its obligatory character' (Habermas 1985: 49–80, 90). This universalistic morality is developed by means of a methodological atheism that prioritises rational argument and empirical evidence, with religious arguments only justified insofar as they are themselves rationalised (Habermas 1985: 89; Mendieta 2002: 12; Stacey 2017a). This approach can be seen to carry over into his later work, such that despite his reflections on the postsecular, despite even his 'awareness' that something is 'missing' from an exclusively secular public sphere, still his solution always amounts to the same ideal of a universal, rational language (Habermas 2008, 2010, 2011; Stacey 2017a).

In this light, the only real difference between the earlier and later Habermas is that his later work shrinks the realm to which his ideal applies. Vanheeswijck (2014) observes that the later Habermas distinguishes between a formal and informal public sphere, with the former applying solely to law-making, and the latter encompassing welfare provision and civil society, and suggests that Habermas is an exclusivist regarding the formal public sphere, but an inclusivist regarding the informal public sphere. From this perspective, research into the postsecular can be said to represent a postsecular paradox, aiming merely to acknowledge religions' role in an otherwise secular public sphere. This perspective offers no space for reimagining the public sphere, but only for recolonising religions into a predefined ideology. Religion is no longer confined to the private sphere, but neither is its public presence fully legitimised.

Although he does not point to this paradox himself, it goes some way to explaining Jim Beckford's dissatisfaction with the postsecular, which he insists connotes nothing new. For Beckford, the renewed interest in religion is less to do with recognising alternative ideas of the public sphere, and more to do with fear of radical Islam and the potential contribution of particular religions to public service delivery (Beckford 2012).

This public policy interest in religion points to another key problem with the postsecular: the concept of the postsecular seems to be more an observation of the continued presence of religion in a secular society than a new way of thinking about the relationship between transcendence and solidarity.

Since the postsecular does not seem to be offering a way of reimagining this relationship, it cannot provide an alternative to a secular public sphere. As a result, following the postliberal logic offered in chapter 1, neither can it challenge the dominance of state and market as means of inculcating solidarity. Instead, this renewed interest can be read in light of a neoliberal shift away from the state and towards the market. Religions are to become key players in the mixed economy of welfare. Religions, Dinham explains, are understood 'as "containers" of staff, buildings, volunteers, networks, values and skills which can be "harnessed" in key community domains' (Dinham 2011: 526).

There is other work coalescing around the idea of the postsecular, however, which seems to offer a deeper engagement with the potential contributions of religion, as well as providing possibilities for reconciliation between religious and secular actors.

Baker's research will prove particularly illuminating for analysing my ethnography. Baker and Skinner (2006: 9) develop the term 'spiritual capital' to indicate how solidarity is motivated by a 'value system, moral vision, and a basis of faith'. Baker and Miles-Watson (2014) make clear that secular people may also have spiritual capital. Drawing on the theory of both Durkheim and Putnam and Campbell (2010), Baker (2013) explores how spiritual capital spreads across a group and from thought into action. Baker pinpoints three categories for study: belonging, becoming and participation. Baker subdivides belonging into three further categories: "sociality (shared social and religious events); feelings of bondedness (empathy); structures of support that are particularly effective when people are going through stressful or difficult times (solidarity)" (Baker 2013: 357). The sense of belonging derived from a shared theological vision is shown to encourage members through a process of becoming. More than elusive concepts such as effervescence and communitas, Baker thus begins to provide a social scientific language for understanding how people are motivated to embark on MacIntyre's journey from humans as they are to humans as they could be. The particular nature of becoming depends on the religion in question. Together, belonging and becoming provide the impetus for participation in public life, whereby religious actors carry out their values for the broader benefit of a religious and secular public.

A couple of issues remain, however. First, the focus on spirituality, while intended to appeal to secular people, is primarily drawn from research into religious actors and ignores how much resistance remains to the concept to spirituality, whether because of its religious connotations, or because of its association with flakiness. The relevance of secular spiritual capital to an increasingly secular population is underexplored. Second, the notion that spirituality provides 'capital' can feel uncomfortable for the purported beholders, for whom spirituality is often perceived as a deliberate juxtaposition to an instrumental, fast-paced and competitive capitalist world. Thus although Baker's framework will be key to my analytical lens, I avoid the term spiritual capital. The research here will also advance Baker's framework, filling the processes he observes with ethnographic content and thus bringing the ideas of belonging and becoming to life.

Alongside this development, a few researchers are beginning to use the term 'postsecular rapprochement' to identify collaborative efforts between religious and nonreligious civic actors (Beaumont and Baker 2011; Cloke and Beaumont 2013; Stacey 2017a; Williams 2015). Although these authors tend to draw on Habermas' more recent writing, they also draw on the thought of postliberal thinkers such as Milbank and Blond, employing theory in interesting ways that open up new avenues for understanding the role of religion. Cloke and Beaumont in particular draw on Habermas' idea of 'crossover narratives' to indicate spaces in which religious and secular narratives converge, and suggest that spaces are emerging for 'reflexive openness to religious narrative' (2013: 19). Williams' work shows that religious and nonreligious actors are equally capable of creatively adopting one another's discourses, as well as embracing the contribution of those discourses. By acknowledging that 'different ethical precepts performatively elicit distinct affective registers' religious and nonreligious actors are able to 'recognise the salience of beliefs-in-action' (Williams 2015: 199). I suggest that this new way of interpreting the postsecular can be used to take Habermas beyond Habermas, demonstrating that a universal, rational language is not only unnecessary but also unhelpful, in that it forecloses the imaginative contribution provided by different religious and secular perspectives.

This same body of research has equally emphasised the role of postsecular attitudes in challenging neoliberal discourses. Williams (2015) explores how religious motivations have been used to challenge neoliberal forms of governance in drug rehabilitation programmes, pointing out that the Christian notion of *caritas*, for example, loosely defined as the virtue of charity, had been employed to keep shelters open for longer than funding would otherwise permit, to understand patients as people, and to recognise that individual self-responsibility alone could not account for the path to addiction.

These recent developments in postsecular thinking seem to lend support to the postliberal perspective, stressing as they do the fundamental importance of transcendence in developing solidarity. Yet the concept of the postliberal may still stand out for two reasons. The first, somewhat ironic given its strong Christian legacy, is that using the term postliberal may provide ways of reimagining the public sphere that move beyond religious/secular binaries. The second is that it offers the reimagining of a clear normative agenda, rendering it less susceptible to the whims of particular researchers: it asserts the possibility of shared transcendence over the liberal claim of irreducible plurality; and it uses this claim to specifically challenge the dominance of state and market.

Beyond Christendom, beyond religion: inklings of a new postliberal transcendence

These developments in postsecular thinking can be supplemented by recent developments in the anthropology of ethics. As I will show, these developments begin to offer pathways and conceptual frameworks that push through the religious/secular, mythic/rational binary, providing ways of recognising what has and has not been lost at the level of everyday understandings and performances of moral responsibility. While, for instance, this literature will provide succour to postliberals by demonstrating the relevance of transcendence, and of virtue ethics for understanding moral responsibility as it is lived, by the same token, the broad and continuing relevance of these categories demonstrates their resilience irrespective of religious and institutional change, and thus that they are not limited to particular notions of transcendence – in the postliberal case, one rooted in Christian theology. According to Lambek (2008: 140) for instance, by stressing the interconnectedness of virtue ethics and Christendom, MacIntyre mistakes 'a general feature of the human condition for a historical effect'.

For Lambek, the turn to virtue ethics 'evades excessive polarizations between the rational and irrational', demonstrating 'how attention to ethics may contribute to thinking through the relation of culture to social action' (Lambek 2010a: 7; see also Lambek 2000, 2010b). Specifically, this is achieved by locating ethics less in abstractions and more in practice and by recognising that rather than there being a distinction between rational and nonrational motivations, instead all practices are rooted in a tradition or narrative (Lambek 2010a: 24). Keane (2010: 67) explains this point in detail, stating that

> morality is not founded on structures of pure reason or on psychological universals but is the product of an encompassing social order, oriented to a distinct vision of human flourishing, and the historically specific habits and disciplines it inculcates.

Keane further suggests that this rootedness in 'historically specific habits' is not the preserve of religions. As Block (2016: 6) demonstrates, secularity too is 'reproduced in the myths, habits, stories and symbols' of a particular time and place.

Yet if Lambek and Keane are correct in this description of ethical behaviour, it remains to ask what happens sociologically when 'a distinct vision of human flourishing' is lacking; that is, what happens when, in a diverse religious and nonreligious society, discrete communities offer discrete visions. To further elaborate this point, it is useful to draw on Pool's (2016: 47) suggestion that 'the capacity to imagine', specifically, to imagine a world of human flourishing 'may be the universal human predisposition that generates behaviour that is called "ethics"'. What happens then, when we are no longer imagining the same things, or when we are no longer, at least explicitly and reflexively, imagining anything at all?

Bloch has identified a similar problem. In order to understand how he frames the problem, it is important to understand Bloch's approach to the study of religion. Bloch controversially suggests that 'religion is nothing special but is central' (2008: 2055). For Bloch (2010: 4), it is not possible to theorise about religion:

> Theory has to be a general contribution to what kind of animals human beings are . . . A theory of religion cannot do that because, as has been argued, religion is a word that can only refer to a series of historically created situations which, although continually changing, have unique and specific genealogies linked specifically to the Abrahamic religions.

Working towards a general claim, Bloch proposes that human beings exhibit both transcendental social and transactional social identities. Bloch defines the transcendental social as connoting the essentialised roles and groups, existing separately from the individuals and sets of individuals that hold them, and thus separately from their transactional power status: a trader, for instance, or politician, is expected to uphold certain ideals irrespective of her position within a hierarchy of power. The transactional social, on the other hand, is the product of continual manipulation, assertions and defeats: that same trader or politician acts on the basis of what will provide her and her organisation the highest yield (Bloch 2008: 2058).

For Bloch (2008: 2057), what gives the transcendental its power is its denial of material conditions. It forms an ideal social imaginary that negates and *thereby* transforms the way we live out our ordinary lives. Bloch (2010: 8–9) suggests that the transcendental social is most readily available in ritual:

> Ritual evokes representations, which are radically different from – but also *derived* from – the representations that govern everyday practice . . . For example, funerary rites are based on an understanding that death is the end of life, but then ritual gets to work on this representation and evokes – in a ritual drama – life after death represented as a negation of the basic representation.

Distinguishing between the transcendental and transactional is useful because it is suggestive of how people live with radical ambiguity, simultaneously carrying two worlds that act as denials of the other. In this way, the transcendental should not, as Marx would have it, be regarded as an illusion that helps people to forget their material conditions, but rather as the creative capacity to imagine a different set of conditions. So even as we distinguish between these two framings, it is important to remember that they are constantly operating and interacting – they are hermeneutically reliant on one another (Bloch and Parry 1989: 27).

Bloch (2010: 10) has also seen how the transcendental and transactional play out in politics:

> This apparent independence from the transformative life of natural people is also true for groups . . . which can be represented as 'one

body' that can comprise not only many contemporary individuals, but also forbears and future members . . . These roles and groups seem to form systems that live in a temporality that negates basic and universal understandings of the passage of time . . . Such nonempirical creations are the products of ritual and the way it transforms everyday understandings to create imaginary representations, which nonetheless have great significance . . . [These constitute] one of the most fundamental differences of the organisation of the social from that of our closest nonhuman relatives, the chimpanzees.

In this way, Bloch provides us with a framework for understanding but moving beyond the role of religion in public life. Moreover, by thus moving beyond religion, Bloch also helps us to subvert our interest in religion: rather than asking how can our current ideological, political and economic structures use religion, we begin to ask how can various ways of imagining society be employed to transform the way that we relate to the world, and what role might religious and secular ideas and people play in this process? Rather than singling out one community as unique and worth capitalising on, we treat all as equal stakeholders in a collective search for solidarity.

Yet Bloch's own formulation of the transcendental social is highly ambivalent. Based on his earlier grounding in Marxism, it might be suggested that Bloch dissolves religion into the transcendental social partly in order to demonstrate that ideational manipulation is not something unique to religions. According to Lambek (2012: 347)

> Bloch does describe the seizing and even ostensible taming of vitality . . . in and through ritual, but he does not moralize about it. Indeed, he critiques rather than celebrates repression, which he sees carried out less for the needs of society or for ethics writ large than for the imposition of an alienating transcendent world on ordinary human life and for the legitimation of social hierarchy.

Notwithstanding Lambek's reading, it is perhaps best to see Bloch as ambivalent on the matter. Elsewhere, Bloch warns of the 'horrendous possibility that the individual will become so embroiled in the short-term cycle that he will ignore the demands of the long cycle' (Bloch and Parry: 27). Moreover, given Bloch is seeking to uncover universal tendencies in his formulation of the transcendental social, it is of no use to simply critique its existence and discard it in favour of some presumably more real society or ethics: back to Marx. Rather, if it is universal, then our question must not be how to discard the transcendental social, but how it should be imagined and, perhaps more radically, who should be doing the imagining.

So while the notion of ethics as explored by Lambek and Keane manages to overcome a polarisation between the rational and nonrational, it seems to ignore distinctions between the religious and the secular, rather than seeking frameworks for overcoming this distinction. In so doing, it neglects to explore what might be lost with the demise of shared religion, even as it acknowledges ethics' being rooted in a 'distinct vision of human flourishing' (Keane 2010: 67). What Pool and Bloch begin to offer, however, are the foundations of one such broader framework, namely the transcendental and transactional social. Moreover, Pool offers a way of reconciling these two schools by suggesting that the ethical imagination is the bridge between the transcendental and transactional social. Ethics is the process by which people seek to live out their visions in the real world (Pool 2016: 49). By aiming to be potentially universal in its application, this framework may offer possibilities for exploring what is missing without prioritising categories such as religious or secular.

Others, including postliberals and including myself at other times, have preferred to use the term imaginary rather than transcendence (Taylor 2004: 23, 2007; Calhoun 2014; Stacey 2017a). I prefer the term transcendence for three reasons. First, I feel that transcendence better evokes the process of ethics as aiming at something beyond the world that we see around us. Second, I feel that the use of the term imaginary potentially calls the ontological status of transcendence into question. Third, and perhaps most importantly, following Pool, I want to reserve the term imagination, employed frequently in this book, to indicate a cognitive capacity to envisage transcendent ideals, and to creatively live out those ideals in the world we see around us, with all of its temptations.

In the ethnographic section, I will seek to build on this theory of transcendence and ethics further still. I will argue that myth is the process by which we articulate the transcendental social: we tell stories of extraordinary events and people that open up a path to a different way of living, and that ethics is the process of emulating, honouring these stories (see also Stacey 2017a). To be clear, I will not be suggesting that distinctive notions of the transcendent, and distinctive myths, must be dispensed with to clear space for the creation of new myths. This I deem impossible and, where possible, violent. Nor do I seek to reduce and eradicate distinctions in the way that people relate to their myths: some do so far more literally, others reflexively, others entirely metaphorically. Rather, I suggest that living well with different religious and secular others requires the ability to suspend one's disbelief in others' myths, putting discursive rationality to one side, and to observe the kinds of ethical behaviours they encourage: what Williams (2015) calls recognising the salience of beliefs-in-action and what I am calling performative rationality.

In the next section, I explore how all this theory links to social change in the Anglo-Saxon West. In particular, I will suggest that while theory is useful in creating frameworks for thinking about the connection between transcendence and solidarity in a changing world, the reality is far messier than any one of the theories discussed heretofore can accommodate. I will then conclude the section by explaining why an ethnographic approach is best for exploring the connection between transcendence and solidarity amidst this messiness.

Social change: a messy religious and nonreligious landscape

Notwithstanding the prophecies of early social theorists, and while accepting the momentous shifts of the Reformation and Enlightenment, religious identity has been far more constant in the Anglo-Saxon West than many theorists allow. Postliberals are right to explore the early ideational roots of contemporary shifts, but observers should not allow this to distract them from the fact that the biggest changes in the religious landscape at the level of individual belief and practice, namely, secularisation and immigration from non-Christian countries, began in earnest not between the 16th and 18th centuries, but in the 1950s and 60s (Block 2016; Brown 2001/2009).

A messy religious and nonreligious landscape

It is moreover worth noting that these changes themselves are by no means wholesale. As Weller explains, the current landscape of the UK is simultaneously 'Christian, secular and religiously plural' (Weller 2006: 6). This same quality can equally be applied to the US and Canada, though in all three cases, there is great disparity between global multicultural cities and monocultural towns and rural areas (Dinham 2009: 1, 28). From this perspective, unfortunately for theorists, politicians and policy makers alike, the question is not simple as to whether religion can be wholesale replaced by some other category as a source of solidarity. Working in the real world is far more complex than this.

Beneath these surface manifestations, there have also been shifts in the way that people relate to religion. Theory in this area is developing rapidly. Davie (1994) first characterised religion in Britain as 'believing without belonging', explaining that while we may identify as Christian, we are far less likely to attend church – a trend which Block (2016) has equally identified in the US and Canada, and particularly in the Pacific Northwest. This idea was altered by Hervieu-Leger, who suggested that people 'belong without believing', that is, they identify as Christian but no longer believe (2006). Exploring further why so many identify as Christian without attending church, Day (2011) suggests that another way of characterising this relationship might be 'belief *in* belonging', that is, identifying as Christian as a marker of one's national or familial loyalty. People do not so much have faith in dogma but in belonging to a particular group or place. In each case, a Durkheimian notion of religion-as-belonging is foregrounded. Yet it seems unlikely that one's Christian identity will act as a reliable predictor of one's sense of solidarity. As Woodhead (2016: 42) points out, retaining a religious 'label' is no longer an indicator of accepting a religious 'package', or even of accepting the authority of religious leaders. Instead, people in the UK, US and Canada exhibit a de-differentiated pluralism whereby they

> draw on select elements of religion that they still find meaningful (eg., life-course rituals, various symbols an narratives), abandon other elements (eg., membership and regular churchgoing), and meld them together with a wide range of other sources of significance.
>
> (ibid)

Moreover, people are 'increasingly likely to engage with spiritual meaning across the various compartments of their life, and not merely in private' (ibid: 45). The reality of religion in the Anglo-Saxon West is messy (ibid: 43. See also Davie 2015; Dinham and Francis 2016).

Is there anything beyond the messiness?

Beyond but perhaps adding to this messiness, it is also important to reflect on cultural norms that cut across religious difference. Williams (1999), for instance, demonstrates a continuing Christian heritage in supposedly secular ideas concerning moral responsibility in the US. Rather than suggesting that this continuing presence is suggestive of the importance of Christian values, Williams (1999: 8) explains that 'the interweaving of religious and moral traditions with American pluralism has produced distinct rhetorics with overlapping and entwined heritages'.

Numerous scholars (Bellah 1967; Gamoran 1990; Gerteis 2011; Gorski 2011; Williams 2013) point to the possibility of civil religion in America, reified in numerous rituals from presidential addresses to the pledge of allegiance. Davie (2015) has similarly pointed to the possibility of civil religion in the UK, especially around the coronation of the Queen, and around her Diamond Jubilee. But Davie is careful to question whether the celebration around this event reflects, or instead demonstrates the attempt to *create* civil religion. Gamoran (1990) offers a possible answer to this question: whether public ceremony reflects or aims to create civil religion, the question is whether the ceremonies are successful. Beaman (2014) perhaps offers a way of measuring this success, namely, on the basis of the tension it produces.

Perhaps shattering the illusion that this civil religion will be the elixir of solidarity, drawing on the work of Durkheim discussed above, Bellah has further observed a process of sacralising the individual in American civic life. Confirming postliberal concerns, Bellah suggests that the sacralisation of the individual has led to a 'self-worshipping materialism' whereby people 'reject all outside obligations' (Frohnen 1992: 150–153). Yet for others, Bellah's pessimistic view is a foregone conclusion based on the narrow questions he asks (Beaman 2016). In fact, it may be that new forms of the sacred are emerging that once again embed people in moral responsibility. Lynch (2012) suggests that in the US and UK, the nation and humanity have become sacred categories that inspire a spirit of moral responsibility. This position seems to be supported by Francis and Knott's (2015) comparison between the Dreyfus Affair in France in the 1890s, and the Rushdie affair in the UK in the 1990s. When a *fatwa* was called against Rushdie for his publication of *The Satanic Verses*, there was a public outcry from the liberal media. Francis and Knott suggest this outcry demonstrates the sacred status of the rights of individual expression in the UK. In terms of the framework I will be developing further down, we might suggest that as much as demonstrating something sacred that is already there, these events show how the sacred is sustained through the development of myths of heroic individuals such as Dreyfus and Rushdie.

Whether this commitment to individual rights suggests much for the prospects of solidarity in terms of social justice, however, seems questionable. Woodhead (2016: 45) suggests that individual choice has become the new moral universal. Wuthnow (2006) demonstrates how myths of self-reliance have become core to American moral responsibility. And Skeggs (2014) reveals how contributing to capitalist value has become core to British moral responsibility.

Building transcendence amidst the messiness: winners and losers in organised religion

Understanding what these shifts mean for organised religion may provide some insight into how to think about the relationship between transcendence and solidarity in the contemporary landscape. Heelas and Woodhead (2005) predict a shift away from dogmatic, institutionalised religious belief and practice and towards more spiritual and independent belief and practice. They suggest that in the future, successful religions will be those that recognise people are less interested in guidance, and instead want to be assisted in self-actualisation. From this perspective, the potential role of religions in guiding moral responsibility seems limited. As Bruce (2006: 43), the leading proponent of secularisation theory argues, 'only a religion that has an authoritative reference point outside the individual is capable of providing a challenge to the status quo' and yet, in a secular society, any organisation that relies on such transcendent legitimisations is doomed to be confined to the margins of society. This difficulty is further confirmed by more recent research, which suggests successful religions of the future will have to act less like states and more like markets; that is, religions can no longer rely on a pool of loyal subjects, but rather must cater to consumer demands (Woodhead 2014).

The reality may be yet more complicated. First, it is unclear whether religious actors themselves are comfortable with the market analogy. Perhaps they regard themselves as having a loyalty, which is nonetheless not unconditional. Second, it may be that what 'consumers' demand is in fact a religion with strong dogma and rigid practice, that is, religion that deliberately challenges the absolute freedom of belief and practice associated with markets.

Contra Woodhead, Berger (1979: 213) famously argued that 'inasmuch as religion rests upon supernatural certitudes, the pluralistic situation is a secularising one'. This point has since been extrapolated to individual organisations within pluralist settings, which become caught in a bind: either they liberalise dogma and offer nothing distinctive from the secular world, or they hold fast to dogma, potentially alienating people. Either way they risk losing members. In this regard, Davie (2015: 12) notices that

> more people opt in to conservative churches than to liberal ones, a pattern which reflects a global trend. It is the conservative forms of religion that flourish in the twenty-first century, and not only in Western Christianity. Simply a glance at the global south, or at the Middle East, or at the Muslim world in all its variety will attest to this fact.

Put simply, 'what happens on Sundays should be different from, rather than an extension of, the everyday' (2015: 13). Pool (2016) offers another explanation for this turn to conservatism: referring to Islam in India, she suggests that the rise in orthodoxy is better explained by a desire for ethical renewal amidst a loss of integrity on the part of secular governments than by any tendency internal to religions confronted with plurality.

Yet Davie also demonstrates that there has been marginal success for new forms of religious expression that speak to the world as it is. In particular, Davie cites the Greenbelt Festival, which, though Christian in vision, welcomes people of all beliefs and all ways of life (2015: 18). In either case, while the growth of conservative forms of religion may demonstrate success in a market situation, speaking to certain sections of a pluralist society, it by no means demonstrates the ability to speak to the whole of a pluralist society simultaneously.

Pink-Dandelion (2016) offers a third way between liberality and conservativism. Accepting Berger's claim that pluralisation leads to secularisation, Pink-Dandelion's research into Quakers in the UK shows that Quakers have managed to maintain relatively consistent membership even as that of other dissenting religions declines. He suggests that one reason for this stability is that while Quakerism has always been liberal regarding dogma, it nonetheless maintains a strong tradition of shared practice. Perhaps then, Pink-Dandelion's research demonstrates that one option for religions in pluralist settings is to shift focus from orthodoxy, right belief, to orthopraxy, right practice.

In exploring how these findings might inflect on our understanding of the relationship between transcendence and moral responsibility at present, we are immediately forced onto shaky normative grounds. If we are interested merely in what is already the case, we can simply reinforce key ideas of transcendence already available: perhaps of our Christian heritage, though clearly not the full Christian 'package' to use Woodhead's phrase; of the nation and humanity; and perhaps indeed of self-reliance and capitalist value. Yet it is in recognising what is the case on the ground that we return to Milbank's critique of the Durkheimian trend in social analysis: if *what* is sacred is only important insofar as it reinforces the social, we may be left with ideas of the sacred that are self-defeating and morally dubious in terms of solidarity. If, for instance, we are to uphold capitalist value as the foundation of solidarity, the basis on which people are included or excluded from our moral community may itself be considered a transgression of solidarity.

The religious landscape in the Anglo-Saxon West is shifting dramatically. Not only is the Anglo-Saxon West now Christian, secular and religiously plural all at once but these categories themselves are becoming less useful as people hold on to some elements of their religion, abandon others, and meld them together with a wide range of other sources of significance. Alongside these changes, certain ideas have attained a sacred status that cuts across religious difference: the nation, humanity, individual choice, self-reliance and capitalist value. In this context, it is useful to explore which religious organisations are growing, and which are declining, in order to understand how the connection between transcendence and solidarity may or may not be successfully cultivated. Yet research in this area has not achieved consensus. It is moreover worth noting that while literature on social change demonstrates how religions develop internal solidarity, it does not speak to solidarity with religious and secular others.

Amidst so much messiness, and indeed so much disagreement about exactly what the mess looks like, an ethnographic approach is essential to understanding how actors on the ground seek to cultivate solidarity. It is not only theories of the connection between transcendence and solidarity that are problematic. This section has shown that even the relatively recent observation of the contemporary landscape in the Anglo-Saxon West as simultaneously Christian, secular and religiously plural is no longer sufficient to capture the complexity on the ground. In the following section, I thus bring theory and social change together to ethnographically explore how civic activists have addressed the connection between transcendence and solidarity in the pluralist context of London.

Ethnography: developing solidarity in a messy religious and nonreligious landscape

The first section of this chapter demonstrated that postliberal theory has an ambivalent relationship with largely secular social theory. On the one hand, there seems to be support for postliberal theory in the form of evidence for a link between transcendence and solidarity. On the other, the very emergence of this theory in a post-Christian world suggests that on some level, the connection between transcendence and solidarity might remain relatively stable irrespective of religious and institutional change. This more nuanced approach is reinforced by literature in anthropology, which provides a framework for understanding what is missing from a purely secular idea of the public sphere without treating religion generally, or any particular religion as special. This point notwithstanding however, I made clear that at the very least *reflecting* on transcendence was core to avoiding the latter's latching onto divisive categories, as well as ensuring that people are empowered and included rather than oppressed and manipulated. The next section sought to grasp the contours of religious change in the Anglo-Saxon West generally, and the UK specifically. It explained that rather than Christianity being replaced in the contemporary Anglo-Saxon West, in fact the religious landscape might best be described as simultaneously (post)Christian, (post)secular and religiously plural. Yet in this radically altering landscape, some ideas do seem to have achieved a transcendent status, cutting across religious difference: individual choice, self-responsibility and capitalist value. The question became whether these ideas were not in themselves anathema to solidarity.

In this section I bring together social theory and social change to ethnographically explore the connection between transcendence and solidarity amongst civic activists in the UK. My review of social theory and social change suggest an almost irreducible complexity in the contemporary Anglo-Saxon West. Yet my ethnographic exploration reveals the ability of people on the ground to reflexively and pragmatically deal with and thrive on this complexity. In the following, I will demonstrate three points that reveal how transcendence and solidarity can be reimagined in pluralist settings. First, I show that transcendence is indeed core to solidarity. Transcendence, I will argue, is articulated through myths: the stories we tell of extraordinary events and people that open up a path to a better way of living. I will suggest that ethics is the process of emulating, honouring, performing these stories. My use of the term 'myth' is not intended to deny the ontological reality of the ideas people live by, but rather to point to the way that they reach beyond logical and empirical evidence to an imagined future. I will explain that this framework holds for religious and secular activists alike. Second, I stress that the rationality of myth is not in its discursive content but in the performances it inspires. By demonstrating that discursive rationality is thus epistemologically subservient to performative rationality, I will challenge the idea that myth can be translated into a secular language. It can be justified in a rational language, but it cannot be thus dispensed with. While this untranslatability may seem a worrying prospect, I further show that my participants are able to relate to their myth reflexively in the context of a messy religious landscape, and suggest that myth, rather than secular rationality, is also the means by which different religious and secular others are recognised – as having a myth, 'a faith' as my participants often put it, of their own. Demonstrating this parity between religious and secular actors, I suggest, provides new avenues for rapprochement between religious and secular activists. It also provides new ways of understanding the growing population of secular people, providing possibilities for reimagining solidarity. The third point I develop is regarding reflexivity. Agreeing with liberal theorists, I suggest that reflexivity is core to solidarity amidst plurality. Yet if myth is core to the construction of solidarity amongst religious and secular actors alike, then reflexivity is not a matter of standing outside of myth to judge it in terms of a secular language, but an ability to recognise the way that myth operates in our lives, to critically explore the myths we harbour and the performances that result, and to openly engage in possibilities provided by myths different to one's own.

As explained in the introduction, I draw on data from four groups indicatively representing key post-war paradigms for framing the relationship between myth and solidarity: Christian, secular, multi-faith and postsecular. I explore their capacity for generating solidarity using Chris Baker's indicators of belonging, becoming and participation. And I extend this by exploring solidarity beyond organisations themselves to the messy religious landscape as a whole. While I suggest that each organisation provides practical means for engaging the messy religious landscape, ultimately those organisations that fit too neatly with any one paradigm struggle to engage the whole landscape, while those that manage to be as messy as the world around them are far more successful. To put it simply, in the current climate of the UK, and I would suggest the Anglo-Saxon and wider West the best strategy for speaking to the whole religious landscape is to be (post-) Christian, (post)secular and religiously plural all at once. I would go further too. Research seems to suggest that it is specifically (post-)Christian, liberal forms of secularism that have become dominant in the postcolonial world, and with them liberal forms of statism and capitalism (Asad 2003; Pool 2016). By pointing to the failure of these paradigms to resonate in the Anglo-Saxon West, as well as to the solutions being developed at the grassroots, it may be that possibilities for resistance can also be transported. Particularly because my focus is less on discursive content than on pragmatic performance, it might be easy to imagine a slightly tinkered model of, for example, (post-)Hindu, (post)secular and religiously plural solidarity in India.

Christians on the Left (CotL)

That for a Christian group transcendence plays a central role in the construction of solidarity may not seem surprising, but the particular way in which transcendence is articulated through myth is instructive both for understandings of how myth operates in relation to solidarity generally, and for demonstrating parity between religious and secular actors.

As suggested by Bloch (2010), for my Christian participants, a transcendental ideal is foundational to their work. As with Pool's Muslim participants (2016), my Christian participants expressed their transcendental ideals through a relationship with God. Ralph explains:

Pretty simply . . . it is a belief that ummm the Christian call is to be a partner in . . . the mission of God . . . which I believe is seeing the restoration, redemption and reconciliation of all things in creation to the creator . . .

If you imagine a ven-diagram . . . there's this kind of sphere of heaven and the sphere of earth and the space where they do intersect and there's this beautiful little intersection where there is love and joy and compassion and justice and mercy and you see . . . little bits of heaven or whatever you might call it in moments that happen in and out of every day . . . and the belief that there will be a day when those two spheres are actually fused and that is, you know this place of perfection, and that is what we are working towards . . .

Christians talk about demonstrating the kingdom, demonstrating that perfection in the way that we live now and living in expectation of it, living in hope of it.

For Ralph 'the Christian' is 'called' to be a 'partner' in the 'mission of God'. Ralph draws strength from an imagined ideal of how humans could be, rather than a rational argument about how humans are. If there is 'evidence' inspiring Ralph, it is in seeing 'little bits of heaven' on earth, that is, little fragments or glimmers that confirm his myth and show possibilities of a better way of living. Ralph's reflection here provides insight into how the transcendental and transactional worlds may be connected. Pool (2016) explains that ethics is the means by which people move from the transactional world to the transcendental world – from the transactional up. She also demonstrates throughout her work how people move from the transcendental down, embodying religious virtues in daily life. Similarly, for Ralph, these 'little bits of heaven', these glimmers inspire him to '[demonstrate] the kingdom' in the way that he lives. These glimmers are events that take on a mythic status: they are not statistical evidence of the kingdom but testimony to it – just enough hope to sustain one's faith.

Ralph's theological commitment is implicit in his explanation of what his organisation is trying to do:

What I desire it to be is a . . . support to each other and a space or resource where people can actually grapple with political issues from a theological perspective.

. . . [There is] a definite desire to create a sense of belonging. So that's . . . why a lot of my time is spent just having meetings with people, having coffee, having lunch with people . . . A lot of it is absolutely about building that space where people can feel they belong . . .

There is a dynamic that happens when you're campaigning together, when you're working together with a common cause, a lot of bonds are formed . . . that sense of common cause – we all know that from sports teams, or from going on a kind of foreign aid trip or something like that: we've gone to a foreign country, we've displaced ourselves slightly so we're in that more liminal space, so we're kind of slightly in need of each other that little bit more . . . it's the difference between community and communitas . . . communitas which is a community that is formed where people have a common purpose and a common goal that they're working towards.

It is worth noting that Ralph's theology is reflexively aware: he is not only aware of the transcendental ideals that drive him and how those ideals should play out, but also of how transcendence *per se* functions. Ralph wants to provide a 'resource' that offers members a 'sense of belonging'. Belonging is constructed through the creation of 'liminal space', and is distinctive in that it is 'formed' around a 'common purpose'. While Ralph's use of the term 'communitas' perhaps does not fit with the formulation of the term offered by Turner and Olaveson, since it fails to recognise the ambivalent relationship between structure and communitas, it does seem to correspond to the notion of *gemeinschaft* employed by Tonnies. This is striking because it suggests that Tonnies' supposedly excessively idealistic take on pre-Modern, rural Europe in fact seems to resonate with actors on the ground in 21st-century London. From here on, I will call Ralph's ideal 'missional community'.

On the surface at least, Ralph's missional community has clear and practical outworkings. I observed how the majority of CotL time is devoted to providing pastoral care to lonely Christian MPs by 'having coffee, having lunch', to prayer and to developing projects. If a particular member is troubled for whatever reason, small prayer sessions will be held in groups of two or three.

The group also holds monthly prayer meetings. It is in these meetings that we see Ralph's idea of liminal space. Attendees are assimilated into the performance of juxtaposing the world that is. Meetings are held in the heart of British political life, often in Portcullis House in Westminster. Opened as an extension of the Palace of Westminster in 2001, Portcullis House provides offices to over 200 MPs. When I first walked in as a young researcher, through the police barrier, explaining I had a meeting with an MP, I felt the aura of power, as if I deserved esteem. It did not matter that I was only there as a researcher; I was taken in by my auspicious surroundings and the sense that somehow I could influence the levers of power. I could read the same aura in those I chatted with; there is a sense of buoyancy, a hunger for influence, and a concomitant tendency to bully those deemed unworthy of power. Portcullis House is a space in which I have been privy to numerous backhanded remarks about the intelligence of certain MPs. I have attended numerous policy meetings in which young researchers jostle for the attention of senior researchers and MPs, and I have sat in the intentionally constructed coves in which MPs whisper. Yet in these very coves is also where Ralph can be found sitting around in his shabby suit, quietly playing his guitar, and saying only encouraging things as he welcomes guests to prayer meetings. Ralph and CotL perform a juxtaposition that pulls on the heart-strings of overworked Christian MPs. Ralph's theology is thus not so much rationally conveyed through argument but rather is performed and embodied in the way that he dresses and carries himself in public space.

One way of considering Ralph's performance is as an act of evangelism. Dave explained to me that he felt the mission of the organisation could change behaviour indirectly. He explained how, by living a distinctly Christian life, he hoped he could change how others behaved:

> We're called . . . in the Bible . . . to be distinctively Christian . . . For example I live in London so I'm not called to be a Londoner, I'm called to be a Christian in London . . . and to live out that life, to live out that example, so I would hope that in my workplace, in my home life, in my community, I live a . . . distinctively Christian life and people will kind of see that I'm living in a different way . . .
>
> And then think, start to think well . . . you know . . . why is he living in that w[ay] . . . or . . . you know, is that an example to follow? They don't necessarily have to um then go "Oh, he's living that way because he believes Jesus is the Messiah and I should go to church and read into that" . . . it's more about actually – how are you living, and can I follow that example? Can I be, kind of, more welcoming to people, more kinda, you know, be more approachable and open.

In this performative evangelism, life itself becomes a ritual: it 'evokes representations, which are radically different from – but also *derived* from – the representations that govern everyday practice' (Bloch 2010: 8–9).

Performative evangelism recalls Robbin's (2015) notion of exemplars. By 'demonstrating the kingdom', Christian activists seek to transcend everyday reality, demonstrating the possibility of living a more moral life. It also recalls Baker's understanding of role modelling: it facilitates the shift from 'talking about morals and principles toward an obligation to live out one's public life in accordance with those principles' (Baker 2013).

It is against this backdrop that prayer meetings are held. If prayer meetings provide a formal space for cultivating belonging, it is in the informal chatter after these meetings that a missional community is formed. Members discuss their ideas and their frustrations with what is becoming of the world. They organise lunches, pub trips and speaking events. What emerges theologically is simultaneously a sense of breaking beyond the power struggle by getting to know one another as an end in itself, creating a sense of interdependence, but also from this basis, developing a shared responsibility to act in the world. For CotL this is perhaps the only criterion of involvement in their missional community: engaging in the world (see Stacey 2016: 185–190). This touches upon Baker's ideas of belonging and becoming as modes of moral freighting (Baker 2013: 359–363). Members feel supported by their membership of the group, and that worshipful reflection helps them turn inwards, as well as obliging them to turn outwards and behave responsibly in the world.

The performance is powerful. Not being Christian myself, I have nonetheless felt the power of this prophetic, countercultural presence, divulging very personal information. In the very heart of a culture of fear and mistrust, especially in relation to personal information, Ralph and Dave provide a space in which people can be human, even if only very briefly. Soon, I felt inclined to offer my support wherever I could – often far more than I could reasonably manage. This created a cycle of inspiration followed by guilt each time I recalled that my first duty was to the research itself.

This recognition led to an odd conversation after an event. I explained to Dave that I was beginning to feel more Christian, but could not call myself one because I did not believe in a God that could intervene in the world. Dave replied: 'Do you believe that the stories of Jesus Christ can be transformative?' This utterly struck a chord with me. 'Yes', I said, almost reverently. 'Well isn't that divine intervention?'

This conversation speaks to two aspects of the relationship between myth and solidarity. First, Dave's part in the conversation speaks to reflexivity on the part of the religious. Clearly theology plays an important role in developing solidarity at CotL. But the beliefs on their own are neither necessary nor sufficient. No matter what any particular member's belief position, they are equally welcome to events and discussion – to shaping a shared theology. When I asked Ralph whether having Christian values is a prerequisite of the kinds of actions CotL sought to inspire, he answered:

> I think absolutely no you don't have to have Christian values but then also that I don't believe in the phrase you have no beliefs whatsoever, I think we all have beliefs, I think we all have faiths . . . for folks to say that they're not, that we're not operating out of a belief system, just because they're not operating according to what we might call a more recognised belief system like Christianity, you know, or Islam, that to be put in a separate category to someone whose belief system that's been cobbled together from different things they've been exposed to . . . and I think that those are both equally belief systems that form their thinking.

Recognising that someone different nonetheless has 'a faith' is the means by which Ralph and Dave recognise that person. The claim that we all have faiths is a deliberate challenge to the Habermasian distinction between religious and rational argument. For Ralph, faith has an ontological status: we all have faiths on which we are acting, and so no discursive mode deserves priority over any other. For Ralph, it is not the case that transcendental ideals have faded in liberal secular societies, just that they have been excluded from, or at least devalued within the public sphere. Moreover, contrary to Taylor (2007: 3, 539–593), this assertion appears to break through the immanent frame, drawing on a transcendent frame: faith is not one option amongst many; we all have faiths, it is just a question of which one.

From within the transcendent frame, the difference between religious and secular people is not categorical but reflexive: 'for folks to say that they're not operating out of a belief system, just because they're not operating according to what we might call a more recognised belief system' does not make sense.

The second striking aspect of my conversation with Dave is the ability of performative evangelism to convince by cutting through the rational. Without having the same beliefs as my participants, I too felt the call to belong to a group who lived out something higher, deeper or set apart from the power struggle around us. Propositional belief in God is not a necessary prerequisite of belief in a particular idea of transcendence, or of a mutual belief between the community and the participant, a belief in belonging, as Day (2011) puts it.

This theological liberality regarding membership also speaks to CotL's understanding of how best to engage with the world. Since faith has ontological status, to put one's faith to one side in political discourse does not make sense. Indeed, to speak as if from nowhere, from a Rawlsian original position, might be considered an act of deceit. Instead, says Ralph, it is more authentic to 'be upfront and say where you're coming from'. When one's faith is on the table, both the faith position and its beholder can be held to account.

To understand how CotL maintains a theological liberality whilst nonetheless offering something distinct from the world as it is, it may be worth returning to Pink-Dandelion's (2016) insight of a shift from orthodoxy, right belief, to orthopraxy, right practice. I have already stressed that the only criterion of involvement in CotL is a demand to engage in the world. As will be explained in more detail in chapter 3, the majority of CotL's campaigning work is directed towards convincing Christians to engage in conventional political processes. CotL is perhaps able to maintain a relatively strong membership by offering theological liberality alongside firm expectations of political engagement. Alongside this demand, as shall be detailed further in chapter 3, CotL is also extremely democratic in its formulation of policy.

CotL can thus be seen to create a strong connection between transcendence, articulated through myth, and solidarity. Myth is specifically not rationally constructed. Not only is the discourse aimed at imagined ideals of how humans could be, but also the discourse itself is secondary to an embodied practice, a performative evangelism. Myth is reflexively constructed and as such can involve those without propositional belief in a God that intervenes in the world. Yet the reflexivity on the behalf of the religious comes with a demand on the part of the secular that they recognise that they too have 'a faith'.

CotL's openness notwithstanding, the messy religious landscape in the Anglo-Saxon West suggests that a Christian message alone is impractical for reviving solidarity. Partly, perhaps, my own openness to the theology was down to my approach of methodologically suspending disbelief, deliberately open to the sway of different ontological perspectives. That it appeals to me does not mean it could appeal to everybody. As the next case study will show, Christianity aside, some people are instantly turned off by even the mention of religion.

Hackney Council for Voluntary Service (HCVS)

At first glance, neither HCVS nor the motivations of its members can be deemed either explicitly or implicitly religious. On my first day in the organisation, when he heard me mention religion, Frank told me, with a smile 'don't ask me about religion, I don't want anything to do with it', and, when pressed, suggested that religion causes conflict. There is certainly no awareness as to having 'a faith'. Instead, Frank appears to be caught in a religious/ secular, mythic/rational binary, assuming his motivations are secular and rational. Yet in the following I will demonstrate that by adopting Bloch's framework of the transcendental and transactional social, it is possible to cut through a religious/secular binary and bring to light shared transcendental ideals articulated in myths and realised in rituals amongst those involved in HCVS.

At first no such ideals seemed to emerge, and members seemed to epitomise Prochaska's (2006: 171) lament that secular charitable activity is motivated by 'altruism, filling spare time, or the need for a more imposing CV', none of which bode well for cultivating a solidarity that is resilient to fluctuations in personal interest. Specifically, members articulated motivations ranging from stories of personal suffering, to making a difference as its own reward, to job prospects. Yet slowly it appeared that, while largely implicit, transcendental ideals were being articulated in stories of personal suffering. These stories acted as myths, and were embodied and performed, only with less clarity than amongst religious actors.

Earlier in this chapter I critiqued the postliberal position by drawing on anthropological literature on ethics. I suggested that although postliberals are right to stress the importance of a shared notion of transcendence with associated practices in developing solidarity, transcendence is resilient to religious and institutional change. Here I am able to contribute to this literature by suggesting that what is lacking in some secular settings is not transcendent ideals, which seem to exist irrespective of the beholder's awareness of them. Rather, what is missing is specifically this awareness – a reflexivity on the part of the beholders that can help them articulate their ideals in myths, critically explore the implications of these myths for their practice, share their myths with others, and place them on the public table where they can be challenged.

Transcendental ideals at HCVS were perhaps best encapsulated in a single word: equality. James told me that 'wanting to work towards a more equal society' underpins all of his work. He also demonstrated a correlative frustration with the failure of the world to live up to this equality. He sees

> lots of examples where it's frustrating that perhaps the progress isn't what you would hope for if you look back to previous decades, you know to decades when I wasn't working in the sector. Or in general, when you're looking at society.

James' stress on equality came about as a result of my own discursive intervention, inquiring as to the ideals that inspire James to be involved in HCVS. This point is particularly worth noting since it demonstrates both the importance of reflexivity, and the ease with which reflexivity can be awakened among secular people with a timely and sensitive intervention.

Once I began to prod in this way, I noticed that equality is mythologised in the stories of personal suffering people tell. John, who is of Indian descent, offers a clear picture of how personal suffering could lead to action:

> I faced so much discrimination, and so much abuse, on a daily basis, but I didn't know that this was going to happen – it was just a shock. And slowly, over the years, I was there over 26 years, so I became their white, though not so white, but one of their brothers and all this. But what happened was, slowly people that were from minority communities came in, and started talking to me, you know, and . . . so I sort of like started helping people, whilst I had all these different shops I had a private business and stuff, and I really liked that kind of work because I saw the difference it made in their lives.

John's personal suffering created a capacity for sympathy that inspired him to help others in his position. His voice noticeably shook when he spoke of being discriminated against. There was a clear sense that he felt he did not belong. It is this feeling of having himself not belonged that inspires John to help others.

There is also a clear sense in which the ideal of equality is performed. 'Addressing local inequalities' is part of the organisation's vision. The HCVS offices are just off of Dalston Kingsland High Street, where the relatively recently arrived, mainly white wealthy digital media "creatives" and students from London's top universities rub shoulders with far longer-term residents of Turkish and African-Caribbean origin, many for whom English is a second or third language. These subcultures in such close proximity seem to display an example of parallel lives. The first two groups are of the most privileged in the country, the latter two the most deprived. The employees of HCVS seem to straddle all of these subcultures: a walk through the offices sees white and black, media-savvy and computer-illiterate, educated to doctoral level and barely to high school level, privileged and deprived, all working in a single organisation. Their mere togetherness is a juxtaposition that invokes an imagined world in which all of these subcultures have equal access to the country's resources. As a local resident, I was struck that HCVS provided my first opportunity in a year of living in the area to speak for an extended period with people of different backgrounds. Equality clearly provides a backdrop for HCVS' activities and, as with CotL's Christianity, its performance becomes a source of inspiration. It forms an imagined world towards which the group is striving, by which the present world is held to account, and by which causes are selected.

The idea of equality seems to resonate with Durkheim's cult of the individual. Contrary to expectations from critics, at HCVS this cult is not limited to merely safeguarding against infringements to fundamental rights but rather involves supporting people in the development of services that contribute to a more fulfilling life. The question remains, however, whether this ideal limits people to push for greater access to resources within a world that is fundamentally lacking in solidarity; that is, what possibilities are provided for thinking beyond the world as it is? This question will be further explored in chapters 3 and 4.

The use of equality as a criterion by which causes are selected was institutionalised in an Equality and Diversity working group. Chaired by the organisation's board of trustees, the group brought together senior management to explore areas of expertise and areas for improvement. Areas for improvement involved identifying communities, such as the LGBT community, that deserved more focus. Through the Equality and Diversity Working Group, equality thus provides a framework for becoming and participation. Equality forms an accepted discourse and there appears to be potential for a shared mission.

Yet because equality is not recognised as a transcendental ideal, no rituals of belonging are established around it. Although equality is articulated in stories of personal suffering and in the diversity of the team, there are no opportunities for formally sharing these stories or for recognising this diversity.

The Equality and Diversity Working Group provides a good example of this shortcoming. Its meetings do not appear as opportunities for creatively reflecting on, constructing, consolidating and internalising the organisation's ideals. Instead they are dry and practical affairs. If the sense of equality pervades the atmosphere, the meetings in which it is explicitly explored are not exactly instances of a 'fiery furnace', forging 'new identities and transformed relationships in the sacred fires of collective effervescence' (Mellor and Shilling 1997: 53). Rather, these meetings are procedural endeavours. The Equality and Diversity Working Group draws directly on policy frameworks and thus appears rationalised and bureaucratic. Further reinforcing its bureaucratic nature, the working group involves only trustees and management. The particular performance of equality thus itself undermines the equality of members. The result is alienation.

This alienation becomes evident, occasionally distressingly so, when working with those on the front line. Staff often suggested their roles were not properly appreciated and that they were not being listened to. One staff member in particular would frequently plead with me: 'Tell them . . . tell the management how important this work is'.

This alienation also impinges on what Baker (2013) calls becoming, since it means there is a lack of clarity when it comes to frontline policy. When I questioned frontline staff about the criteria by which they accept and reject groups, the first answer was always, proudly, 'we don't reject anybody'. On the one hand, this insistence on acceptance once again points to how embedded equality is, but it also demonstrates how vague the idea is.

The lack of awareness and coherence also manifests in missed opportunities for developing solidarity outside of the organisation. There are few concerted attempts to spread the idea of equality to other groups and people, such as to progress and develop the culture.

In the key practices in which equality is spread to external groups – in bespoke surgeries and workshops for those trying to develop community enterprises – it is framed as a means of meeting statutory requirements or applying for funding. The idea of equality is not treated as an ideal to be discussed and critically explored, but as a bureaucratic procedure to be navigated. People were told to think inclusively, since this was more likely to achieve funding. Unlike CotL's 'kingdom of heaven', equality becomes less an idea of how humans could be than a procedural dictum of how humans must be, with rigid accompanying rules in the form of a policy framework to be followed. This procedure suggests a discrepancy between the equality that inspires staff and the procedures and practices around equality and diversity derived from legislation. If there are differences here, it would be useful for these to be brought to light and critically explored. As an intermediary between state and grassroots action, HCVS finds itself implementing procedure without fully reflecting on it. Moreover, this lack of reflection means there are no criteria for deciding whether there is correspondence between the ideals of the organisation and the ideals and practices of those it seeks to help. Bureaucracy thus serves to foreclose the capacity to articulate myth by replacing creative reflection with obedience to rules. This tendency of bureaucracy to constrain creative reflection will receive further attention in chapter 3.

At first, HCVS seemed entirely secular and void of any frameworks reminiscent of religious groups. Staff seemed motivated by personal grievances that inspired a sense of sympathy for others, or because serving others makes them feel good. A shared sense of transcendence had no connection to solidarity. But considered through the lens of the transcendental and transactional social, it became possible to see that equality is a transcendental ideal, and stories of personal suffering are the myths through which that ideal is articulated.

This tendency to operate around the idea of equality demonstrates that those that pay no attention to religion may nonetheless act within a frame of ideals that unreflectively take on similar functions. Equality operated like a transcendental ideal, having the potential to inspire and organise the group, and to challenge the way they carried out their practices. At the upper levels of the organisation, the idea was critically explored and a kind of missional community formed. On these grounds, it seems inaccurate to suggest we are living in an immanent frame wherein politics is legitimised not by transcendent ideas but by social contracts. It might be more accurate to suggest, as Schilling and Mellor have, that behind seemingly self-referential, contractual behaviour, there are underlying pre-contractual ideas (Mellor and Shilling 1997: 58). Perhaps then, when the old gods die, new ones emerge to replace them.

Yet despite the potential of equality to act as a transcendental ideal, there were many elements in which its function had not been realised, and possible contradictions emerged in the way staff carried out their work, selected groups to work with, and developed the capacity of those groups. The difference, then, between religious and secular worldviews is not categorical but reflexive; HCVS are not lacking in myth by virtue of their secularity, but by virtue of their reflexivity. Yet reflexivity is fundamental. If transcendental ideals, the myths through which they are articulated, and the performances through which they are embodied emerge irrespective of our attention to them, it is better that they are out in the open where they can fully inspire belonging and becoming, as well as be critically challenged. In this case, the adage that where old gods die, new ones emerge to replace them, needs amending. Instead, where old gods die, new gods emerge half-formed and require critical cultivation. It is not that secular myths are not possible, but that secular culture may foreclose possibilities for thinking critically about the way in which transcendental ideals shape and misshape our myths and our practices.

If the notion of equality as reified at HCVS may lack the clarity required to inspire secular actors, it is equally questionable whether it can cut through religious difference. On the one hand, although there appears to be a lack of religious literacy within the organisation, so long as groups frame their actions based on secular goals, there is also no discrimination on the grounds of an organisation or an individual being religious. This appears to be secularism at its best. Yet two points are worth noting. First, this lack of religious literacy means that it can be difficult for a religious organisation or individual to navigate the appropriate discourse surrounding what counts as a secular goal. There is no recognition that religion itself may be a disenfranchised identity requiring of concerted efforts of inclusion. More fundamentally for the point of this book, operating through this religious/secular, mythic/rational lens forecloses recognition of the unique contribution that religions and religion-like ideational frameworks may offer in developing solidarity.

Faith-based Regeneration Network (FbRN)

Perhaps ironically, as an organisation concerned with the role of faith in the public sphere, the primary transcendental ideal at FbRN too appears to be a secular notion of equality. Like secular actors at HCVS, FbRN seems to draw on the Durkheimian cult of the individual: a person *as a person* has the right to be included in the public sphere. The adoption of this ideal at a multi-faith organisation might suggest that equality has the potential to act as what Cloke and Beaumont (2013: 19) call a crossover narrative. Yet the following case study will complicate this hopeful interpretation. It may be that equality represents an organically developing ideal that cuts across religious and nonreligious differences. But the prominence of this idea in the multi-faith setting does not indicate the organic flourishing of a shared ideal. Instead, it demonstrates the dominance of the liberal secular paradigm in the ways that people, including religious people, imagine public roles and organisational structures in diverse settings. Equality is drawn primarily from a policy and funding agenda, rather than from the creative insights of the many faiths contributing to FbRN itself. The experience with HCVS demonstrated that the passive reception of transcendental ideals from policy agendas can be damaging in itself. In this section, I show that doing so can be particularly problematic when a secular government casts its agenda into a messy religious landscape, seeking to utilise faith as a resource. This situation is problematic enough for serving the ends of the secular government, let alone for understanding and addressing what is missing from a purely secular idea of the public sphere. In the following I highlight this failure through a critical discussion of the substance (or lack thereof) of multi-faith as a transcendental ideal, the lack of myths through which it is articulated and of performances through which it is actualised. Dinham (2012: 586) has stressed that

> In the end, the multi-faith paradigm . . . has no religious creed, buildings, explicit practices, or formal leaders . . . Multi-faith practices risk constituting a parallel world running alongside 'real' faith communities, seeming to respond to policy hopes but unable to bring constituencies of faith with them.

Indeed, I demonstrate that members of FbRN have no distinct vision for how multi-faith might offer an alternative to a purely secular idea of the public sphere. I credit this to an inability to envisage a public sphere beyond secular reason. Even as they have their own faith position from which they critique the degradation of public ethics, members question the place of their faith in public, considering secularity the only means of ensuring inclusivity. I suggest that this inability to think beyond the secular negatively impacts on the power of the organisation to develop processes of belonging, becoming and participation. Rather than drawing on multi-faith, whatever this may mean, members draw on their own faith for motivation.

A former secularist himself, Gary turned to faith later in life, recognising its capacity for rediscovering solidarity in contemporary society. In this way, Gary's position reflects Pool's (2016) observation that the turn to faith is as much a matter of reimagining 'public ethics' more broadly than it is a denial of plurality. This personal journey is reflected in his analysis of the degradation of public ethics:

> One of the great gaps in our society is the absence of the trade union movement, which, in the 70s, was still very strong. Ummm and which was still a force which could inspire people. It's hard, now, to talk about the Labour movement, the trade union movement, as something that would inspire people. Now, if it exists at all, it's just about protecting certain rights. But not about inspiring people . . . to take action in the world . . .
>
> I think disenchantment with other voices in the public square, disenchantment with politicians, journalists, with others, and you're looking for, you know, who is there who is talking about public ethics and it . . . seems to be, well faith communities.

Gary's thinking not only lends support to the postliberal suggestion that the loss of a shared sense of transcendence leads to a retrenching in communal identities with claims to rights, but also cuts through both Tonnies and Durkheim's differentiation between mechanic and organic solidarity. For Gary, one must draw on mechanic ideas to develop the organic solidarity associated with trade unions. What has been lost is a sense of inspiration and enchantment. Gary's position seems to be evidenced by research from Dore (2002), which suggests that focusing on the rational self-interest of members alone has led to unions losing middle-class members as workplace social security improves. It is faith groups that can re-enchant people in public ethics and shared responsibility. Gary also thinks policy makers recognise this role. In a manner reminiscent of Putnam and Campbell's (2010) research, faith is regarded as the last bastion of social capital, and as having an important role to play in rebuilding it. Faith is also regarded as having the ability to restore public trust in institutions more generally.

Yet notwithstanding Gary's own faith on the one hand, and his insistence on the importance of faith in rebuilding solidarity on the other, he seems to operate within a secular imaginary that forecloses his appreciation of the rich contribution of faith. In my time at FbRN, it always felt quite uncomfortable asking how the organisation might transform society, since such an agenda seemed to be perceived as antithetical to the only limited answer that could be given: 'all faith communities participating fully in civic life'. Here I recalled the postliberal concern that rather than challenging the *status quo*, left liberals seek greater inclusion in an already unjust system. I found it constantly surprising that despite being creative, intelligent and critical as individuals, *as members of FbRN*, there was a collective failure of imagination about what it was they were trying to achieve. Faith is considered vital to developing solidarity, even as its role within the organisation itself, in defining its agenda, developing belonging, transforming the public sphere, is relatively neglected.

The problem this analysis emphasises is the same as that identified at the beginning of this chapter as dogging much of social theory: while members of FbRN recognise that something is missing from a purely secular public sphere, they nonetheless cannot think beyond secular reason to creatively reimagine the relationship between myth and solidarity in pluralist settings.

This lack of imagination comes across in staff's motivation for working with FbRN. Dominic, for example, was primarily motivated by his Zoroastrian faith. He claimed that this faith could not be separated from multi-faith action, since the former demanded the latter. Yet despite a lot of questioning, Dominic failed to acknowledge a distinction between working with fellow Zoroastrians to engage in multi-faith work, and drawing on a distinctly multi-faith myths, whatever these might look like. From this perspective, the idea of multi-faith does not appear to have traditions or narratives of its own that draw members in; rather, multi-faith seems to be primarily recognised as a policy paradigm. That the multi-faith agenda is shaped by a policy paradigm is reminiscent of the shortcomings observed at HCVS – a fitting similarity given that both the equality and diversity and multi-faith paradigms were both developed during New Labour governments under the same principle of social inclusion. In the context of this policy paradigm, multi-faith is seen as an opportunity to develop skills and contacts. Multi-faith is less a means of challenging a purely secular idea of the public sphere than an invitation for greater involvement within that sphere.

This shortcoming cannot be put down entirely to the multi-faith concept itself, however vacuous this may turn out to be. Rather, as with HCVS' engagement with equality, in part the lack of motivation around multi-faith needs to be put down to a lack of opportunities for reflexively developing the concept. Very little space or time is devoted to the inclusion of others in the development of theology, and no obvious sense of belonging emerges. From my limited time at the organisation, no such opportunities arose, except where these were created by me through critical questioning.

The absence of these opportunities for cultivating meaning and belonging is especially pronounced when one hears Claire's attitude towards FbRN. For Claire, although she is motivated by her faith to undertake social action, her work in FbRN is not part of that "I personally have a faith commitment, but I do quite a lot of other things in relation to that, and FbRN is primarily work rather than a faith expression." Despite being inspired to engage in multi-faith work, in the case of Dominic, or mono-faith social action, in the case of Claire, both appeared to be engaged with FbRN on a primarily instrumental level, whether to serve the calling of their own faith, to address the skills deficit of that faith, or simply for the money. This point is underscored by the fact that both were leaving the organisation as funding ran out.

The lack of imagination regarding the possibility of shared transcendental ideals in the context of plurality is all the more surprising since my interactions with individual members of FbRN, rather than the organisation itself, offer a number of practices that point to such an imaginary. These practices take the form of transparency and translation, multi-faith myths, breaking down the distinction between religious and secular narratives, and dispensing with myth altogether.

I asked Gary whether, in seeking to develop solidarity, he appealed to stories of his own faith, or tried to find common experiences:

> Both. I think it's both. When I go into a room full of people, I can talk religion and I can talk, you know, from my own experience, you know, whatever kind of room full of . . . an organisation, mixed bunch of representatives, you know, I can talk from a position of someone who's actively involved in a religious [tradition]. I talk about specifics, I, my experience, because it's my experience, but I also do have a broader experience, which has been through working with people from other faith traditions and people from no faith tradition.

Gary clearly sees his faith as a way of starting conversations. In some sense, Gary is placing faith in others to understand him from his context, and to translate into their own context those ideas that make sense. The Habermasian translation proviso is turned on its head: it is not the role of the speaker but of the listener to translate.

Yet this same translation process can also be seen the other way around. When I spoke to members about my experiences with people of other religious and secular backgrounds, they took delight in drawing out similarities and differences, translating their myths into the context of others. In this sense, the act of translation might not be perceived as an act of oppression. Rather than forcing ideas into a language in which they no longer make sense, it is a creative experience. Perhaps what is important in this regard is not so much the stipulation to translate, but the power relations involved in the translation process. Oppression arises when one feels the need to translate one's faith into a language that undermines that faith, simply in order to receive funding or legitimacy.

The process of transparency and translation is just one means by which members of FbRN seek to speak to the messy religious and nonreligious landscape. Alongside transparency and translation, individuals also offered multi-faith myths that draw on overlapping narratives between different faiths. Gary, for instance, was particularly excited about how the notion of hospitality inspired anyone of an Abrahamic faith:

When I say the word hospitality to any one [of an Abrahamic faith] their brain will immediately go to the story of Abraham, and the tradition that his tent was open on all sides so that he could welcome strangers coming from all directions. So all I need to do is write the word hospitality and immediately they're going into a mode of thought . . . it's about strangers, it's about people coming from different directions.

For Gary, the word hospitality acts as a repository of memories, ideologies and obligations that can inspire people of certain traditions to act. Hospitality is a common denominator, an overlapping consensus or crossover narrative that provides a space for talking about solidarity. Looking at this strategy in the context of the messiness of the real religious landscape however, the problem is that it is questionable just how many myths and performances are *already* shared. Equally, one must question whether those myths that are already available and widely accepted are not simply replicating the public sphere as it is, rather than transforming it.

The third practice I want to highlight is the frame by which FbRN broke down barriers between religious and secular narratives, namely, faith. Like Ralph at CotL, Gary tried to open up a wide umbrella around the idea of faith. This meant both being open to minority faiths, and broadening the concept of faith.

For Gary, 'who's a faith, who's not a faith, who's allowed in, who's not allowed to be in . . . we just don't get involved with things like that'. Gary's approach appears to contradict the Schmittian idea championed by Mouffe that outsiders must be created in order for a political identity to be formed (Schmitt 1922/2006; Mouffe 2007). Instead, the political process is one of bringing the other into the fold. While FbRN sees faiths as a last bastion of social solidarity, it nonetheless takes a deliberately ambiguous stance on what faith is.

In terms of opening up to secular actors, Gary summarised for me the kind of message he has been trying to give at secular events:

It's not just faith people who have a belief system, we all do, you know, sometimes it's explicit, sometimes it might be driven by a faith tradition, sometimes it might be driven by a political understanding of the world, but we all, if we're community workers, trying to do some good, or trying to do something, nearly all of us, either consciously or less consciously, we are motivated by some kind of worldview, ideology or belief-system, and . . . at the very least we should be honest to ourselves and try and understand what it is for ourselves but much more, to use that in a positive way in the work that we're doing. You know I'm a very proud [laughing] I'm a very "out" Jew.

In his generalisation of the idea of faith, Gary was also suggesting that honesty about one's faith, and acting upon it were intimately linked. This position is also demonstrated in a reflective practice tool developed by FbRN: it suggests that 'most people operate on a day-to-day basis' with a 'theory-in-use', which may be 'unconscious' and 'quite distinct' from our 'espoused theory', that is, 'the conscious answer we give when someone asks us what beliefs or ideas shape our work'. They go on to suggest that 'without beliefs and ideas our work is groundless' (FbRN 2012). Enabling religious and secular actors to develop a level of reflexivity regarding their own deep commitments is fundamental to solidarity. It is ironic then, that FbRN has failed to apply this same idea to its own ideals.

On top of this lack of reflexivity, what remains problematic about this value-generalisation around the idea of faith, considered universally, is that, as was evident in the discussion of HCVS, there remains significant hostility towards the idea of faith. While perhaps this hostility can be overcome through education, and the improvement of literacy, the question remains whether it is not more productive to begin in a place that is less contested, and less evocative of prejudicial sentiments – particularly if Bloch is right in stressing that religion is not a category with potentially universal resonance but a geographically and historically specific idea. Despite being broad in its interpretation of faith, FbRN is nonetheless seeking to impose an umbrella, rather than inclusively develop shared ideals through the sharing of myths.

The final practice involved dropping narrative altogether. In answer to how faith might transform the public sphere, Dominic tells me:

> Frankly I don't agree that in multi-faith work you should be promoting your faith. Frankly what you're doing is going down the road of proselytising. And that's dangerous because multi-faith is based on trust, bonding, bridging and linking. You're initially bonding, and then you're developing trust, and you're coming together to do some work for the common good.

Multi-faith is not a creed in itself, but rather is used as a stepping-stone for facilitating the good work of people of faith. Moreover, the multi-faith environment is not an appropriate place to be talking about faith, since to do so risks creating friction within the group. As already stated, what emerges is a paradox whereby those most interested in faith as a last bastion of social solidarity nonetheless fail to find creative ways for faith to reimagine the public sphere.

FbRN fails to provide a level of reflexivity regarding the transcendental ideals leading the organisation, the myths through which these ideals are articulated, and the performances through which they are embodied. As a result, there is a clear lack of belonging, becoming and participation. As funding began to run out, staff slowly left. They did not give up voluntary work altogether, but returned to their own distinct communities. This seems to reflect a wider trend amongst multi-faith organisations, of which FbRN was one of the last (Dinham 2012). As I watched this happen, it became apparent that with no clear vision of what multi-faith is, no sense of belonging, becoming or participation could be developed. Instead, multi-faith appears as a funded project that has run its course. This observation links well with Dinham's (2012) point that there is no multi-faith religious creed. I would perhaps be less pessimistic, and suggest that while there is no multi-faith religious creed at present, given the umbrellas constructed by Gary, just one person, it is not inconceivable that a concerted effort from like-minded individuals could drive a movement. Each of Gary's strategies had the potential to be fleshed out and given a greater opportunity to flourish. A good example of this comes from numerous case studies offered by Beaman (2017), in which individuals tell stories of positive encounters with people of different religious and secular backgrounds. There is perhaps scope for imagining such stories of positive encounter themselves becoming multi-faith myths.

Although individual members of FbRN developed a number of practices for navigating the real, messy religious landscape, these appear inconsistent, and it is questionable how powerful each could be in developing belonging, becoming and participation. The overlapping consensus sought in ideas like hospitality is limited to terms already agreed upon. It thus arguably fails to see metanarrative and indeed language itself as a creative process for transforming the world we inhabit. The process of breaking down barriers between religious and secular actors through the use of the term faith remains limited, since faith as a term, no matter how broadly conceived in the abstract, can inspire hostility, as reflections from HCVS demonstrated. Most strikingly, dropping myth altogether denies the place of ontology and its reification in creative language in reimagining who we are and why we are here. If social actors drop myth, it is worth asking whether, rather than reimagining the public sphere and its problems, actors may end up seeking to solve problems that have already been defined for them by somebody else.

Taken together, all of these potential pitfalls seem to be indicative of an organisation operating within a secular, liberal frame. Where there is difference, it must be put to one side rather than creatively overcome. The organisation draws from traditions that are already present as if they are immutable resources, rather than creatively and inclusively building new myths. What seems to be lacking from FbRN, ironically, is a creative process of inclusive ideational construction reified through transformative action. From this perspective, as I will suggest in chapter 3, it might be suggested that multi-faith organisations risk furthering a secular agenda by co-opting faith groups into dual binaries of religious/secular, religion/politics.

London Citizens (LC)

Thus far we have seen how CotL, a Christian group, is able to clearly imagine the relationship between transcendence and solidarity, and articulates transcendence through shared myths that are equally discussed and performed, but cannot relate this to the messiness of the religious landscape as a whole. We have further seen how HCVS, a secular group, displays inklings of a connection between transcendence and solidarity, but lacks the reflexive awareness necessary to critically develop the articulation of ideals through myths and, in so doing, develop belonging, becoming and participation. And we have seen how FbRN, a multi-faith group, failed to imagine how multi-faith might offer a vision for transforming a purely secular idea of the public sphere. I suggested that this failure of imagination risked furthering a secular agenda by co-opting faith groups into dual binaries of religious/secular, religion/politics.

LC offers potential for overcoming these binaries, demonstrating, more comprehensively than FbRN, practices through which transcendence and solidarity can be developed in ways that not only respect but thrive on plurality.

LC articulates its activity as 'working from the world as it is, to the world as it should be'. In this manner, LC reflects Bloch's framework of the transcendental and transactional social. The world as it should be is an imagined ideal of how the world could be ordered and how humans could behave. And this world is constructed in deliberate contradistinction to the world as it is. This is best seen in the following story.

In May 2012 I was sat in a somewhat stuffy room on the second floor of the new Osmani Centre building in Whitechapel, a place in which religious plurality and globalisation are unavoidable. One can stand amidst radical belief and practice diversity, amongst first-, second- and third-generation immigrants, in view of the skyscrapers of the City of London. I was there for a London Citizens Training Event, and sat with 60 people from numerous backgrounds, all with an interest in the public good: middle-aged white male vicars, young North African Muslim female community activists, secular Jewish university students.

We were sat on plastic chairs in a semi-circle, cheated to face a group of three young community organisers dressed in suits without ties – what I call politician-casual.

This diverse group of people is being asked to come up with some words we might associate with the world as it should be: 'Equality', says a young Afro-Caribbean woman. 'No more poverty', says an older white man. 'Respect', says a young man of North African descent.

When enough words have been shared, we are asked to imagine how to get from the world as it is to the world as it should be. We are asked to focus on small, winnable goals. Each of us currently works in an institution. We are asked to consider what we could do in our institution to take a small step in moving from the world as it is to the world as it should be. What began as an abstract but inspirational performance became a concrete set of tasks. Later, I ask one of the community organisers about this task:

> This idea of taking the world as it is, to the world as it should be, what does that mean? What is that world that should be? Are we all thinking about the same world?

Aaron: Definitely not. We're not all thinking about the same world. I don't know if we're even thinking about a world. Because we've not experienced that world. I mean it's the way I think about it. I mean what we do, on the training, is to say, everyone think about the way you think the world should be, and some words that are associated with that world. And they tell you some words and they tend to say things like peace, justice, love, equality, happiness – those kind of things. We've run that course a hundred or more times and those are the same words that come up. We kind of use it to show this diverse group of people that there's enough in common in the way the world should be that they can act together.

But I think if you were to paint with any kind of detail or texture it would become quite difficult because their reference point, they tend to be using certain religions, certain texts, certain ideologies perhaps, that they subscribe to, and they're lifting those words, lifting some of those abstractions I suppose, to offer something towards the common idea of what the world should be. And so while we do talk about the world as it is and the world as it should be, the way we actually move people towards action together, is to find stories that are clearly unjust. And those stories as they're told by the one who's suffering them, everyone feels them in their gut.

We often find ourselves motivating around challenging injustice, and then we come up with a reasonable, winnable statement or goal. We come up with a reasonable goal, which is a good thing, a step in the right direction, a step towards the world as it should be.

Six points are important to take from this story. The first is that the organisers reflexively construct a transcendental framework, drawing on the ethical imagination, appealing to the as-if or subjunctive capacity of the participants to consider a different, better world towards which they are working. This shared imagining of how the world should be trumps rational argument in developing consensus. Second, rather than emphasising any particular ideal, consensus is developed through a generalised transcendental framework, that is, transcendence as such: the world as it should be. Third, this consensus is not rationally constructed but embodied and performed: attendees find a shared identity in their shared desire for peace, justice, love, equality and happiness. We see the beginnings here of a performative postsecularism whereby deconstructing the rational content of shared ideals is less important than the performance of sharing ideals. Fourth, this framework inspires participation not only amongst people of very different religions, but also amongst those of no religion. These training sessions act as a ritual, taking people apart from their ordinary lives in which they may not meet with those of such diverse backgrounds, creating a liminal space in which shared action appears possible. A sense of collective effervescence or communitas develops. Sitting in a semi-circle, we are able to listen to the organiser and observe each other simultaneously. Observing people visibly different from ourselves espousing the same core ideals is an emotive experience that draws us out of our individual and communal identities, creating a sense of shared humanity with shared purpose. Fifth, my use of the term consensus is somewhat precarious. The point to focus on is that achieving consensus as to a fully articulated possible world is considered impossible, and the attempt to do so is considered not only dangerous, but also counterproductive and unnecessary. LC simultaneously seeks to develop solidarity around transcendence as such, the world as it should be, while nonetheless recognising the messiness of the real religious landscape, the world as it is. This exemplifies a crucial development in the connection between myth and solidarity in religiously plural settings: while some notion of transcendence remains core to shared action, to flesh out the rational content of transcendence is not only potentially divisive, but may distract from small, winnable goals. So long as people are aware that they are working together towards a shared world, these actors are free to draw on their diverse religious and nonreligious backgrounds in moving from the world as it is to the world as it should be. Finally, in order to avoid a retrenching along faith, race, nation, gender or economic status, the myths through which shared ideals are articulated are primarily new myths of suffering. The real power is finding stories that are clearly unjust, that people feel in their guts. This development of new myths that can appeal to all participants proves particularly important in bringing people of very different backgrounds together. LC organisers recognise through practice that the way to challenge divisive myths is not through rationally deconstructing those myths, but by providing counter-myths that inspire a sense of solidarity.

One such story of personal suffering comes from Aaron himself. When I ask him if any particular values motivate him to act, Aaron explains that:

> I've never been one for values as they exist in particular words . . . The experiences I've had which are meaningful to me . . . Growing up . . . the massive gulf between the environments, the chances and the choices, the quality of life that different friends of mine had from different sides of the divide. So some of those friends were growing up in a council estate in Clapham Junction, on the 15th floor, with a single-parent mum who worked all the time, and a younger sister that they cared for. And they went to a school where sometimes the classes were so disrupted that you couldn't really learn. But they really wanted to learn, you know, he was a conscientious student, good footballer, but, you know, for him to make a success of himself in academia was taking a super-human effort on his part, to balance all the things that he had to balance. And then, I think of other friends I had, who were growing up in a 2 million pound mansion house in Dulwich Village, and they went to a private school, and when they turned 17 they got bought a car, and if they were selling weed they were doing it out of that car to kids with very little risk to themselves. So I guess you could say, yeah that's

equality, I believe in equality, I believe in equality of opportunity, you know, those things. But those words aren't particularly . . . I don't hold them up, it's more the experiences.

Aaron shows a reflexive awareness that the transcendental ideal that he aims at is equality. In this Aaron shares his motivations with members of HCVS and FbRN and equality again appears as a crossover narrative. But Aaron is clear that it is the myths through which this ideal is articulated that inspire solidarity – not the rational content of equality. Through retelling, these experiences become an embodied performance of solidarity. With this level of reflexivity, Aaron is able to push through the religious/secular, mythic/rational binary by developing and enacting his own secular myths.

Aaron's ability to tell his story so succinctly is shared amongst all members of LC, and is derived from a practice considered core to the organisation's work: one-to-ones. Exploring the nature of one-to-ones can help us to understand a level of reflexivity on the part of LC that, unlike HCVS, allows them to carry their ideals into embodied practices that inspire solidarity.

Ivereigh (2010: 57) has described one-to-ones as 'an exercise in hearing each other's stories, and finding out what we each care about'. The telling of these stories itself creates a sense of ritual whereby transcendental ideals are performed, and an alternative to the world as it is can be offered:

> because contemporary society does not allow people time to listen to others' stories, their hopes and fears – at least not outside a narrow circle of friends and family – we have lost the habit that would have been natural to previous generations.
>
> (ibid.)

One-to-ones act as a ritual that awakens people to their own ideals and the stories through which these are articulated.

Now it is also worth noting that one-to-ones are a method of luring people in by sharing vulnerabilities. As Katrina, an experienced organiser, put it to me, 'It was only after the training that I was able to look back on my first conversation with an organiser and realise I'd been one-to-oned'. I will reflect further on the manipulative aspects of some LC tactics, and the implications for solidarity in chapter 4. Here the point I want to focus on is that one-to-ones are a deliberate process of constructing stories that inspire, and of unlocking the 'self-interest' of one's interlocutor so as to appeal to this self-interest in future collaborations. But the reflexively constructed nature of one-to-ones does not make them less authentic. Partly, this is because these stories still draw on real emotional experiences that drive the beholder to act. But more fundamentally, a different idea of truth is at work. Like training sessions, one-to-ones point to the development of a performative post-secularism: it is not simply that we perform processes of belonging with people of different religious and secular backgrounds, but that performance itself is key. Stressing performance implies a different approach to ontology and epistemology, whereby the truth of a narrative is not derived from its corresponding to an objective world, from its rational content, but from the kind of performances it inspires.

One-to-ones create a connection between the world as it should be – the transcendental social – and the world as it is – the transactional social. While the telling of one-to-ones is aimed at inspiring people to act in the interests of the world as it should be, they are drawn from difficult experiences in the world as it is. One-to-ones are thus simultaneously a means of reflexively constructing myth to develop belonging, becoming and participation within the group and, by engaging with the world as it is, a pragmatic basis for engaging the messy religious landscape.

A similar process of developing myths that both construct belonging and becoming and appeal to the messy religious landscape can be found in the veneration of great figures. In my time at LC, a number of key individuals were rendered exemplars, from self-identifying community organisers like Saul Alinsky, Ed Chambers and Barack Obama, to great people of history such as Mahatma Gandhi or Martin Luther King. Exemplar status was cultivated through discussion of these figures, of their many sacrifices or their meteoric rise to positions of status or power. These figures and their deeds would be discussed on journeys to and from meetings, and sometimes their biographies would be handed from one member of staff to another, as a prize for hard work, as a birthday or Christmas present, or simply as a gesture of goodwill. These figures again recall Robbin's (2015) notion of exemplars; they seem to transcend transactional reality and demonstrate the possibility of a more ethical way of life, thus aiding actors in the process of becoming more ethical themselves.

As at CotL, this exemplar status was also cultivated by, and attributed to, people working at present. Organisers would tell stories of their prowess, with one telling me how he managed to recruit four dues-paying members in one afternoon, having recently completed a pub lunch. More frequently, organisers would talk of their sacrifice: their inability to see friends, the many hours they had worked without pay, the fact that they were giving up their weekends.

By constructing these secular exemplars, organisers also gained an understanding of religious exemplars, albeit from within the framework of their own secular myths. This led to a process of *bricolage* whereby secular organisers reflexively drew on the stories of characters they recognised as religious to draw inspiration for their own stories.

This reflexive awareness became key to developing parity between religious and secular citizens. When seeking to recruit Jews, Christians or Muslims, organisers would often mention that Jesus Christ or the Prophet Muhammad were heroic community organisers. They would draw parity between their own myths and those of others, creating the possibility of shared myths across religious and nonreligious difference, as well as in the process further deifying great community organisers and themselves; if Jesus and Muhammad were community organisers, so Alinksy, Obama and Aaron are just the latest prophets. Rather than appealing to people purely on the basis of the efficiency of community organising as a practice, or else on purely secular reasons, organisers developed an element of multilingualism, drawing on myths to create a sense of parity between actors from very different backgrounds.

This multilingualism has to be quite fluent. LC organisers often have to *ad lib* translate the rationale of their work into the myths of those they want to bring on board. At one training session, we had just been introduced to the concept of one-to-ones, when a vicar put up his hand and took umbrage with the use of the term self-interest, which, he explained, constructed the world and people's motivations as entirely instrumental. He rounded off his tirade by asking, 'What, please tell me, is my self-interest?' Without missing a beat, the organiser who had first brought the vicar on board replied 'bringing about the kingdom of heaven'. This ability to navigate the myths of those they wanted to bring on board was common amongst LC organisers. This ability inverts Habermas translation process, placing the burden on secular actors to make their ideals tangible to religious actors. We might call this process a suspension of disbelief.

This multilingualism also legitimises organisers in steering people away from theological conflict to shared needs in shared spaces. Sarah tells me of a time she was trying to bring together Jews and Muslims to campaign for safer streets in their neighbourhood. In the midst of the campaign, there had been an attack on Israel by a Palestinian. At first, disagreement between the two groups seemed interminable, and it seemed the campaign would not go ahead. But then Sarah offered a very simple argument: 'Okay', she said, 'you may not be able to agree on Israel and Palestine, but you can agree that this street needs better lighting'. This very simple point brought the two groups back together, reminding them of the very practical achievements they had already made. Sarah told me that she used the same strategy when trying to assuage conflict between groups with differing political ideologies, which often flare up during election periods. Sarah's simple insight demonstrates how theological and ideological conflict can be overcome by drawing people back to shared needs in shared spaces. That these shared needs are available speaks to Knott's (2009) point that on some level, people of different religions in a single area will often share more in common than with people of the same religion elsewhere. The focus on shared needs in shared spaces demonstrates what might be called a pragmatic secularity of place: actors are pressed to recognise that 'religion is no more than a secondary concern' given the needs in their area (Lee 2015: 19).

It needs to be stressed, however, that this multilingualism is not without controversy. I came across numerous secular activists who were entirely turned off by LC on the basis of what they saw as 'religious favouritism'. A number of LC meetings, for instance, are held in churches on the grounds that they have a big capacity and can often be used without charge. But little consideration is given to the discomfort this may cause to secular activists. Others express awkward feelings regarding LC's 'cult-like' behaviour, which they feel reproduce the worst aspects of organised religion. In this sense, the very rituals here being positively reviewed cause some people discomfort.

Notwithstanding these concerns, I suggest that the work of LC demonstrates the complex but pragmatic ways in which an organisation can revive a relationship between myth and solidarity in a plural world. Partly, what LC shows is that in a plural world, the particular narrative we choose is less important than the processes through which it is cultivated. Yet in order to get to the world as it should be, LC recognises that people must work with the world as it is. In particular, this means offering what I called 'a pragmatic secularity of place', whereby people are steered away from theological and ideological conflict to focus on shared needs in shared spaces. Perhaps this must include explaining to secular actors the practical advantages of meeting in religious buildings. In order to be effective in a messy religious landscape, I have made clear that pragmatic secularity needs to be supplemented with a level of religious literacy, that is, an ability to navigate people's individual theologies and translate one's arguments into a language one's interlocutor can relate to. This must include an appreciation of the concerns of secular people. But members of LC, including secular members, are also doing more than merely demonstrating skills of translation: they are also creatively navigating a diverse world of stories and developing a porous pastiche of prophetic stories that inspire them. It is this complex intertwining of (post-) Christian, (post)secular and religiously plural attitudes that makes LC so well suited to the messiness of the real religious landscape. It is this complex intertwining that I have elsewhere called 'performative postsecularism' (Stacey 2017a).

Conclusion: reimagining the relationship between myth and solidarity in pluralist settings

This chapter opened by suggesting that postliberal and liberal theory alike risk reproducing a religious/secular, mythic/rational binary that forecloses possibilities for reimagining the relationship between transcendence and solidarity in religiously plural settings. I said that this binary was problematic for both religious actors, since they become excluded on the basis of their failing to meet secular standards of rationality, and for secular actors, since the complex ways in which they construct transcendence are overlooked. The point of this chapter, I explained, was to seek an alternative.

I opened the section on social theory by exploring Comte. While Comte's call for a religion of humanity seems unrealistic given the messiness of the real religious landscape, I suggested that it provides a useful starting point for thinking imaginatively about what a post-Christian connection between transcendence and solidarity might look like at the level of society. I then pitched Tonnies as Comte's opposite. I suggested that Tonnies reproduced a subtraction story from Christendom to modern instrumentalism, being too idealistic about the past and too pessimistic about possibilities for reimagining the connection between myth and solidarity in the present.

Between these two extremes, I argued that the creative thinking of Durkheim, Turner, Anderson, Bellah and Habermas had emerged. These thinkers explored the possibility of founding transcendence in the individual, in the nation, in the economy, and in communicative action. Yet I argued that these thinkers brought numerous problems of their own, whether reducing the sacred to the social and thus leaving no space for ethical considerations, relying on a cult of the individual that seemed questionable in its capacity to develop solidarity, or reproducing a religious/secular, mythic/rational binary.

I then turned to two recent developments: postsecular rapprochement and the ethical turn in anthropology. I suggested that theories of postsecular rapprochement demonstrate how religious and secular actors themselves had offered possibilities for pushing through a religious/secular, mythic/rational binary by developing crossover narratives, and by paying less attention to ontological or epistemological difference, and more to the positive results of various myths, religious and secular, as they are performed. And I suggested that the ethical turn in anthropology cuts through the religious/secular, mythic/rational binary by suggesting that tradition and narrative always provide the basis of ethical action. This discussion also provided a way of understanding that something is missing from a purely secular idea of the public sphere without treating religion generally, or any particular religion as special, namely, using Bloch's framework of the transcendental and transactional social. Together these developments demonstrated how theorists too often pay attention to the difficulties in reconciling abstractions, rather than to the complex ways in which people on the ground pragmatically navigate difference in the search for solidarity.

I then explored this theory in the context of social change. The key point was that social theory is too simplistic to grapple with the reality of what is really happening on the ground. While theories emerge that move the connection between transcendence and solidarity from a Christian, to a secular, to a postsecular frame, the reality is that both the landscape as a whole, and individual people within it, are often simultaneously (post-)Christian, (post)secular and religiously plural. I encapsulated this idea in a phrase: the messiness of the real religious landscape.

I considered that one way of exploring how best to engage with the messiness of the real religious landscape is to ask which religions have proved most successful within that landscape. This approach proved problematic, however, given scholarly disagreement. Some suggested that liberal religions were the most successful. This seemed problematic for reimagining the connection between transcendence and solidarity, since a religion that offers no higher authority than individual beliefs and lifestyles might only reflect, rather than transform the public sphere. Others suggested that conservative religions were more successful. This suggestion seemed problematic since while such groups may create a strong sense of internal solidarity, as well as offering a distinctive vision, they may struggle to engage the messiness of the real religious landscape.

Finally, I drew on Pink-Dandelion's research into Quakers to suggest a possible third way: rather than focusing on orthodoxy, right belief, organisations may inspire a strong sense of belonging and becoming by focusing on orthopraxy, or right practice.

My ethnography aimed to draw these two studies together by analysing how the connection between transcendence and solidarity has been imagined and performed by four groups indicatively representing four paradigms: Christian, secular, multi-faith and postsecular. A number of key concepts emerged in the process. In particular I stressed that if transcendence is key to solidarity, then myth is key to how transcendence is articulated.

My exploration of CotL demonstrated that transcendence acts as an imaginative ideal that is articulated through myth, related to reflexively and primarily performed. The idea of spreading myth through performance I called performative evangelism. I stressed that performative evangelism not only created a sense of liminal space around the performers, creating possibilities of belonging, but also inspired others to undergo processes of becoming more ethical beings themselves: what I called 'missional community'. Finally, I suggested that the reflexive manner in which members of CotL carried their myths, alongside their stress on performance, assisted them in appealing to people of different religious and secular backgrounds. I suggested that this approach spoke to Pink-Dandelion's stress on orthopraxy as a means of developing solidarity in the messiness of the real religious landscape. I stressed, however, that notwithstanding their reflexivity, the Christian narrative so central to CotL would inevitably alienate people of other religious and secular backgrounds.

My exploration of HCVS shed further light on the notion of reflexivity. I said that while members of HCVS seemed to operate out of a religious/ secular, mythic/rational binary, their motivations seemed to confound this binary. I suggested that secular actors operate out of transcendental ideals, in the case of HCVS equality. I thus claimed that the distinction between religious and secular motivations is not categorical but qualitative: it is not, I said, by virtue of their secularity that secular actors lack critically constructed myths and associated performances, but by virtue of their reflexivity. It is this lack of reflexivity that thus hampered HCVS' ability to construct processes of belonging, becoming and participation.

At FbRN, although members saw faith as an important resource for developing solidarity, they could not offer clarity as to how faith might be employed in the public sphere to generate solidarity. Instead, their position appeared to be one of opening up a secular public sphere to draw on faith as a resource. This seemed the more surprising because individual members of FbRN offered practices that seemed to offer alternatives to a purely secular idea of the public sphere. I suggested that this failure of imagination risked furthering a secular agenda by co-opting faith groups into dual binaries of religious/secular, religion/politics.

My exploration of LC offered opportunities for overcoming these binaries while not only recognising but thriving on plurality. I argued that by distinguishing between the world as it should be and the world as it is, LC is able to stand outside of parochial notions of transcendence to offer a reflexively constructed framework of transcendence as such. This broad umbrella allows people to rediscover what is missing from a purely secular idea of the public sphere without treating either religion generally, or any particular religion as special. Emphasising this idea of transcendence as such, LC organisers use the notion of the world as it should be to curate a performance of shared concern, while assiduously avoiding fleshing out the rational content of the world as it should be. I explained that to focus on this rational content would not only create potential conflict, but would also distract social actors from small, winnable goals. Yet I also demonstrated that to flesh out the rational content of the world as it should be would miss the point. It is not rational argument but emotive stories that form the core of motivation amongst those associated with LC. From this perspective, performance one again became key: focusing on performance allows people to pay less attention to ontological or epistemological difference, and more to the positive results of religious and secular myths in practice. Once performance is treated is key, it also became clear how people were able to develop *bricolage*, drawing on various myths to inspire performances of solidarity. These myths are often contradictory in terms of rational content alone and instead find convergence through the performances of solidarity they inspire.

At the beginning of this chapter I suggested that since myth is evident equally amongst religious and secular actors, the question is not whether myth has a role in public life, but what kinds of myth and how and by whom they should be constructed. The evidence from my case studies supports this case and offers a possible answer to the question of how and by whom myth should be constructed in pluralist settings.

The key point I have been trying to make is that the transcendental social is articulated through myth: we tell stories of extraordinary events and people that open up a path to a better way of living; and that ethics is the process of emulating, honouring, or as I prefer, *performing* these stories.

Myth seems to be a way of taking hopeful acts and stories to gain a positive spin on the human situation, on the possibility of a better way of living. Kahneman (2011) has said that humans make poor statisticians: we tend to extrapolate from anecdotal evidence to general rules. Perhaps my exploration of myth shows that this predilection for poor statistics is essential to the human capacity to imagine a better way of living: finding hope in those little moments of goodness that Ralph calls 'little bits of heaven' – moments that in common parlance we say 'restore our faith in humanity'.

If myth can be a way of restoring our faith in humanity, then what those operating from within the religious/secular, mythic/rational binary perceive to be the constraints of myth, ontological and epistemological, may actually be key enablers of the ethical imagination.

Indeed, and perhaps counter-intuitively given Habermas' suggestion that religion must become reflexive if it is to have legitimacy in pluralist settings, it is specifically religious actors that seem to display reflexivity regarding myth and secular actors that seem least equipped with this reflexivity. Yet this idea is only counter-intuitive from the perspective of a religious/secular, mythic/rational binary. If religion is held to have a monopoly on myth, and myth is considered irrational, then secular reason becomes the standard of reflexive awareness. But if secular actors too seem to operate on the basis of myth, then to lack reflexivity regarding the way that myth operates becomes problematic, not only for mutual understanding between religious and secular actors, but for the self-understanding of secular actors and their ability to develop processes of belonging, becoming and participation.

My exchange with Frank at HCVS points to where this lack of reflexivity might come from. Frank seems to have quite neatly imbibed the myth of liberalism outlined by so many scholars, namely, that to believe in anything too strongly is dangerous (Asad 2003). Rather than being merely a subconscious secularist, Frank might be better characterised as a subconscious liberal, asserting that any belief held too strongly is liable to lead to violence. Caught in a religious/secular, mythic/rational binary, Frank's attitude illustrates something essential about liberalism itself and the worldviews of those living within it: liberalism is that myth that denies it is a myth. Instead, it is grounded in a supposedly purely rational interpretation of what humans are capable and, more importantly, incapable, when they live side by side with people of different beliefs. As the myth that denies it is a myth, liberalism forecloses the possibility of reflexivity about the myths that drive us.

My experience at HCVS demonstrates that this rationality myth is its own worst enemy. By grounding ethics in clearly defined rules, rather than in character, people are led to follow the letter of the law, but not its spirit. Instead, myth is just that spirit behind the law, offering stories of inspiration as to how we should live. To disobey a law is to disobey an external constraint, but to disobey a myth, if it is believed in, is to deny one's own character.

My exploration begins to confound the liberal idea that we are incapable of living side by side with people of different beliefs. It demonstrates that the role of constructing myth is not, as Comte might suggest if he were alive today, for postsecular priests, but for ordinary people. Better than theorists, ordinary people seem to be able to cut through abstractions, simultaneously reflexively constructing their own myths that inspire a better way of living, and recognising the parity between their myths and those of other people. Where inclusive spaces are provided, people are able to embrace the messiness of the real religious landscape. They do so by suspending their disbelief and judging myths less by the ontological or epistemological differences they indicate and more by the performances of belonging, becoming and participation they tend to produce. Reimagining the connection between myth and solidarity may not require a rationally constructed idea of postsecularism, with clear rules, perhaps of inclusion, to be followed. Instead, perhaps what is required is a creative and embodied, performative postsecularism aimed at developing the kinds of characters that can thrive on plurality in the search for positive myths about the possibility of a better way of living. The implications of this performative postsecularism for the state and the market will be the focus of chapters 3 and 4 respectively.

3　Myth, solidarity and the state

If there is to be a shared sense of transcendence in a world of radical diversity of belief and practice, it will come from the curation of inclusive spaces in which people of all religions and none can reflexively recognise, draw on and share their own myths; find synthesis between their myths and those of others; cobble these together; embody them; and explore them through the performances they inspire. How to reconcile this fact with the political landscape facing us at present? People retrench into faith, race, nation, gender and class. They hold onto and sow myths of division, seeking to empower themselves and their identity through the construction and rejection of some dangerous other. And this alienation seems underscored by, if not directly attributable to, a politics that thinks ordinary people unworthy of trust, consumed by dangerous myths, a self-fulfilling assumption that facilitates and then confirms its own rule. In short, how can we envisage a functioning relationship between myth, solidarity and the state in spaces of radical diversity of belief and practice, in a world in which neither the state trusts the people, nor the people the state? This chapter seeks to answer this question.

As explained in chapter 1, postliberal theory suggests that the perceived impossibility of shared transcendence led to the construction of the state as a means of rationally adjudicating between the various and conflicting demands of disparate individuals and communities. The state then comes to impose a paradoxically de-normativised, rational idea of solidarity that not only fails to inspire people, but that also undermines the traditional resources of solidarity that are already available in intermediary institutions by challenging their legitimacy. I explained that this view is disquieting, since either we seek to revive a shared Christian outlook, which seems neither desirable nor possible in a religiously plural context, or we take a de-normativised anti-statist stance, which might end up being indistinguishable from neoliberalism. Such an association would be anathema to postliberals who regard neoliberalism as the culmination of the right liberal project, undermining solidarity by reifying purely economic incentive to the centre of human motivation.

Chapter 2 then suggested that its oscillation between Christianity and secular rationalisations led postliberal theory to unwittingly collude with liberal theory in the construction of a religious/secular, mythic/rational binary. More than simply suggesting that this binary emerges when we undermine or undervalue the rationality of religious narratives, a point already well established in sociology (Fitzgerald 2011: 11–14) and anthropology (Asad 2003), I stressed that the binary may also emerge when we undermine or undervalue the mythic strength of secular narratives. More importantly still, I suggested that this binary neglects the parity between religious and secular narratives, ignoring shared normativities that are already available and foreclosing opportunities for creative encounters between people of radically different belief and practice backgrounds.

This chapter draws this critique into an exploration of postliberal ideas of the state. As with chapter 2, I slowly develop a complex conversation between postliberal theory and lived realities by: placing postliberal theory into dialogue with predominantly liberal social theory; placing both of these into dialogue with the recent history of social policy in the UK; and, finally, exploring original ethnographic research to demonstrate how policy in the UK is reflected in the lived realities of activists.

As explained in chapter 2, because postliberal theory is normative rather than simply empirical, the aim of creating a conversation between this theory and reality is not to credit or discredit the former. Rather, the idea is to ask whether postliberalism may have resonance in terms of what can be observed about the state and its impact on lived realities. Where crediting or discrediting comes in, however, is when those normative accounts rely on assumptions about the state that can be empirically explored. Hence I focus on the empirically explorable claims that the modern liberal state arose in the context of the perceived impossibility of solidarity rooted in a shared notion of transcendence, and that this construction of the state itself undermines the possibility of shared transcendence. The claim I move to make in this chapter is that while it seems inaccurate, or at least a claim in need of major nuancing, to suggest that "the state", whatever that is, arose in the context of a lack of transcendentally anchored solidarity, still it does seem plausible to suggest that the modern liberal state potentially undermines the possibility of such solidarity by failing to believe in the capacity of ordinary people.

Rather than entertaining postliberal ideas by giving space to authors that clearly fit their critique, I focus on those predominantly liberal social theorists that demonstrate a degree of ambivalence: theorists that have recognised the importance of religion in the construction of the state, but who, in the face of religious plurality have sought to replace religion with secular narratives and procedures. My exploration of these authors will lead to a critical reappraisal of the postliberal position, once again placing the religious/secular, mythic/rational binary front and centre. I will suggest that, confronted by religious plurality, social theorists cast religion as hegemonic and as prone to inciting violence, and the secular as capable of emancipating individuals from the control of religions and peripheral social groups and redirecting these newly emancipated individuals towards a potentially universal basis for solidarity. Yet, challenging postliberal and predominantly liberal social theory alike, more recent research suggests that a mythic element is always present, and that the question is not whether the state should be religious or secular, but how, where and by whom its mythic component should be constructed.

Literature in social policy paints a similar picture. The shared religious history of the Anglo-Saxon West outlined in chapter 2 contributed to a shared political landscape. The late 19th and early 20th centuries saw the political landscape dominated by the development of a Protestant-driven capitalist entrepreneurship combined with extraordinary charitable activity. In the post-depression and post-war years, capitalism was tempered by a social democratic consensus which involved – much more fundamentally in the UK, to a lesser extent in Canada and still less in the US – empowering unions, undertaking largescale industrial projects and expanding welfare provision. This consensus was underpinned by a Christian spirit of association and involved co-opting charitable institutions into the auspices of the state. Yet with the rise of secular discourses in the 1980s and 90s, this solidarity was undermined, such that in an age in which the state is now under threat, there is very little spirit left to draw on.

The social democratic consensus of the 1960s, confronted with the fall of the Berlin Wall and the supposed 'end of history' has given way to a neoliberal consensus in which the role of the state is radically called into question by both left and right (Judt 2010). This shift is particularly demonstrated by 'Third Way' socialism whereby parties of the traditional left – British New Labour in the UK, the Democrats in the US and the New Democrats in Canada – recognise the inevitability and primacy of capitalist economics. Even those who still hold onto the state as the key source of solidarity are confronted with what has been called the progressive's dilemma: how to maintain egalitarian ideas about social justice as well as a relatively open attitude towards migration and migrant integration (Kymlicka 2015). Alongside this, the power of the state increasingly pales in comparison with global market forces to the extent that it has been suggested ours is a time of interregnum, in which the rulers no longer can rule and the ruled no longer wish to be ruled (Baumann 2012). This shift has been met by disillusionment on the part of large swathes of the population, who no longer believe in the ability or credibility of mainstream politics to answer the problems they face. Both nonconventional political protest movements and anti-globalisation populist politicians and parties are on the rise across the globe.

These problems are exasperated by the fact that religion has diversified and changed in many complex ways since we last paid attention. No longer can religious leaders – archbishops in the UK and Canada, theologians and popular preachers in the US – call a wide populace of Christians to social action (Dinham 2014). Not only are there fewer Christians, but those that remain are less likely to believe in hierarchy (see chapter 2).

Yet today, new spaces for engagement between people of all religions and none do seem to be opening up, both within and beyond the state. So the question becomes, what role can the state play in encouraging these spaces and the actors in them?

At this point my ethnographic findings step in. These findings suggest three key ideas. First, operating within the state is not inherently destructive of mythic ways of relating to the world. Even from within the state machinery it is possible to maintain mythic narratives of solidarity that challenge the processes of rationalisation that undermine human relationships. This is partly because actors recognise that the boundaries between state and society are far more blurred and porous than theories allow (Gupta 2006). Actors within the state are able to use this porousness to their advantage, bringing in actors from the outside. Yet processes of rationalisation and neoliberalism remain widespread. In this context, the second key idea is that if people within the state's sphere of influence do not have reflexively constructed, mythic narratives of their own, their ideational framings become 'up-for-grabs' as Taylor puts it, and they have no counter-narrative with which to challenge processes of rationalisation and neoliberalism. Indeed, they end up being complicit in imposing these processes upon grassroots activists. This idea becomes more striking when the state insists on these processes even as it recognises and seeks to involve religions as important retainers of solidarity. As a result, rather than creating the dynamic relationship between state and religions envisaged by some thinkers, processes of rationalisation and neoliberalism end up colonising and being imbibed by religious actors, who then impose these same processes on others, thus undermining idiosyncratic framings and performances of solidarity. Third, and building on findings from chapter 2, it is not necessary to consider this a zero-sum game. It is perfectly possible to envisage a state able to simultaneously acknowledge the importance of mythic elements of solidarity, and to empower and enable inclusive, independent exploration of myths and the kinds of performances they entail. Those working within the state need to place faith in the evidence available at the grassroots.

It must be made clear that what I end up arguing for is not a simplistically idealist understanding of either solidarity or the state. Rather, I suggest that the transcendent component of solidarity in relation to the state has been too often neglected, treated as impossible, or regarded as something that the state imposes in order to maintain pernicious control. I want to suggest that while this ambivalence about transcendental solidarity in the face of plurality is important, the consequence of neglecting the former, far from providing succour from hegemony, is to allow hegemony to go uncontested, or else allow solidarity to atrophy. I do counterpoise the mythic against the discursively rational, treating the former as a safeguard against excesses of the latter, but two disclaimers are important: first, as with chapter 2, my notion of the mythic pushes through a religious/secular, mythic/rational binary, suggesting that the rationality of myth is found less in its discursive content than in the performances it inspires; and that both religious and secular actors and institutions are capable of reflexively constructing the mythic narratives that inspire performances of solidarity. Second, the point of myth is that it ignites *people*. Emphasising any particular myth is of secondary importance to the processes by which it is constructed: of the people, for the people, by the people. Any conception of either solidarity or the state, mythic or rational, is not only liable to hegemony but to failure, if it does not creatively involve the people in its construction.

Social theory: constructing the state

The key theorists challenged by postliberals are Hobbes, Hegel, Marx, Durkheim and Weber. Here, I leave out Hobbes since his writing so neatly exemplifies the postliberal critique as to render discussion a waste of the reader's time (see chapter 1). In terms of the other theorists, much as postliberals have suggested, the defining context is religious plurality and conflict. In this context, theorists seek to establish the state as the sole vestige of solidarity. The key component that I want to add to this narrative is the construction of a religious/secular, mythic/rational binary, whereby religion is regarded as irrational, mythical, ritualistic and, since every individual has a different take on religion, prone to inciting violence, and whereby the secular is perceived as rational, capable of emancipating individuals from the control of religions and peripheral social groups and redirecting these newly emancipated individuals towards a potentially universal basis for solidarity. Yet two points are in order. First, each of these thinkers shows a greater degree of sympathy for the important role of myth in developing solidarity than postliberals acknowledge. Paying attention to the processes for constructing solidarity that these theorists have emphasised is thus crucial to redeveloping solidarity in a religiously plural context. Second, later theory challenges the religious/secular, mythic/rational binary, suggesting that the mythic component is always present, providing the state with a means of social control. On the basis of this proposition, it is suggested that the question is not whether the state should be religious or secular, but how and by whom the mythic component should be constructed.

Re-anchoring solidarity in rationality: mutual self-interest and the founding of the state

Hegel exemplifies the ambivalence towards religion found in predominantly liberal social theory. Avineri (1972) contests that any exploration of Hegel's theory of the state must begin with his glorification of the Greek polis for 'its integration of the religious and the political into one totality' (ibid: 31): 'each individual . . . had "the picture of the state as a product of his own energies"' (ibid: 20). Yet notwithstanding this glorification, Hegel is clear that the polis represents a moment in history to which we cannot, and should not hope to return (ibid: 22). We cannot return to the polis because the introduction of Christianity has raised our subjective consciousness – unlike past religions, Christianity emphasises the autonomy of the individual subject (ibid: 225). And we should not hope to return to the polis since, for all its shortcomings, not least the emergence of unfettered self-interest, subjective consciousness creates the possibility of a more ethical polity, whereby people are not integrated into the political system out of ignorance of their own subjectivity, but rather because of their subjectivity (ibid: 226–228). Yet in order to achieve the necessary level of consciousness, it is eventually necessary to move beyond even Christianity, which is based on feeling rather than rationality, and which tends to treat 'worldly interests' with 'indifference' (Hegel 1821/1991: 291). The truly self-conscious individual will thus move beyond religion to recognise the universal, rational basis of solidarity, namely, the parity between her own self-interest and the interest of society at large (Avineri 1972: 87; Hegel 1821/1991: 290–296). This newly integrated polity is what Hegel calls the *sittlichkeit*, or ethical life. The role of the state is to educate citizens into their role in this new ethical life (Avineri 1972: 99, 101–104, 124).

For Milbank, Hegel's analysis is normatively insufficient (Milbank 1990/2006: 168). This is because any pretension of genuine reconciliation is always undergirded by self-interest: 'Personal striving is really in the interest of collective purpose, and yet Hegel defines this collective purpose precisely in terms of the making to coincide of public and private interest' (Milbank 1990/2006: 171; see also Jailobaeva 2007: 5). Because human self-interest is ultimately unavoidable, the true *sittlichkeit* can never be achieved. Hence, suggests Milbank, Hegel comes to stress the importance of policing and punishment as means of forcibly cultivating solidarity.

It may be contended that Milbank misunderstands Hegel, placing too much emphasis on Hegel's ideas regarding the state proper and not enough on Hegel's ideas about the role of corporations in acting as intermediaries between the state and the individual. Avineri (1972) points out that Hegel consistently warns against the encroachment of an overbearing state (44–49; 101–103; 171–172). Moreover, for Hegel it is also in corporations that individuals become educated in the universal (78, 160, 162, 164–168). Hegel emphasises an ongoing hermeneutic between the state and corporations and between corporations and individuals. Yet at whatever level we look, the focus on enlightened self-interest remains. The role of corporations, for instance, is for individuals to realise that their own self-interest is connected to those that share their trade (164–168). It is moreover, worth noting that Milbank himself comes to rely on these same secular rationalisations in his own discussions of the state (see chapter 1). Thus it might be better to amend Milbank's critique: the problem is not so much that Hegel legitimises state violence but rather that his notion of solidarity is only valid insofar as individuals really do see their own interests aligning with those of others and the state as the best vehicle for realising these shared interests. Insofar as solidarity is rooted in rationality alone, then when either of these criteria are compromised, people opt out – a development Dore (2002) has recognised in the trade union movement.

Based on findings from chapter 2, Hegel's shortcoming might be better understood from a slightly different perspective: not as normatively insufficient, but as empirically insufficient. Hegel constructs a religious/secular, mythic/rational binary, casting myth as an unnecessary component in developing solidarity given the development of reason. Having first glorified the Greek polis and the role of myth, Hegel later stresses that the emergence of subjectivity, and consequently religious pluralism, demands that religion be separated from politics. Yet this is all for the better, since anyway only reason can bring about the *sittlichkeit* (Avineri 1972: 72, 169, 193). I contend that Hegel is too optimistic about reason, too negligent of myth, and too pessimistic about the possibility of instantiating inclusive processes for constructing myth in pluralist settings.

A standard reading of Marx offers two key revisions of the Hegelian perspective. First, he suggests that rather than acting as the fulfilment of ethical life, the state always reflects particular interests: in the case of capitalist societies, the interests of the bourgeoisie (Hay 1999). Although the socialist state will provide a necessary step towards the process of integrating the individual into ethical life, once this new way of being is achieved, the state will no longer be necessary (Ollman 1977). Second, far from merely rejecting myth, Marx rejects the ideational as a means of achieving solidarity. It is not simply that myth loses its role to the ongoing development of reason, but that ideas themselves are always shaped by material conditions, and thus the search for ideological, or what I have been calling 'transcendental' solidarity is a distraction from the search for material solidarity. Instead, material solidarity informs transcendental solidarity. It is only in recognising that communist society will be materially better that the individual begins to reintegrate herself into society.

The Marxist narrative is challenged by both Durkheim and Weber. By Durkheim, primarily on the Hegelian grounds that state and society may develop a symbiotic relationship in which the interests of both society at large and particular groups can be represented; by Weber, on the grounds that the transcendental remains fundamental to energising social action.

For Durkheim, the state plays a dual function. First, it emancipates individuals 'from the control of peripheral social groups and local allegiances as well as from the hold of the church' (Badie and Birnbaum 1983: 14). Second, having thus emancipated individuals, the state then re-comports individuals towards the public good. Yet Durkheim's state will not comport individuals towards the public good by means of control. Rather, it does so by cultivating the same critically engaged public by which it will be held accountable. Palumbo and Scott (2003: 377) demonstrate that this ideal is expressed in education, which should be aimed at developing moral individuals, and in professional organisations such as trade unions and guilds. As to the latter, Durkheim is quite clear that these must be formed outside of the state:

> A society made up of an extremely large mass of unorganised individuals, which an overgrown state attempts to limit and restrain, constitutes a veritable sociological monstrosity. For collective activity is always too complex to be capable of finding expression in the one single organ of the state. Moreover, the state is too remote from individuals, its connections with them too superficial and irregular, to be able to penetrate the depths of their consciousness and socialise them from within. This is why, when the state constitutes the sole environment in which men can fit themselves for the business of living in common, they inevitably 'contract out', detaching themselves from one another, and thus society disintegrates to a corresponding extent. A nation cannot be maintained unless, between the state and individuals, a whole range of secondary groups are interposed.
>
> (Durkheim 1902/1984: liv)

By thus emphasising the importance of these secondary groups between the state and the individual, Durkheim fits quite neatly with postliberal theory. Yet Durkheim makes clear that it will be for statesmen to formulate the policy for developing secondary groups (Durkheim 1902/1984: l). Moreover, these groups will in turn become the means by which the state itself is transformed:

> Now that the commune, from being the autonomous unit that it once was, has been absorbed into the state just as the municipal market was absorbed into the national market, may we not legitimately think that the corporation should also undergo a corresponding transformation and become the elementary division of the state, the basic political unit? Society, instead of remaining what it is today – a conglomerate of land masses juxtaposed together – would become a vast system of national corporations. The demand is raised in various quarters for electoral colleges to be constituted by professions and not by territorial constituencies. Certainly in this way political assemblies would more accurately reflect the diversity of social interests and their interconnections. They would more exactly epitomise social life as a whole.
>
> (Durkheim 1902/1984: liii)

What Durkheim offers then, is a state that develops a critically engaged public, that encourages that critically engaged public to develop secondary groups, and that is in turn constituted by representatives of these groups. For Durkheim these secondary groups are not only legitimate settings for cultivating solidarity, not only provide opportunities for critically engaging the masses in the cultivation process, but also become central to the modern state.

Thus far, Durkheim sounds entirely materialist in his analysis of solidarity, though as a reading of chapter 1 will attest, not too far from postliberals themselves (Coser 1984: xviii; Marske 1987: 4). Yet as has already been detailed in chapter 2, Durkheim later develops a notion of the cult of the individual, wherein the human person enjoys a sacred status such that she derives sympathy from others solely on the basis of her being human. In this light, we may regard Durkheim's stress on secondary groups as spaces in which this sympathy is developed (Chriss 1993: 6; Coser 1984: xxiii). Durkheim (1902/1984: lii) draws on studies of Roman corporations and Christian guilds, both of which integrated religious and professional aspects, to suggest that in secondary groups 'there arises a warmth that quickens or gives fresh life to each individual, which makes him disposed to empathise, causing selfishness to melt away'. Like Hegel, Durkheim suggests that through secondary groups, the state and society may develop a symbiotic relationship in which the interests of both society at large and particular groups can be represented. Yet rather than these groups merely developing a rational recognition of collective self-interest, Durkheim sees these groups as creating the possibility for a cult of the individual which contains within it 'all that is required to take the place of the religious cults of former times' (Durkheim in Marske 1987: 11).

Two points are worth making. First, by suggesting that secondary groups will form the basis of the cult of the individual, Durkheim remains a materialist. By changing material conditions we will change minds. Second, much as with postliberals, Durkheim risks wishing for a shared myth so deeply that he finds one. The sacred is both ontologically real and normatively essential – it is the source of ethics. As such, it cannot, it must not decline but can only change. At this point three further points arise. First, as chapter 2 attests, old religions are not dying as Durkheim suspected. Rather than theorising a way for these to coexist, Durkheim is simply adding another to the mix. Second, if the cult of the individual does exist, which is certainly questionable, it is important to question how it is cultivated. It may be that this cult draws its strength from other mythic narratives. Third, if a cult of the individual is primarily defined by its rendering of the human person sacred, then little seems better to judge its resilience than its ability to challenge what Weber called the *de*humanising process of rationalisation. Findings in the current chapter will suggest that this cult, at least on its own, is not sufficiently robust to withstand these processes.

While Durkheim and Weber show some agreement on the power of ideational factors in influencing social change, Weber's understanding of the role of the state in cultivating these factors in a pluralist setting is less optimistic and, as a result, more cynical.

Like postliberals, Weber lamented a lost connection between politics and the church, which had not only ensured a connection between the ethics of responsibility and the ethics of conviction, that is, between a deontological ethics of ideals and a consequentialist ethics of outcomes, but also, through local churches, had connected individuals with their community (Palumbo and Scott 2003: 273). In exploring a modern alternative, Weber chose to speak separately of politics and bureaucracy (compare, for instance, Weber 1919 with Weber 1922/2006). While the role of the former was to provide charismatic leadership such as could motivate public energy, the role of the latter was to provide processes of rationalisation such as could ensure the impartial and efficient running of public services.

In politics, Weber envisaged the cultivation of a minority of heroic individuals that would not be restricted by bureaucratic processes, and who compete for hegemony, accountable only to democratic procedures. Here Weber takes a Nietzschean perspective. He recognises the power of myth, but assumes that any notion of a shared myth is really only that which serves those in power (see also MacIntyre 1981/2007: 26). Weber thus forecloses the possibility of multifarious individuals acting on the basis of different and conflicting myths to nonetheless work together to challenge rationalisation (Horowitz and Maley 1994. See especially chapters from Warren and Beetham).

In some sense bureaucracy was to provide a buffer between the essential but precarious will of charismatic politicians and the policy making process. It is against this position that MacIntyre (1981/2007: 86) offers his strongest critique. Yet Weber was nonetheless ambivalent about bureaucracy. It is first of all worth noting that because all significant historical changes result from ideational factors, or values as Weber prefers, Weber ironically regards secular-scientific thinking as a value in itself that has shaped modern bureaucracy – albeit a value that on principle excludes values (Kalberg 1980). Weber (1922/2006) thus explains that bureaucratisation is the process of paying as little attention to individual human circumstances as possible (ibid: 56); that it mechanises creative human processes, creating an iron cage that alienates intellectuals and activists from their work, in the same way that factories alienate labourers (ibid: 59); and that by co-opting activities once undertaken by communities, it makes into organised, rational action (*gesellschaftshandeln*) what was once community, or social action (*gemeinschaftshandeln*) (ibid: 62). The result is that the more impartial and efficient public services become, the less engaging they will be for the public, and, especially when these services are concerned with helping the disadvantaged, the less empowering they will be.

Kalberg has suggested that, for Weber, purely bureaucratic procedures cannot cultivate ethical action:

> Action cannot be understood as simply an adjustment to "given" realities, whether daily routine or bureaucratic statutes, as manifest in practical, theoretical, and formal rationalities . . . Instead, according to Weber, *action motivated by values* and resistant to and counterpoised

against environmental moulding by interests has been of the greatest historical consequence.

(Kalberg 1980: 1170)

Yet notwithstanding this constraint, Weber (1922/2006: 62) suggested that the longer bureaucracy remains, the more dependent on it people become, so that the idea of removing bureaucracy in order to reignite social action is a fantasy. The state must be involved in whatever solution is offered, even if, indeed, especially if the solution is a smaller state. So we return to Marx.

In some sense the Weberian ideal came to fruition in 20th-century Europe, but the result was that the charismatic leaders overpowered bureaucratic and democratic processes. Far from seeing religious, irrational myth replaced with secular rationality, the rise of fascism in Germany and Italy, and of socialism in the former USSR saw a melding of utopian ideologies with myths of race and nationhood. A number of scholars (Anderson 1983; Badie and Birnbaum 1983, Finer note 37) thus suggest that the state has always required a non-rational element. Anderson (1983) especially sees the myth of the nation as the key source of state power, as well as state-inculcated solidarity from the 18th century to present.

Anderson's thinking sheds light on an ambivalence that emerges in theory that cuts through the religious/secular, mythic/rational binary to recognise the continuing power of myth. On the one hand, the capacity of the state to conjure myth is dangerous, since it may incite violence against those that do not belong. On the other hand, any state requires an imagined community from which it draws legitimacy and into which it casts policies.

Mann (1986: 23) similarly places religion and ideology in the same bracket, and offers a similarly nuanced picture. For Mann (1986: 23), although ideology provides a means through which the state gains control, still: "People are not manipulated fools. And though ideologies always do contain legitimations of private interests and material domination, they are unlikely to attain a hold over people if they are merely this." In Mann then, we begin to see a renewed awareness not only of transcendental solidarity per se, but also the potentially positive role of the state in constructing such solidarity through the development of myth and ritual.

Yet notwithstanding their revalorisation of myth, social theorists continue to push myth out of the public sphere. The ambivalence demonstrated in Hegel remains in contemporary thinkers such as Habermas. In chapter 2 it was already suggested that Habermas recognises the importance of myth in developing solidarity. Yet insofar as the state is concerned, Habermas tell us that "Democratic legitimacy is the only one available today. The idea of replacing it or complementing it by some presumably "deeper" grounding of the constitution in a generally binding way amounts to obscurantism" (2011: 24). As stated in chapter 2, Habermas distinguishes between two realms: the formal and informal public spheres. In the formal public sphere, by which Habermas intends parliaments, courts and public bodies, 'the potential truth contents of religious utterances must be translated into a generally accessible language before they can find their way onto the agendas of parliaments, courts, or administrative bodies and influence their decisions' (2011: 25–26). In the informal public sphere, however, of religious bodies, pressure groups and NGOs, myth should be allowed to flourish and even influence the critical social questions that are debated in the formal public sphere. Habermas thus reproduces the religious/secular, mythic/rational binary, insisting that whatever the consequences, a small section of the state must always be reserved for the secular.

The return of transcendence: democratising ideology

It was in the context of the rise of new ideologies that neo-Marxist thinkers such as Althusser, Gramsci and Freire began to offer an alternative. These thinkers saw religion and secular ideology alike as equally threatening to solidarity. The question for them was thus not whether the state is religious or secular, but how, where and by whom transcendental aspects ought to be constructed. Althusser and Gramsci provide nuance to the Marxist narrative, while Freire turns it on its head.

Althusser (1971/2006) demonstrated how the ideational control of the state is developed in churches, schools, families, the legal system, political parties and trade unions – what he calls ideological state apparatuses. Althusser thus interrupts the idealisation of these intermediary institutions offered by Hegel and Durkheim. Rather than reflecting a symbiotic relationship between the state and individuals, intermediary institutions may provide the means through which the state controls individuals.

Gramsci similarly explores how the state exerts ideational control. Taking a Nietzschean approach whereby ideology merely reflects the set of conditions conducive to the success of the beholder, Gramsci explains that the state constructs and imparts 'hegemonic' narratives that safeguard the status quo. These are imparted through political discourse, but also through cultural and educational institutions (Bates 1975). For Gramsci, it is only by bringing proletarians within the state machinery that the hegemonic narratives can be challenged and the wider public conscientised (Gramsci 1971: 10). With this renewed focus on the role of ideas, Gramsci is able to rescue Marxism from a religious/secular, mythic/rational binary that, as I suggested at the beginning of the chapter, neglects myth and therefore gets colonised by myth.

Freire takes these ideas a step further, suggesting that no revolution undertaken from the top-down, that is, implemented by the state, can ever truly inculcate solidarity and empowerment, since to do so is always an act of imposing a way of being and thus alienating people from the construction of their own destiny (Freire 1970/1996: 47–48, 66–67, 76–79). Instead, true solidarity can only emerge when educators stop speaking *to* the oppressed and instead seek to speak *with* the oppressed, conscientising them to take charge of their own destiny. This approach does not rule out the state, but rather calls on statesmen to abandon the path of instilling cultural norms in favour of critically enabling people to explore these norms themselves.

Together Gramsci and Freire begin to provide insights into a new manner of conceiving solidarity: not as inculcated by either church or state, but through the discursive construction of norms in a radically inclusive manner.

This position has been reawakened today in the work of Bretherton (2015), who suggests that religious and ideological notions of the state may be of less importance than theorising the processes whereby people of radically different belief and practice backgrounds cooperate in the pursuit of common goods. Bretherton envisages a 'consociational body politic' wherein religious and secular narratives and actors sit side by side in agitating for higher wages or safer streets, embracing and exploring those parts of one another's narratives that create unity, and putting to one side those aspects that create disunity.

Thus predominantly liberal social theory has always been aware of the importance of transcendental solidarity. And yet, in the face of plurality, the transcendent becomes constrained, either ontologically or geographically. Either mythic elements must be dropped (since any myth implies particularity and therefore exclusion of the beholders of other myths) with the result that myth is replaced by rationality and individuals are united only insofar as they rationally recognise a shared interdependence; or the many myths are supplanted with a new one, namely, of the geographical nation; or else the two are combined, such that individuals are rationally aware of their interdependence with others within a certain geographical area. The role of the state in lending support to any particular myth is considered inherently exclusionary and dangerous. The state plays a role only as architect of rationally recognised interdependence. Only insofar as it is the symbolic carrier of the myth of a nation does the state have a legitimate role in constructing imagined solidarity. Yet nationhood too is a double-edged sword: on the one hand inspiring the greatest acts of solidarity, on the other hand responsible for the greatest atrocities of the 20th century.

Taken together, Althusser, Gramsci, Freire and Bretherton begin to offer an alternative picture: although the state may be potentially hegemonic in its casting of ideas, the answer is not to dispel of the transcendent, which is anyway impossible, but to critically question how, where and by whom the transcendent ideals are constructed.

Thus far, however, we have focused on the state as if it is entirely autonomous in shaping society. Alternatively, Abrams (1977/1988) suggests that as important as any actual power that the state may have is the belief on the part of the people as to the power of the state. This line of thinking will become central to my own ethnography.

Social policy: (de)constructing the state

From a look at social theory, there is a sense of being caught in a bind. We must accept the postliberal argument that a shared sense of transcendence is central to a state capable of energising solidarity, and therefore that such an outlook must be revived and reconnected with politics. Or we must take a materialist or rationalist approach, neither of which, even for most proponents of these approaches, are capable of developing solidarity on their own.

Yet theory can take place in a kind of abstract laboratory to which the real world is neither privileged nor constrained. Unlike the world of social theory therefore, the world of social policy has tended to be far more pragmatic, recognising the complexity of changing and overlapping narratives. As detailed in chapter 2, in the Anglo-Saxon West the shift from a Christian, to a secular, to a religiously and nonreligiously plural society is neither uncontested, clean nor complete. Instead, all of these narratives coexist. And it is out of and into this complex landscape that social policy is drawn and cast.

Transcendental sources of the state

The last section demonstrated that the vision of a secular state drawing from a rationally recognised interdependence amongst citizens to deliver social justice was theorised at least as early as the late 18th century with Hegel. Yet the reality is that the development of the modern welfare state beginning in the 19th century, and advanced most comprehensively in the 1950s, depended on Christian narratives, people and resources, even as it re-appropriated these for what might be recognised as secular institutions and policies. Prochaska shows that in the 19th century the majority of social services were provided by the churches or by friendship societies, underscored by, and promulgating a shared spirit of association (2006: 9).

But the post-war years saw great changes. Social scientific, bureaucratic and economically interventionist approaches were all gaining traction. In the UK, these developments were epitomised by Fabianism, which suggested social scientific bureaucracy could solve social ills. This approach was consolidated under wartime planning from 1939–45, which gave unprecedented powers to bureaucratic institutions. In this context, charity came to be seen as outmoded (ibid 2006: 152). Still, at this time it remained Christian arguments that underpinned the development of the welfare state, with Archbishop William Temple claiming of the Beveridge Report that it was 'the first time anyone had set out to embody the whole spirit of the Christian ethic in an Act of Parliament' (quoted Barnett 2001: 29). Albeit to a lesser extent than in the UK, the post-depression New Deal and post-war Great Society programs in the US drew on Christian, and primarily Catholic discourses for the development of largescale industrial and welfare projects (Duncan and Moore 2003). At the same time in Canada, the Presbyterian-dominated Social Service Council of Canada 'was a powerful force in guiding the popular mind towards an acceptance of the state's wider responsibility in fostering the general welfare of society' (Christie and Gauvreau 2001: 198)

Secularisation of the state

It was not until the 1960s that governments began to drop Christian discourses in favour of secular discourses. In the UK, Dinham and Jackson (2012: 273, 274) refer to the '*deliberate* marginalisation of religious socialization', and note that this was especially evident in the valorisation of 'social work as a competitor to faith-based philanthropy'. Wuthnow (1989: 108) and Eisgruber (2006: 459) have both observed similar developments in the US and Canada, though Vanderwoerd (2011) stresses that this process has been over-emphasised by implicitly secular social scientists whose neglect of the role of religion in developing social work is tantamount to writing religion out of social welfare history.

Once the machinery of the state was in place, the state quickly came to regard the people with suspicion, undervaluing and undermining their capacity for ideational solidarity. According to Prochaska:

> While British governments of both right and left enlist the citizen volunteer when it suits them, they have rarely had much regard for charitable independence, in part because voluntary campaigners openly criticise government policy.
>
> (2006: 163)

This research seems to support Weber's suggestion that by co-opting activities once undertaken by communities, the state makes into organised, rational action (*gesellschaftshandeln*) what was once community, or social action (*gemeinschaftshandeln*). Prochaska adds that even where more recent emphasis on voluntary association has been authentic, because the rise of the secular state undermined religious and voluntary organisations, there was no spirit of association left from which to draw:

> The New Right, with its reversion to the language of the minimal state and the need for voluntary endeavour, echoed sentiments that had been little commended since the heyday of Victorian liberalism. But such sentiments were being voiced in a world that had lost its Christian underpinnings. Thatcher's millionaires, unlike the Colmans, Rathbones, or Cadburys of the past, had other things to spend their money on than their fellow citizens.
>
> (2006: 161)

Indeed, Prochaska claims that by the late 1940s, 'with collectivism in the ascendant, the payment of taxes had become the primary civic duty' (2006: 149).

So the notion that the modern liberal state undermines transcendental solidarity seems to have real purchase in social policy. The state first displaces religion by establishing its own legitimacy on contractual grounds. It then challenges the legitimacy of religious activities in the civil sphere, which it first supplements, then either replaces or co-opts. In the process, religion loses its social significance, and its cultural capacity to motivate social action (Gill and Lundsgaarde 2004). The result is that even where bureaucrats now awaken to the idea of social action as integral to human flourishing, if the state is removed, it may be confronted by a lack of appetite (see chapter 1).

Woodhead (2012) offers her assent to this idea too, suggesting that if the secular state ever did offer a transcendent source of solidarity, people have recently become disillusioned with this idea, leading to a turn back to religion. We might add that this turn can be seen equally amongst academics (Habermas 2010) and the wider public, some of whom are responding in interesting ways: some turning back to religion, others accepting religious identities on a level playing field in the search for a common good (Beaumont and Baker 2011; Cloke and Beaumont 2013; Williams 2015).

Secular ideals of the state

The picture of the state offered thus far is one of a monolith undermining what it means to be human. This picture must be balanced against views of the state as building a shared spirit of association. To shed light on this view, I briefly return to theory.

Richard Titmuss regarded taxation and redistribution as a beautiful and efficient means through which a whole nation can enter into a process of gift exchange (Titmuss 1971/1997). MacIntyre has denigrated this position as legitimating the interests 'not of workers, but of managers and technocrats' (MacIntyre in Knight 2005: 267). Still, seeking to avoid a crude endorsement of statist utilitarianism, Titmuss advocates a symbiotic relationship between the state as administrator and individuals as voluntary suppliers.

Badie and Birnbaum (1983: 30–31) explain that a similar view was held by the neo-functionalist social theorists, for whom the state is seen as providing an integrative function against the worst atrocities of industrialisation and differentiation. For neo-functionalists 'the welfare state is the end result toward which political development leads in all societies' (Badie and Birnbaum 1983: 27). For Parsons, in its most advanced form, the state is to guide social action, while for Eisenstadt, the aim of the state is to redirect private goals towards the public good (Badie and Birnbaum 1983: 32–33). In order to play this role, the state distinguishes itself from civil society, acting as a neutral arbiter between multifarious groups, and challenging intermediary institutions so as to establish a primary 'allegiance to the nation' and thus a direct relationship between itself and citizens (Badie and Birnbaum 1983: 35–37).

MacIntyre's point holds however, since there is little regard for the empowering of people. Prochaska can help to elaborate this point:

> As Max Weber pointed out, 'bureaucracy inevitably accompanies modern mass democracy in contrast to the democratic self-government of

small homogeneous units'. In compensation for the decline of rival sources of democracy, politicians and social commentators sought to replace the sense of community, which people had built up in the past out of family life and self-governing local institutions, with a sense of national community, built out of central bureaucratic structures and party politics. In passing social legislation, government acted in the name of freedom, progress, and social justice. The beauty of such abstractions perhaps blinded the public to the dangers of overburdening the state. Despite the warnings of the liberal economist Frederick Hayek and others, there was relatively little public debate over the insensitivity of central government to the periphery. It was not a strong current in political discourse to argue that effective social reform might come from below, from local institutions that derived their energy and legitimacy from openness to the immediate needs of individuals and communities. The more the government expanded its role into areas that were formerly the responsibility of families and voluntary institutions, the more it reduced the scope for individual service and social interaction.

(2006: 163)

As the bureaucratic state expands and co-opts, it slowly undermines social action. Yet at this point it is important that postliberals do not undermine their own project. Critique of the state in the absence of either a cultural impetus for solidary action or institutional support as alternatives might easily collude with neoliberal ideology, critiquing the state on the grounds that it inhibits individual autonomy.

Moreover, even if this point is addressed, three fundamental points remain. The first concern is expressed by research suggesting that the state plays a key role in founding, sustaining and supporting social action. Skopcol has argued that 'organized civil society in the United States has never flourished apart from active government', which 'nurtured and rewarded voluntary associations' (1996: 23). The second concern is regarding the 'postcode lottery': welfare policies in the Anglo-Saxon West were initially set up in response to enormous gaps in welfare provision at the grassroots, in terms of both quantity and quality. Repealing the state risks reproducing these gaps. The third concern is that in a globalised world, in which companies may have more wealth than states, it is nonetheless only states, and collections of states, that have the power to confront such companies and to stand up for social justice. The state is constantly in danger of co-opting and undermining social action. But it is also the only institution big enough to provide universal services, support struggling voluntary associations, and stand up to global companies.

The reality of the state in the Anglo-Saxon West

It is moreover worth noting that there have actually been a number of initiatives from governments in the Anglo-Saxon West over the last 50 years that grapple with deep ideas of human flourishing. It is important that postliber-als engage with these projects, since although they have had many problems, or perhaps because they have, they are able to contribute vital information as to how to take the project forwards. In the following I shall summarise a number of such projects in the UK during the post-war period.

The late 1960s and 70s was a time of reawakening to the shortcomings of the state. 1968 was a year of 'revolt, rebellion and reaction throughout the world' (Popple in Ledwith 2005: 11). Although such rebellion was often more focused on race, capitalism and war than on statism, it may have influenced self-reflection on the part of the establishment as a whole. 1968 also saw the publication of the Gulbenkian Report, which recog-nised that 'participation in decision-making about every aspect of life is of fundamental importance to human flourishing' (Dinham 2014). 1969 saw the introduction of the Community Development Projects (CPD) 'amidst the emergent crisis in social democracy and the perceived threat of disaffection and dissent' (Shaw 2003: 362). Although these projects drew on the a-structural 'cycle of transmitted deprivation' theory with the intention of lifting families and areas out of poverty, project workers were given enough freedom to 'reject this reactionary theory in favour of radical/structural Marxist analyses of discrimination' (Ledwith 2005: 11). This shift was best observed in the publication of *Gilding the Ghetto* (CDP 1977) and *In and Against the State* (London Edinburgh Weekend Return Group 1980), which claimed that the government ignored the structural causes of deprivation such as 'bad housing conditions, redun-dancies, lay-offs, and low wages' and that 'state welfare workers were locked into a set of social relations that operated against working class interests by "protecting capital from our strength"' (CDP 1977: 4; Shaw 2003: 363). With government unable to control the narrative of CPDs, funding was withdrawn.

Dinham suggests that this cycle was repeated in the 1990s and 2000s with New Labour's New Deal for Communities (NDC). In a tellingly entitled article *Empowered or Over-powered?*, Dinham suggests that NDC placed too many constraints on communities:

> [T]he prescription of general floor targets and the speed of development required is undermining the community development commitment to empowerment at local people's pace and causing a sense of exclusion amongst local people from the programme.
>
> (Dinham 2005: 309)

Again, even the best-intentioned policy can struggle to hand over the kind of power local people require for a sense of ownership.

Similarly, the Big Society agenda, which was introduced by the Conserva-tive part of the coalition government, suggested a renewed interest in the ability of local people to take control of their own lives. Yet not only has the Big Society failed to produce organisations willing to make structural criticisms, but also it has been perceived as a cover for structural changes in terms of reduced social spending.

A major outcome of the Big Society was the commissioning of a community organisation to develop local capacity. While this commission was widely expected to be secured by London Citizens, it went to a new umbrella organisation named Locality. Bunyan explains that:

> [O]ver the course of the tendering process and since the decision was made about the organization deemed best equipped to spearhead the community organizing initiative, there would appear to have been a significant shift in emphasis in terms of the style and approach that is to be adopted.
>
> (2013: 129)

He suggests that

> [T]here is a danger that the initiative as currently conceived will perpetuate unhelpful narratives and assumptions about the nature of poor and disadvantaged communities and fail to politicize such communities in building collective power capable of challenging the existing order.
>
> (Bunyan 2013: 131)

Each of these attempts to cede power from government to local communities has led to a recoiling. What states often fail to grasp is the paradox at the heart of how community development workers often wish to operate: in and against the state. By co-opting voluntary activities, states fail to appreciate the importance of self-determination in the process of social action.

Yet it is worth stressing that the way the state is imagined by those on the inside plays a crucial role in the way that the state develops. It has been suggested, for example, that the US is a 'one-myth' political culture. So pervasive is the myth of negative liberty, that is, individual freedom from institutional control, that it subconsciously shapes all political judgements (Forbes 1987: 290–291, 294). Perhaps this hegemony explains Hall's (2006) observation that even the most statist of US policy programs – Hall focuses on the New Deal but we might include the Great Society and Obamacare – have placed an emphasis on local control and collaboration with business and civil society. Thus the problem is not the state *per se* but the particular manner in which the state is envisaged.

Returning to the UK, where the state has taken a direct turn towards involving religions, the impact has been similarly ambiguous. In the early 2000s, the New Labour government came to recognise the importance of faith communities in delivering social services and developing more cohesive communities. In particular, this included the development of multi-faith organisations.

Dinham questions whether multi-faith organisations are really equipped to play the role of reviving a shared spirit of association, given their tendency is to draw on the goodwill of faith actors that are already in existence, drawing especially on those with 'openness and readiness already to engage with people different to themselves' (2012: 579). He adds:

> To this extent the multi-faith paradigm remains a construct of policy hopefulness. In terms of hope for what, the fit between the vision for a multi-faith society and being a multi-faith body is one in which the New Labour government turns out to have been unambitious anyway – largely limiting its hopes to making efforts to accept there is plurality and preventing people from falling out with each other; and harnessing faith groups to provide services.
>
> (Dinham 2012: 586)

Chris Baker (2009) goes a step further, suggesting that more than merely failing to enthuse already existing constituencies of faith, government policies have often undermined the 'spiritual capital' of these constituencies by forcing them to frame their work in a rational, secular language.

In the context of theory and policy, the key question becomes how the state can reinvigorate solidarity without imposing itself on already existing sources of solidarity and thus undermining them. One point worth noting is how transcendental sources have been undermined by a set of policies that have sought to rationalise welfare services. In the study of religion, it has been suggested that this process of rationalising ideational aspects leads to a decline in membership (Berger 1979). The research explored here suggests this point might be extended to politics: in its tendency to rationalise solidarity, the state potentially undermines solidarity.

In light of this dual context of secularity and neoliberalism, more recent research coalescing around the notion of postsecular rapprochement begins to show a reawakening to the role of religion, not simply as a resource but also as offering alternative logics that can challenge the state and the market in the way that the public good is defined and ways of working towards it developed (see also chapter 2). Far from casting religion as a special category, moreover, this research demonstrates ways in which people of all religions and none can work together in redefining the public good (Beaumont and Baker 2011; Bretherton 2015; Cloke and Beaumont 2013; Dinham 2014; Williams 2015). Perhaps paradoxically, this research demonstrates ways in which a neoliberal policy climate in which the role of the state is increasingly challenged, social actors may come together to redefine the public good, thus providing new discourses from which the state can be reinvigorated. It is in the context of this research that I turn to my ethnography.

Ethnography: the state imagining the people, the people imagining the state

Skopcol (2008) has suggested that any sociological or anthropologcal study of the state must take into account the policy culture in which groups and individuals are formed. Put simply, what the state already does and has been known to do inevitably influences people's expectations of the state. For this reason, the policy considerations developed in the last section become a key lens through which I analyse the ideas and actions of my research participants. The narrative I have offered is of a move from a Christian socialist state, to a secular socialist state, to a multi-faith neoliberal state, and finally I anticipated the emergence of postsecular activism.

The central thrust of the last section was that the state in the UK has tended to tread an ambivalent line between representing and developing ideas and actions associated with solidarity, and co-opting and disempowering the groups it seeks to work with. By way of uncovering the contours of this line, this section will take each case study in turn, seeking to understand the connection between transcendent sources of solidarity and the state. I ask how the transcendental ideals informing politicians and policy makers shape their understanding of ordinary people and, in turn, how the ideals of the people inform their understanding of the state. Put simply, I ask, how does the state imagine the people, and how do the people imagine the state?

This is where I return to Abrams' work (1977/1988) mentioned above. Contrary to attitudes offered in both theory and policy, from inside the machinery of the state, where the state imagines the people, it is experienced as human. It is, after all, a machine full of humans with all of their flaws and redeeming characteristics: sometimes with agendas, with stresses and anxieties, at others with compassion. This human quality was experienced especially in the rooms and offices associated with developing what Weber regards as inhumane bureaucratic procedures. These are the spaces in which imaginations run wild and passions burst forth, in which people's true characteristics surface. To regard the state as a piece of machinery is to deny these human aspects, to sweep the bad under the rug and to undermine the good. Instead, it may be better to question whether the *people* who *perform* the role of the state are doing so in ways that are empowering. In this sense, I go beyond Abrams (1977/1988) to suggest that, in part, the influence of the state is reliant on the way that those within the state imagine the people. So I ask, what kinds of narratives are they drawing from? Christian? Secular? Multi-faith? Postsecular? How do these narratives shape the way that they imagine the people? As drawing on myth or secular rationality? As already solidary and simply in need of empowerment, or as potentially divisive and incapable of collective action? How do these approaches impact on the capacity of people to act in solidary ways? On the other hand, following Abrams, the actions of those within the state may be futile if they are misread by the people they intend to serve, and so I ask: how do the people imagine the state, or, following Mitchell (1991), how do the people imagine the distinction between themselves and the state?

The organisations with which I worked are ideally located to offer comparative findings on both how the state imagines the people and how the people imagine the state. Each organisation, to various degrees, demonstrates what Gupta (2006) has called 'blurred boundaries' between state and society. Each organisation operates simultaneously inside and outside of the state, with the result that participants now play the state, now the people, and, caught constantly navigating the ambiguities and ambivalences between the two positions, provide both reflexive and unconscious reflections of their situation.

Christians on the Left (CotL)

Chapter 2 reflected that the difficulties associated with being Christian in the context not of a secular politics, and a secular socialist politics at that, had led to a reflexivity on the part of staff at CotL, a reflexivity that simultaneously gave greater strength to their personal myth *and* greater understanding of those who did not share in their specific myth. In terms of staff's relationship with the state, this strength gave staff the awareness of when their narrative was being challenged by the state and the conviction, courage and resources to challenge the state from within. Understanding this strength is key to understanding how CotL navigates the ambiguities associated with being simultaneously close to the state and challenging it.

CotL developed conterminously with the Christian-inspired welfare state in the UK. Alongside the likes of Titmuss, as well as the neo-functionalists, CotL regards the bureaucratic mechanisms of the state as fundamental to addressing the kinds of fragmentation and injustice that necessarily occur as a result of industrialisation and differentiation. Yet rooted as it is in Christian socialism (Norman 1987), CotL regards socialism not only as a political ideology, but also as a lifestyle commitment. It thus sees its dual role as critically speaking to the state while encouraging Christians to be more involved in politics, that is, developing a connection between policy and lifestyle (see also Stacey 2017c).

Notwithstanding its history, a cursory glance at CotL's manner of operating might seem to suggest that its staff imagine the people as insignificant, thus fitting well with a Weberian model. CotL is situated within the British Labour Party headquarters in the heart of Westminster, includes over 40 Members of Parliament in its membership, and the majority of its campaigns involve lobbying the Parliamentary Labour Party to bring about changes in law or policy. In explaining why he wants to encourage more Christians to be involved in politics, Ralph insists that when it comes to any major decision that will impact on the majority of the population, 'you bet your life these things will be decided in dull committee rooms'. Here Ralph appears to endorse the dominance of bureaucratic process, and to accept that action on the outside of this process is of less significance. This endorsement would appear to support MacIntyre's critique that this approach favours managers rather than workers. Yet here it is worth recalling my discussion in chapter 2 of how Ralph performatively juxtaposes himself against his political surroundings. For Ralph the bureaucratic process is not something to be overcome but transformed: by bringing in people with strong ties to a community.

Weber laments that bureaucracy forces actors and actions to become instrumentally rational. Findings at CotL may turn this suggestion on its head. Value-rational actors transform bureaucracy, imbuing values into instrumentally rational institutions and actors. Here then, Ralph's philosophy seems more in line with Gramsci. The necessity of bureaucracy in a mass democracy cannot be overcome. But what can be changed is the culture governing that bureaucracy.

Weber's problem was in regarding bureaucracy as a monolithic transformation that excluded the possibility of value-oriented action. Hence Weber speaks of those with unified value systems along remarkably similar lines to Bruce (see chapter 2), that is, as if they will be consigned to exist on the margins of modern society. But the continuing presence of value-oriented actors at the centre of political life, though admittedly in a minority, suggests that the revalorisation of value-oriented action is possible within existing political structures.

Moreover, far from merely bringing a different type of person into the centre of bureaucratic power, CotL seeks to change how bureaucratic power functions. The great difficulty for CotL is how to make bureaucratic politics more relational. As one member put it to me:

> I think government would be very different if it worked in a more relational way but I don't know . . . it's difficult to do it, because we can do that on a one-to-one basis, whereas the government has to do that for 70 million people . . . it's a difficult thing to do . . . you'd have to have a hell of a lot of civil servants.

From inside the machinery of the state, it can be very difficult do envisage a relational way of engaging with 70 million people.

This seeming chasm between those making policies and the wider populace perhaps speaks to a further point: from inside the machinery of the state, it is not the state but the public that seems impersonal and remote. Even considering the relatively small membership of CotL – about 1,000 compared with the Labour Party's 500,000 – the key question was always how to better engage members. I would often sit behind my computer screen trying to imagine the technological or bureaucratic innovation that might build a bridge between the Westminster team and the wider membership. From an office in Westminster, "the public" feels a long way away.

How to bridge this distance might be as much a matter of transcendent orientations and associated practice as technology. A perfect example is *Labour Neighbours*, which sought to simultaneously reform local parties by turning them from being election-winning machines to social action galvanising machines, and to encourage more people to get involved in local party politics. Local party organisers were to change their activity, becoming more like community organisers. Rather than taking centrally devised policies and selling them to constituents, organisers would ask constituents what were the biggest problems they faced and encourage them to be involved in formulating a solution. Dave explained:

> [The party is] organising more . . . around communities . . . rather than just being an election-winning machine. I mean, it was a very good election-winning machine. But people have kind of moved on from that. I think the general population want a bit more than that, we've had the kind of recent loss of trust in politics because politics has become more . . . professional . . . rather than actually looking at addressing real concerns and problems and issues . . . and the party's now moving towards a more issue-based model of not just wanting loads of people to deliver more leaflets because there's an election in May . . . it's more about kind of year-round campaigning and year-round problem solving.

What emerges here is an idea of service irrespective of power, with parties working for local populations, whether or not they are winning elections: 'We need to show that we want to serve people whether or not we are in power'. This way of looking at conventional politics, reforming it from within, turning it inside out both by bringing outsiders in and by shifting the culture of those within to make them focused on collectively solving problems, demonstrates the ways in which critiques of the power of the state and recognition of its necessity might be reconciled. MacIntyre's critique of the power of the state in terms of its tendency to co-opt is dissolved because here the party behaves more like a community organisation empowering local people and institutions (MacIntyre 1981/2007: 103).

CotL's relational stance was further highlighted in their encouraging me to undertake policy construction in empowering ways. The key practice in this regard was the Parallel Policy Review whereby CotL members were asked to develop policy suggestions that could be fed into the Labour Party's policy review process. I asked members to take an A2 sheet of paper and divide it into three sections. The first section was entitled 'The Good Life'. Here members were asked to write down words or phrases they might associate with the good life. The second section was entitled 'Obstacles in the Contemporary UK'. Here members were asked to write down aspects of political, social and economic life in the UK that might stand in the way of certain people achieving the good life. The third section was entitled 'Policy Solutions'. Here people were asked to propose policy ideas that might enable people to overcome or diminish the obstacles that stand in the way of their achieving the good life. The initial results of these in-person workshops were then placed online, where the wider membership who had been unable to attend in person were asked to offer their comments. In this way, a centralised policy process was opened up without changing the structure of the organisation. Members felt as though they were playing a role in constructing the policies by which the country might one day be governed.

The CotL stance is indicative of an organisation that imagines the people as solidary and as capable of taking power into their own hands. Two points are worth noting, however. The first is that this way of imagining the people is framed within a Christian narrative that is anathema to many. As Ralph puts it, 'It's hard to stand up and say I'm a Christian'. It is difficult to envisage CotL providing an umbrella frame that would inspire solidarity amongst people of radically different belief and practice backgrounds. The second point is that despite their best efforts to involve members, still the latter's imagining of the state was so negative that it could be difficult to involve them.

When undertaking the Parallel Policy Review, the whole team was enthused with developing a project that offered real opportunities for people of all backgrounds and from all over the country to get involved. It was therefore with some surprise that I received an email from a member one day accusing me of 'London metropolitan elitism' in developing the review process. That was certainly the first time I had considered myself a Londoner, let alone part of any elite. As a researcher nonetheless operating on the inside, I was hurt, as were those with whom I shared the email. Again, this reflects the disparity between the way that the state is imagined by those on the inside and the way that the state is imagined by those on the outside. Yet more importantly, the anger was indicative of a sentiment that is difficult to overcome: the state cannot claim to embody solidarity if its processes are perceived as being developed, whether from the left or the right, with little involvement from those they intend to serve.

Similar sentiments can be found when CotL seeks to involve civic activists in parliamentary politics. Ralph reflected on the kinds of comments he often heard:

> Politics is just a dirty game they're all in it to make . . . I don't want to be part of that pantomime where I have to check in my brain at the door . . . like at prime minister's questions. The fact that actually the way that I'm seeing change happen at grassroots level is actually far faster and more effective than anything I could do from a centralised position, a legislative position . . .

CotL is thus confronted with a key political conundrum of our time: the state may be the best means of acting in the interests of solidarity. Yet by appearing to work closely with the state, CotL potentially alienates its members, who have become disillusioned with the bureaucratic processes associated with the state.

Hackney Council for Voluntary Service (HCVS)

HCVS offers a diametrically opposed picture. It is important to remember that HCVS was chosen as the representative of secularity on the basis that the latter is often subconscious or implicit, rather than a basis on which to develop solidarity. Transcendental factors are not systematically put to one side but rather rarely even occur to those involved. In chapter 2 I demonstrated that by replacing religion with the transcendental social as my analytical lens, I was able to push through a religious/secular, mythic/rational binary in order to say that rather than lacking in a transcendental outlook, HCVS was lacking in reflexivity, giving little official time to the consideration of the transcendent ideals that guide their work. In terms of its relationship to the state, this lack of reflexivity led to behaviours that seemed to contravene the implicit values of workers.

HCVS is an intermediary infrastructure organisation, meaning that it is often funded by the state in its core task of developing civil society by offering resources to community groups. Yet in its work in this regard, the organisation was often seen to impose bureaucratic processes on community groups, thus collaborating in the building of Weber's iron cage. This point was most glaring in a project responding to a case in which a paedophile had taken advantage of his position of authority in a tenants and residents association (TRA). The result was that Hackney Homes commissioned HCVS to list every TRA in the area, and, taking six TRAs every three months, to meet with the board of directors and check that they were following the proper health and safety procedures.

When I went on a walk-along for one of these meetings, I was struck by a sense of deprivation, made the more alarming by its being so close to where I lived. As is often the case in London, in Hackney, within a minute's walk, one can encounter great wealth, great poverty and everything in between. Standing outside a community hall beneath a high-rise estate, waiting for the chair of the TRA, my colleague Kirsten and I were chatting when suddenly small rocks began to hit the ground around us. Although the conversation was slowly interrupted by tense pauses, we continued, pretending nothing was happening. Then I was hit in the head by a small rock. More shocking than painful, we decided to take shelter under a canopy. When eventually the chair arrived, an awkward, middle-aged, 5-feet-4-inch, 15-stone, tired African-Carribean woman, Kirsten explained why we were waiting under the canopy. The chair knew immediately what was going on. She swiftly went round the back of the building, up a flight of external stairs and onto the roof of the community hall and began reprimanding what turned out to be 10-year-old children. These were not her children, but it was clear that she had authority over them – the tower-block matriarch.

By this time, our senior colleague John had arrived. Returning from the roof, the tower-block matriarch introduced herself as Elizabeth as she welcomed the three of us into the community hall. John asked if we could have a quick look around before things were discussed. He noticed there was no health and safety poster on the wall. 'We never had one', Elizabeth explained. John looked concerned, and asked if we could get out a table for the meeting. Together we put up a collapsible table and placed some chairs around it. 'We'd better wait for the treasurer to arrive before starting', said John politely, as he sat himself down by the side of Elizabeth. 'It's just me', she replied, shrugging. The point was made wryly, suggesting that it was always just her running the show, and that she was aware others ought to be involved. One sensed a confrontational atmosphere brewing. John asked if it would be possible to arrange another meeting when the treasurer could be present. Learning that this would be difficult, again, he furrowed his brow, and decided to move on.

John took out a list of procedures that TRAs were supposed to follow for hosting community events. He began by asking Elizabeth if she had a list of attendees for past events. She shifted in her chair and her eyes seemed to ask, 'Are you serious?' But it was clear John would not be capitulating by relaxing his matter-of-fact gaze. In a sense he was stuck in a bind. These were the rules that Hackney Homes had listed. There had been no negotiation process regarding what the rules should be. But if the point of this process was to empower community activists such as Elizabeth, it was not having the desired effect. Rather, she looked increasingly like a child who had not done her homework.

> 'When you have events, who's at the door?' asked John kindly.
> 'What do you mean?'
> 'Well, when you have events, is there someone at the door with a list of who's invited and checking names of people who come in?'
> 'No', chuckled Elizabeth.
> 'Well in the future, you will need someone to be at the door at events', said John with a tone that was friendly, but almost patronising.
> 'But if we manage to get other adults to come down, they're going to want to come into the party – not stand at the door'.

The conversation continued in this way as John progressed through his list, through the absence or presence of first aid kits, a petty cash float, a safe, criminal record checks and more. On about two-thirds of the list, Elizabeth was found to be lacking, and she was asked to confirm that she would have these items and procedures in place by the next time John visited. After about 30 minutes, we folded up the table and left a demoralised Elizabeth to lock the hall.

As we walked out, I asked if this was a common experience. John said that it was, and explained that in almost every TRA he visited, responsibility for maintaining community activities was the burden of just one, usually female, enthusiast. John did not mention that despite having strong activist values himself, in his capacity as a representative of local government, he might be overburdening the one person in the community willing to give what little time she had. There appeared to be a lack of appreciation for the implications of what he was doing. This whole experience was so striking because John himself experienced alienation when managers imposed values and procedures upon him. Now he was unwittingly stifling local activists in the same way.

When I interviewed her after a number of other such trips, Kirsten said:

> I don't think it's useful, that's the thing. First of all, it's almost an impossible task. And that's an issue because it means it's just never gunna get done. And I just think that, yeah it makes sense to have [the policies], in case something is happening. You know, if God forbid a child is hurt at a community event, you know these policies would be in place to refer to. But the question is, how seriously really do you think the management committee is going to take these policies? You know, I think, just from talking to them, that they're all earnest people that want to help, but they're all working 40 hours a week, plus kids, plus their own lives, and so more likely than that these policies are going to be filed away somewhere and never looked at again.
>
> I saw one of the TRAs, I don't know what the word is for it but basically, okay you're not implementing these policies, you're not cooperating . . . we're going to take your community hall and shut down your TRA – and they did.

The response to a crisis was to implement a heavily bureaucratic set of procedures that residents had not the time, the capacity, or the energy to follow, with the result that some simply gave up and consequently were closed down. This process demonstrates the way in which statism can emerge as a self-fulfilling prophecy. As soon as the state takes on any level of responsibility, it becomes accountable. This accountability then becomes in itself an impetus for greater state control, since if the state is accountable for issues that arise, it must do all that it can to ensure that issues do not arise.

What is most striking is that no effort was made by the organisation to take on the commission to audit TRAs in a critical way, perhaps using the commission to both deliver what the council wanted *and* develop the capacity of TRAs. These projects indicate the unwitting construction of impersonal bureaucratic procedure, which places parameters around some activities and obstacles in the way of others. The organisation enables the construction of these procedures, since it is able to reach communities that the state otherwise could not. From this position, the state imagines the people as in need of bureaucratic procedures to ensure that they act in solidary and responsible ways.

If CotL have too narrow a narrative from which to inculcate solidarity amongst radical belief and practice diversity, HCVS do not seem to have such a narrative. Not only are they not generating new constituencies of solidarity, but some of their practices unwittingly undermine the constituencies that are already there.

What is striking about the comparison between CotL and HCVS is that whereas CotL is situated within Westminster, speaks to a large constituency, and has the potential to influence the levers of bureaucratic power, HCVS is situated in the centre of Hackney and is geographically capable of having personal conversations with individuals and groups. And yet it is CotL that places the greater emphasis on relational politics. This suggests that material proximity to bureaucratic power need not sway the values by which one operates. The structure of the state is of less significance than the transcendent orientations of those within the state: how do they imagine their role, and how do they imagine the people? Perhaps more importantly, it suggests that in the absence of a firm counter-narrative, the ideology of bureaucratic management can easily spread from central government to local authorities, to individuals, even those that perceive themselves as activists. This finding fits well with what DiMaggio and Powell (1983: 151) have called 'mimetic isomorphism': organisations whose 'goals are ambiguous' come to model themselves on the organisations on which they are most dependent, in this case the state.

Employees of HCVS rarely criticised the state *per se*, but a strong critique did emerge regarding the cynical use of language associated with community empowerment as an excuse for cuts in funding. In my short time at the organisation, unused desk space, old computers and part-time staff made it quite obvious they had experienced setbacks from these cuts. Talk of declining public spaces was a theme of casual conversation. I was told how everything from health services to luncheon clubs were being forced to merge. Institutions that used to serve as hubs of community within walking distance of residents had now become mere services for delivering needs, to which people had to travel by public transport. Governments were perceived as being out of touch with the kind of help and support community groups require. John explains:

> [A] couple of years ago when Big Society happened, and the whole ethos around that from what I understood was to enable local people to take local action. Okay? To help a small number of people helping each other. That was one of the angles of Big Society, okay? Localism. Localism helped to arrive . . . with a direction. These are government strategies that came out, okay? Perfect because that would give, you know, legitimacy to our work. We will help those groups to sort of sustain services and everything. But no not really: it was like, 'yes local people to help themselves, literally help themselves' and not really . . . get any help from us. If they need help from us then . . . we'd have to charge them. But then they didn't have any money in the first place.

John is critical of the way the state uses localism initiatives to remove funding from the infrastructure organisations that provide support to local people. John feels that the situation has been exasperated by the rise of the Internet, which he feels is perceived as nullifying the place of infrastructure organisations.

. . . it's come together with the progression of the IT world and the Internet. And, you know, and the misconception of a lot of huge funding bodies that, do we need infrastructure? Because actually community groups, what they need they can get it for themselves . . . through the Internet. Why is there a need for human contact? And they really are questioning whether there's a need for human contact; whether people can just work on, solo, on their own, and just get what they need and get on with it. But obviously communities are . . . you know obviously the focus for us is a lot of communities whose language is – English is not their first language and they're struggling to sort of actually adapt to this life, and what we do is provide them with the comfort of discussing, negotiating, for me directing them, to specific areas of evidence of why what they're trying to do makes a difference.

For John, a bigger state, or at least greater levels of funding at the national level is a prerequisite of greater localism. In turn, a bigger state at the local level, in terms of staff designated to assist grassroots activism, is a prerequisite of such activism. From this perspective, infrastructure organisations are not the enemy but the facilitators of local empowerment. Removing infrastructure organisations would proliferate the inequality that already exists, since those with the most advantages already, in terms of IT, administrative, financial and language skills, will be those that are most likely to receive funding. In a number of workshops with John I discovered that the majority of those he met with were extremely passionate about the way they might contribute to their community, but unable to effectively fill in an application form, let alone run a business. Of course this perspective must be compared with the actual role performed by workers in infrastructure organisations, which I have already suggested can in fact be disempowering.

As an intermediary organisation, HCVS is caught in an awkward position. Staff often find themselves carrying out bureaucratic and neoliberal policies that directly undermine their values, even as they convey an awareness that this is happening. Paley (2001: 146) has called this phenomenon the 'paradox of participation' to indicate the way that the very process of the state's involving civil society actually undermines the latter's ability to critique and pressure: one cannot criticise a process in which one is complicit.

I want to finish on a more hopeful note. One way in which staff considered themselves as challenging the state was by actually competing with it for resources. James told me:

I dunno I mean it's kind of interesting how well the charity sector's positioned I think is quite interesting in comparison to where local authorities are positioned now and where they're going to be positioned in the future as they experience more and more cuts. I think actually the charity sector in many ways is in a better position than local authorities. Right because you're going to receive central funding rather than via the

local authority, is that . . . we can get local authority funding, central
funding, lottery funding, you know we can apply for funding from lots
of different pots.

It might be stressed that James is adopting a neoliberal discourse whereby
the state is just one amongst many organisations with the potential to use
public funds to deliver services. The very right of the state to define the
policy agenda is being called into question. Yet James' calling the state into
question also reflects ways in which members of HCVS are perfectly aware
of the ways in which they have been co-opted and, just as soon as political
and economic opportunities arise, will seek ways of resisting. Specifically
because the state is called into question, James' critique could also be seen as
the beginnings of a cultural shift whereby members of HCVS see themselves
as state-funded but not state-controlled, that is, whereby CVSs become a
meeting point between the state, business and civil society.

HCVS thus provides an interesting case. On the one hand workers appear
not to notice when they are imbibing the logic of bureaucratic management
and imposing it on local activists. On the other hand, they have strong personal values about local activism, which they feel current policy frameworks
are undermining through cuts in funding. This ambiguity speaks to the problem of lacking a clear transcendent ideal by which the organisation and
its employees are guided. Moreover, it speaks to how the lack of this ideal
renders HCVS unable to cultivate a membership on the basis of which they
might challenge and withstand changes in policy. Yet shifts in policy and
funding paradigms seem to be instigating a new-found confidence, which,
steered in the right direction could place CVSs as the cultural, financial and
geographical basis for profound societal changes that go beyond binaries
of state and market. It is just such a possibility that I explore in chapter 5.

Faith-based Regeneration Network (FbRN)

Developed within the multi-faith, neoliberal policy paradigm outlined in the
previous section, FbRN might make for an interesting middle road between
CotL, where strong ideals articulated through myth become a means of
reforming the state from within, and HCVS, where a lack of reflexivity as to
transcendental ideals seems to lead to contradictory practices, in particular
the complicit reification of the power of the state. Chapter 2 suggested that
FbRN was caught in a bind between the critical faith positions of individuals and the secularity of the organisation. Here I show how this same lack
of reflexivity leads to FbRN being co-opted by, and indeed reproducing, the
ideologies and practices of the state. On the one hand, as individuals, actors
see the re-emergence of faith to the centre of politics as a means of challenging neoliberalism and individualism. On the other hand, as representatives
of the state in a multi-faith neoliberal organisation, they imbibe a secular,
neoliberal logic, and tend to imagine the people, in particular people of

faith, as constantly on the threshold of conflict, and as amenable to financial incentives.

Gary seemed to see the state as upholding secular values:

> I think the state funds things that . . . I mean this is a secularist argument . . . any organisation that gets funding by the state has to . . . meet the same criteria . . . and, if for example, any organisation allows exclusion, and if that organisation is therefore not able to meet that criteria . . . .

One can read in Gary's attitude not only the assertion of the state as being the most appropriate arbitrator of which groups should and should not receive funding, but also the expectation of secularity on the part of the state in the way it makes its decisions. The state is held up as key to arbitration and solidarity in a plural world. The way that Gary, a person who sees faith as fundamental to reinvigorating the public sphere, imbibes a secular logic makes the state's power to enthuse the public with ideas seem particularly striking. FbRN seems to fit with Althusser's critique, acting as an ideological state apparatus that imbibes the logic of the state and uses this as the frame by which it imagines the people.

Gary's use of the term 'secular' here does not imply rationality, much less neoliberalism, but staff did seem to similarly laud the state for upholding these aspects too. Staff admired the way the state was able to avoid questions as to what constitutes the public good by deferring such discussions, and the arguments these entail, to the local level. As Claire explained:

> When the government was funding FbRN, the idea that they wouldn't fund certain projects unless they were multi-faith, so it was almost about removing any issues about a dominant faith group in a community by saying 'sort it out amongst yourselves and then we'll give you the money'.

Once again it is striking that individuals with a strong sense of personal faith, and who from this position critique capitalist culture, nonetheless when performing the role of the state regard the people, including people of faith, as motivated by rational incentives such as money. By holding money to communities as an incentive, the government is deemed capable of shaping diverse communities towards the discovery of new understandings of the public good. Yet on this level also, there is no data to suggest that the link between government money and multi-faith cooperation is causal, and it may be, as Dinham has suggested, that the money attracts groups that are already working within, or at least comfortable with the idea of, a multi-faith framework. It is moreover worth noting that for Milbank, solidarity created through financial incentive may not be solidarity after all; rather, it constitutes what Milbank calls a pseudo-*sittlichkeit*: people are incentivised by their own self-interest to collaborate (Milbank 1990/2006: 167). When the money runs out, perhaps the collaboration will too. This notion of the pseudo-*sittlichkeit* is exemplified through the inability of FbRN to maintain staff in the absence of funding. As explained in chapter 2, in my time at FbRN, the organisation was losing government funding. As a result it was losing staff. Although staff gave up a lot of their time to volunteer for organisations representative of their own faith tradition, they did not see FbRN as such an organisation. As Dinham predicted, the multi-faith policy paradigm was failing to bring constituencies of faith with it. Since no multi-faith narrative emerges, in the absence of funding, the organisation begins to disintegrate.

In part due to the loss of funding, staff did appear to be disenchanted with traditional authority. Gary told me that funding was dependent on the whims of particular governments. He claimed that changes in funding and priorities were almost always derived either from ideology or from religiously illiterate reactions to security threats. He would laugh at how arbitrary the process was for choosing groups and people to work with: it was a question of who knew who, and what kind of taste a particular politician or civil servant had. From this perspective, FbRN were in some sense upset about a lack of bureaucracy: personal knowledge and relationships seem to guide who gets funding, rather than impartial procedures.

London Citizens (LC)

Thus far it might be suggested that it is those actors closest to the grassroots that place the least faith in the solidary capacity of the people – a damning indictment. Yet LC offers a very different picture. The last chapter proposed that LC represents the beginnings of a performative postsecular framework for solidarity. LC recognises the importance of transcendence in developing solidarity, and yet it cultivates solidarity in such a way as to include people of all religions and none in the process. In this section, I demonstrate that this ability to bring people of all religions and none together in search of solidarity is rooted in a fundamental faith in the abilities of ordinary people. Indeed, I go as far as to suggest that LC regard the people themselves, rather than the state, as the body politic. Yet this does not mean that LC flouts conventional politics altogether. Instead, they see the state as having vital power for distributing resources. The point is that without direct involvement from the people, beyond merely voting, the state cannot have legitimacy. The state is imagined as a vital resource of positional power that only gains legitimacy by drawing on relational power.

Perhaps the single idea all organisers share in common as to the world as it should be is that of a world in which all people from all backgrounds are equally engaged in a purer practice of politics. If anything, it is this dream of diverse people coming together in solidarity to take action that provides the meta-myth that ties together the many disparate myths inspiring the various groups and individuals involved with LC. Employees often stress how disillusioned they are with conventional politics, which includes local and university politics, and how they have found a home at LC for the politics they grew up imagining. Emily explains:

> I went along to one meeting and the group of people there were just so off-putting. They were interested in talking about all the MPs that they knew, and how they were all related to an MP, and their dad was an MP, and I'd never even met an MP before, you know. I'd read about it in a text book at school, I didn't have any connections. I just found the whole thing not what I was expecting and not really about people or change, it was about elite stuff, and I just couldn't really get involved. I then set thinking about 'well what do I enjoy and do I want to be involved with?' And an opportunity came up that was about going to Uganda to do voluntary work over the summer holiday.
>
> I came back certain that I wanted to do international development. [But] at the time my mum was banging on and on about how there's no need for me to go to Africa, what a waste of money and air miles: I grew up in South Wales and my mum was a journalist, and when I was a kid we'd be driving our little Nissan Micra up into the valleys and she was reporting on the impact of closing the mines on families, where people were ripping up the floorboards to burn firewood because it was so cold, they couldn't afford heating, and she was trying to get me to understand you didn't need to go away. And genuinely to shut her up, I went, 'Fine, I will volunteer in London'.

Eventually this story led to joining LC. Emily had always been politically engaged, but was turned off by what conventional politics turned out to be like. Emily distinguishes between 'elite stuff', which involves networking and jostling for power and a purer form of 'politics', which involves 'community, people, making an impact'. Just as in chapter 2, she draws on myths of great people, in this case her mother, that drive her to perform a particular kind of politics, devoid of self-serving attitudes and bureaucracy.

This yearning for a purer form of politics is, for almost every organiser one speaks with, quenched by big LC events in which conventional politicians, those embroiled in 'elite stuff' are held to account by ordinary people. Aaron tells me the story of the big event that made him sure he would become an organiser:

> The experience that comes to mind is of the 2004 mayoral assembly, where there were a couple of thousand people from London Citizens there, and Ken Livingstone and Steven Norris were contesting the election, and I was just blown away because it just felt right; it was politics as it should be done, it was people whose voices that you don't normally hear in public political life speaking out meaningfully about the things

that they cared about, and decision-makers, the mayoral candidates, the professional politicians were responding to them with some kind of balance of power, giving them yes or no answers. And it was whooping and cheering, and it was a very diverse hall, and it felt like London, felt like the way things ought to be.

In some sense what makes these events so effective seems simple. The first point is clearly a matter of power: people are disillusioned with conventional politics and politicians and see them as dodging questions and out of touch with ordinary people. Having the power to bring politicians into a room and force them to answer difficult questions 'with some kind of balance of power' imbues those present with an aura of power: more so than journalists, more so even than leaders of opposite parties, these ordinary people have created the pressure that induces a politician to give a straight answer. Yet the question remains as to where this power comes from. In chapter 2 I drew on observations at LC to speak of five forms of convergence between people operating according to different sets of myths. The first was a process of constructing a generalised transcendental social framework: talking about the world as it should be. This involved the development of liminal spaces, separate from the world as it is, in which people from very different backgrounds can experience a sense of collective effervescence as they perform the realisation of shared ideals. The second was the process of reflexively constructing a story that is judged less in terms of its rational content than in terms of its ability to inspire performances of solidarity. The third was a form of *bricolage* whereby acting together with people of very different backgrounds allowed people to observe the kinds of performances produced by a very different set of myths. This created a deep respect, which then inspired people to share and draw on and embody one another's myths, whether of Jesus, Muhammad or someone's friend. The fourth was a process whereby people, particularly organisers, learned to translate their own myths into the language of other myths in order to appeal to people of different backgrounds. Rather than seeking a shared rational content, they acquired a multilingualism to speak to numerous myths. The fifth was the process whereby stories of people from different backgrounds acting together became its own myth. The great events of the past become the myths of the present. The big LC events draw together all five forms. They are enacted by people who have undergone the training process, whether together or separately and who have come to learn the power of one another's myths. They are deliberately and thoughtfully constructed, with stories of suffering being developed in the process of finding and energising potential delegates, and the best stories arranged in a particular order to garner the highest possible emotional response. They incorporate aesthetic styles from the numerous groups represented at the meeting: Jewish and Hindu instruments, evangelical choirs. Most importantly, they are the culmination of a long process of working together, listening to the suffering of people from numerous backgrounds, collaboratively developing a list of demands for change in a neighbourhood or city. It is this huge energy derived from so much solidary work brought together in a single moment that offers attendees a power to be bold in front of politicians they once feared, and which turns these events into the myths of the present.

These events underscore the core of LC's understanding of power: not positional but relational. 'A leader', goes the mantra, 'is a person with followers'. In developing its networks of power, LC is careful to select leaders who can bring large numbers of people to events where pressure is placed on people in positional power, from politicians to national and regional managers of multinational businesses. It is by focusing on relational power that LC is able to create this sense of empowerment amongst a diverse group seeking change in their neighbourhood. It is fundamental that activity remains at a grassroots level in order to ensure that people continue to feel that politics is something that they can influence rather than something that is done to them. Yet relational power is always developed with the simultaneous aim of inspiring collective self-responsibility amongst ordinary people *and* challenging those with positional power. Thus even as it shifts the analysis of power to empower ordinary people, LC still recognises state power as a key target of campaigns. Morally redundant as it often appears in practice, the state is still recognised as a key mechanism for delivering social justice. This is achieved by pressuring the state to recognise relational power.

The work of LC suggests that it is possible to revive a shared sense of transcendence with real implications for solidarity. But in a plural world, the particular narrative we choose is less important than the processes through which it is cultivated. Baker, et al. (2015) have referred to this process as an act of curation. Rather than imagining the role of an institution as instilling a shared sense of transcendence, its role becomes to create a safe and inclusive space in which people can share the myths that inspire them, and demonstrate the implications of these myths for performance.

Of course, it might be suggested that LC only maintained this luxury because it primarily positioned itself outside of the state. Yet it is in this role that we might begin envisaging the state: not as drawing on a shared outlook, whether religious or secular, and imposing it from above, but rather as curating shared spaces. And, contra Habermas, this might happen at all levels: in parliaments, in local government, in town halls, schools, churches, mosques, synagogues, gurdwaras or whatever. I suggest that it is in these spaces that people will redevelop a shared outlook with implied actions. The way to revive engagement in old institutions like the state is to make them look more like the new religious and political movements addressing local problems with global implications. These movements cultivate a sense of solidarity by empowering members to collectively construct shared ideals and to make decisions based on these ideals that will impact on their lives.

Conclusion: reimagining the state reimagining the people *or* the state as curator of performances of the postsecular

In chapter 2 it was stressed that a reflexively understood notion of transcendence is core to solidarity, and that transcendent ideals, articulated through myths can be observed equally amongst religious and secular actors. It was moreover suggested that just as myth has been shown to have a performative dimension, so too may collaboration across differences be performative. In this sense, the need for a rational consensus is less important than the need to put faith in people, orchestrating ways of putting them into contact with those of radically different belief and practice backgrounds, and facilitating processes of mutual learning as to how a particular set of myths about the world translate into action.

In this chapter, I showed that a reactionary response to religious plurality has led social theorists to construct a religious/secular, mythic/rational binary, reaching for rationality as the only safeguard against either hegemony or conflict, and leading to a construction of the secular, rational state as the only means of achieving solidarity amidst belief and practice diversity. I suggested that this development is worrying since it forecloses the possibility of transcendentally anchoring shared political goals. I then explained that while this approach came to policy later and with less impact than often considered, still eventually the Christian grounds of welfare were undermined by a drive towards secularisation and rationalisation. The new secularised, rationalised narrative of the state did very little to withstand a new shift towards neoliberalism. It was in this context that religion again became important, only this time to serve a neoliberal policy agenda. Finally, I explained that more recently researchers had begun to identify processes whereby actors of all religions and none are coming together to redefine the public good in ways that offer new possibilities for the state.

I then drew on ethnography to explore solidarity and the state in relation to these four stages in policy, what we might for shorthand call Christian socialist, secular socialist, multi-faith neoliberal and postsecular activist. At CotL, where actors worked within the machinery of the Labour Party to simultaneously challenge the decisions of the Party and bring civil society actors into politics, I showed that by imagining the people as capable of taking charge of their own destiny without descending into disagreement, the organisation was able to devise inclusive processes for changing the culture of the state generally and policy development in particular. I worried, however, that this process was primarily cast in terms of a Christian myth that could not appeal to everybody. At HCVS, where actors were intermediaries between the state and community groups, I suggested that the imbibing of a religious/secular, mythic/rational binary led them to disregard discussions of transcendent sources of solidarity, resulting in the absence of a reflexive myth that could withstand a Weberian model of bureaucratic management.

The point is not merely or only that the lack of a strong myth renders people susceptible to manipulation by the dominant ideological paradigms, but also that the failure to develop such a myth makes it difficult to energise members of the wider public. Without such public support, without an army of volunteers, institutions must shape their practice to suit the demands of funders. The people were imagined as in need of rules and procedures that could ensure efficiency, and as motivated by rational incentives. At FbRN, where actors were intermediaries between the state and faith groups, I suggested that, counter-intuitively, a similar problem emerged. While individual actors had a strong sense of how their personal faith challenged the status quo, as workers within the organisation, in performing the role of the state they adopted a secular, rational imaginary of the world and of people.

Thus although Weberian dystopias are not an inevitable consequence of bureaucracy, in the absence of transcendent sources of solidarity, actors within bureaucratic machinery potentially undermine their implicit values by adopting rationalist, dehumanising approaches to communities, paying more attention to procedure than to empowering people to engage in solidary activities in their own idiosyncratic ways. At first, this seems a worrying conclusion in settings of radical belief and practice diversity such as the UK. In the absence of unifying myths, a rationalist approach seems the only alternative.

Yet work with LC, which primarily positioned itself outside of the state, demonstrated that processes for developing modes of value-rational decision-making do not need to be drawn from a clear and unified vision, but that rather the process of construction itself cultivates the possibility of solidarity and resistance. It may be possible to formulate a transcendental framework that simultaneously challenges a purely rational, instrumental approach to the world and includes actors of all religions and none. By imagining the people as capable of overcoming differences to act in the interests of social justice, LC was able to develop a sense of solidarity amongst participants.

These findings were confirmed in exploring how the people imagine the state. The primary finding pervading all of the case studies was that actors feel caught in a bind, between disillusionment with how the state appears to behave and their ideal of the state as a key source of solidarity. All participants considered the ideal of the state as fundamental in addressing issues of social justice. Moreover, the state was regarded as a key guarantor of these actions being inclusive of people of all religions and none. In reality, however, they felt that the state failed to represent the ideas and practices they associated with a better world. CotL suggested that this bind is best overcome by bringing disillusioned people into the machinery of the state. HCVS began to regard themselves as a potential challenger to the state, being in a more dynamic position to receive funding and help the local community. FbRN were not only dependent on the state for survival, but also did not develop faith constituencies of their own, with the result that they could not envisage a different way of acting. LC were diametrically opposed to FbRN in structure: independent of the state and able to develop a mass following. The result is that they subvert conventional understandings of power, focusing on developing relational power, but they do so in order to challenge and influence the positional power of the state.

In order to reimagine the state in the 21st century, we also need to reimagine the people as neither religious nor secular but as capable of collectively exploring the world they want to bring about. Like Hegel and Durkheim, it seems that social actors within the UK are keen to regard the state as a key source of solidarity. Yet while this construction of the state works conceptually, often their work seems to be undermined by the state in reality. The tendency amongst social theorists to, in the face of religious plurality, construct a religious/secular, mythic/rational binary whereby the secular transcends the realm of difference is not only counterproductive, but also unnecessary. The process is considered counterproductive because, contra Marx, myth, and the state's role in producing it, continues to play a role in actors' orientation towards social justice; and, developing MacIntyre and Weber, seeking an imaginary that stands outside of myth to implement rational procedures tends to reify the people as potentially violent and in constant need of stewardship. Instead of seeking to eject myth from the work of the state, it seems feasible to envisage the state as operating in a manner between Gramsci and Freire: bringing social actors of various backgrounds into the state to develop countercultural myths that bring new issues of social justice to light, as well as encouraging people on the ground to undertake similar processes.

In policy terms, it is neither feasible nor perhaps desirable to reinvigorate a Christian myth with concomitant actions such as philanthropy and volunteering. Yet without any sense of transcendence the state does appear to undermine social action. Here I offer a simple answer: the role of the state is to curate spaces in which ideas of a better world can be discussed and concomitant practices developed, that is, to be a curator of post-secular performance. By encouraging the myths of various groups, religious and nonreligious, the state can ensure that the countercultural ontologies depicted in chapter 2 can constantly reawaken new and dynamic understandings of solidarity. By imagining people as capable of sharing their ideals and developing performances of solidarity without descending into conflict, and ensuring the process is inclusive, the state can facilitate processes of ideational synthesis and action. Pragmatic suggestions as to how to do this will be offered in chapter 5.

4 Myth, solidarity and capitalism

If there is to be any sense of shared transcendence today, it will be developed at the grassroots through the sharing of myths. The state still has a role to play, I have argued, but less as the diviner and disseminator of shared myths and more as a curator of safe and inclusive spaces in which myths can be shared and developed. Yet from the discussion thus far, it would seem that the only blockage to shared transcendence is either the messy religious and nonreligious landscape, or else the dominance of the secular, rational state. To leave the analysis here would be to ignore the ways in which the search for a shared sense of transcendence is shaped and misshaped by economic life, a life which for at least the past 200 years in the Anglo-Saxon West, and today almost ubiquitously across the globe, has been defined by a particular strand of capitalist ideologies and practices, ideologies that, I shall suggest, are often defined in deliberate contradistinction to transcendence, and practices that squeeze people for leisure time, let alone time to spend in contemplation of their deepest-held ideals.

At least as much as the demise of Christendom, the sudden collapse of the Soviet empire in the late 1980s and early 1990s has precipitated a breakdown in imagined possibilities for an alternative future. Left-wing governments across the Anglo-Saxon West spent the late 1990s and early 2000s carving out a "third way" between socialism and capitalism that has widely been perceived as a capitulation to capitalism. The 2010s has seen a crisis in left-wing politics, oscillating between a post-war socialism that no longer resonates with the wider public and third way politics, with which most on the left have become disillusioned. As Anglo-Saxon capitalism becomes more deeply embedded, a central paradox emerges: people seem increasingly divided by class just as ideologies and practices cut across class divides. If once it was the advantaged that seemed excessively focused on accumulation, today encouraging the spread of accumulation to the disadvantaged is core to the survival of the capitalist system. Anglo-Saxon capitalism seems increasingly to influence Europe and, via institutions such as the World Bank and the IMF, developing economies. Although the future will be determined partly by the economic prospects of China and with it Asian strands of capitalism, at present the Anglo-Saxon model continues to influence a deregulation 'reform' agenda in Asia (Dore 2002). This chapter seeks avenues for a different kind of reform within the Anglo-Saxon West itself and, by extension (whether by limiting the appeal of the current model, or else by exploiting its networks of influence) the wider world. It explores how transcendence can be reimagined and rearticulated through the sharing of myths in capitalist contexts.

As explained in chapter 1, postliberal theory seeks to return to the theoretical underpinnings of the current crisis to facilitate ways of imagining an alternative future. It treats the rise of the state and of capitalism as two sides of the same coin: left and right liberalism. Just as the loss of a shared sense of transcendence leads left liberals to argue for a strong state to reconcile people to one another, so it encourages right liberals to argue that people can only be reconciled to one another through the hidden hand of a capitalist market. These philosophies also collude: in the absence of a shared sense of transcendence, the only shared interests can be those essential to all humans, namely improvements in security and wealth spread as widely as possible. Thus the argument emerges that by all acting in their own economic self-interest, each tends to promote the good of others, namely, by increasing overall wealth.

This focus on economic growth also precipitates the downfall of socialism: it turns out that capitalism is better at economic growth, and so socialists are left with nothing but to accept capitalist economics whilst supplementing the latter with redistributive principles – the third way (Stacey 2012: 185).

Postliberals themselves are concerned not only with the structural inequality that capitalism creates, but with the self-interested behaviours – greed, acquisitiveness and competition – it encourages, since each of these tend to undermine solidarity. Yet chapter 1 explained that the postliberal alternative is primarily drawn from a Christian idea of transcendence, or else betrays its own arguments by dispensing with transcendence altogether. And chapter 2 demonstrated that this attitude reproduces a religious/secular, mythic/rational binary. More than simply undermining religious and secular narratives alike, the postliberal problem is one of failing to imaginatively grapple with the complexity of the messy religious and nonreligious landscape, which cannot be characterised as merely Christian or secular (see also Stacey 2017a).

This chapter draws this critique into postliberal ideas of capitalism, exploring transcendent sources of an alternative future that take account of the religious and secular plurality of myth and solidarity. I thus, in turn, place postliberal theory into dialogue with sociological and anthropological critiques of capitalism; both into dialogue with a historical exploration of economic change in the Anglo-Saxon West broadly and the UK specifically; and each of these explorations into dialogue with ethnography.

As with chapters 2 and 3, my exploration of social theory will not reproduce postliberal arguments by reviewing the work of scholars they extensively critique. My aim is not to dispute their reading of these scholars.

Rather, my exploration of literature will critically complicate postliberal theory. In support of postliberal theory, it will suggest that there is clear evidence that societies preceding and outside of the rise of capitalism display an entirely different set of social and economic relations. In this sense, the capitalist myth cannot be considered uniquely natural. It will moreover demonstrate that myth is core to the way that social and economic relations are constructed, and that a capitalist hegemony can alter personal and social self-understandings, in particular promoting rationalised time, the reduction of values to value, and competition.

Finally, it will highlight research that places myth as core to overcoming capitalist hegemony. Myth, I will argue, is always inherent to our economic outlook. To put it another way, no economic system can cut through myth or culture to fit neatly with how we are, because cultivating myths with implications for action is central to how we are. Thus to assume that myth can be cut through is to reproduce the liberal myth that there is a way of living without myth. Moreover, all myths will entail an element of control. There is not a particular system that is more natural and therefore less prone to myth and coercion. Instead, we need to think creatively about means and outcomes. What are our transcendental ideals? How are these realised in the myths we tell of where we are heading, and in the rituals and practices, the means by which we get there?

The section on economic change will then explore how capitalist myths have played out in economic policy and practice in the Anglo-Saxon West generally and the UK specifically in the post-war period.

Dore (2002: 12–13) points to three attributes of Anglo-Saxon economies: First, adversarial relations between capital and labour are not only dominant in theory but also in practice. In the late 1970s and early 80s, there was still an emphasis on social responsibility, which implied responsibility to stakeholders as much as shareholders. Today the priority is on shareholder value (see also Vos 2011: 300). Second, unions are steadily losing both membership and power, particularly as corporations innovate to selectively broaden the concept of shareholding to include the more dynamic employees, thus assuaging their impetus to rebel. Third, inequality is not considered problematic in itself and as a result is higher than in more coordinated capitalist economies such as those of Scandinavia and Continental Europe.

The embedded liberalism of the Anglo-Saxon West is partly characterised by a long history of free-market economics. Yet as Dore's description suggests, and as chapter 3 detailed, the immediate post-war period provides a definite interruption. Thus what is now referred to as Anglo-Saxon economics is partly bound up with what others call 'neoliberalism'. I find the term 'Anglo-Saxon economics' useful because it conjures the ideological history developed in this book, and is suggestive of why neoliberalism should find such a comfortable home in the Anglo-Saxon West. Yet given its popularity, I for the most part use the term 'neoliberalism' for the sake of conceptual clarity.

As if continuing the story from chapter 3, I will briefly reflect on the strong connection between shared myth and solidarity in the immediate post-war period, with the foundation of the welfare state. I will then detail how the rise of neoliberalism shifted the connection between myth and solidarity. I will stress that exploring the connection between myth and solidarity that arises under successive Thatcher governments in the UK, Reagan governments in the US and Mulroney governments in Canada should not be treated as anathema. And this for three reasons: First, although there is a clear decline in sentiments core to a past idea of solidarity, to ignore the new myth, the new idea of solidarity, at the foundation of neoliberal thinking, is to submit to capitalism. I have already stressed that myth is implicit in how all people form their motivations (chapter 2) and their politics (chapter 3). To ignore myth is to fall into the vortex of the liberal myth itself, as detailed in chapter 2, namely, that the liberal myth broadly, and in this case the right liberal, or capitalist myth, is actually not a myth but is purely rational and, as such, incontrovertible – a fault that might be read into third way socialism. Second, on inspection there do turn out to be aspects of capitalist and neoliberal thinking that do inspire solidarity, however problematic these sentiments may (or indeed may not) turn out to be in practice (Bear 2015: 22). Think, for example, of how EU farming subsidies have been criticised by those seeking a fair deal for Africa. Third, if we can accept that myth and solidarity are key aspects of human motivation, then only by unlocking the ways in which these play out in capitalist settings can we hope to truly understand people and (if we so desire) convince them to change.

I then turn to ethnography. Chapter 2 has already outlined the key factors contributing to the connection between myth and solidarity in pluralist settings. With this in mind, it might seem this chapter takes us back a step. Yet the purpose of this chapter is not to explore whether and how a capitalist myth contributes to solidarity amongst my participants. Rather, the purpose is to explore two factors: first, how my participants' myths entangle with capitalist myths, such as rationalised time, the reduction of values into value and competition. Where my participants' myths are substantial, I suggest, the entanglement is complex, and where they are weaker, less so. Where my participants' myths take an overt stance against capitalism, the entanglement will be tense, and where they do not, less so. Second, I explore how my participants' myths shape and are shaped by historical relationships and structural arrangements associated with capitalism. What constraints, I will ask, does living within a capitalist system itself place on the ability to challenge capitalism?

By exploring these two factors, I am able to explore how the connection between myth and solidarity in pluralist settings already developed in chapter 2, as well as its impact on ways of imagining the state developed in chapter 3, relates to ways of imagining and engaging with capitalism. This makes a particularly interesting contribution to studies of capitalism because it demonstrates how its logics spread into what might be considered the last bastions against capitalist logic in Anglo-Saxon societies, namely, settings in which people are seeking to develop solidarity. Much as with anthropologists exploring the spread of capitalism outside of the Anglo-Saxon West, exploring the spread of capitalism into settings within the Anglo-Saxon West where its myths seem antithetical reveals deep insights regarding how capitalist myths alter social and personal self-understandings, as well as possibilities for resistance.

As already suggested, I will point to three key features of myth and solidarity in relation to capitalism: the rationalisation of time, the reduction of values into value, and competition. Time will be treated as the most significant of these. I have already referred to the idea that the transcendental social is in a sense timeless; it points to ideals that are perceived as eternal and thus not subject to social change. While chapter 2 treated this point as merely heuristic, and focused primarily on what specific transcendental ideals were at work, this chapter demonstrates that capitalism brings this aspect to the fore. Capitalist time undermines that which is timeless both ontologically, since living in a world in which time is entirely rationalised makes anything timeless harder to imagine, but also practically, since being forced to rationalise one's own time leaves little time remaining for consideration of timeless ideals. For activists, a key aim is to restore time for leisure, for family, for friends and, crucially, for solidarity.

My exploration of economic change shows how this theory has played out heretofore, as well as how these developments lay the scene for understanding my ethnography. In particular, I stress how political parties of the left have often been complicit in legitimising capitalist myths.

My ethnography then stresses how the rationalisation of time is a key theme for my participants' struggle with capitalism. As such, time provides a key crossover myth by which religious and nonreligious actors alike are able to resist capitalism. Yet it stresses that these narratives do not merely spring up of their own accord (cf. Bear 2015: 155). It shows how those without a level of reflexivity as to how myth shapes discourse and practice are particularly vulnerable to capitalist myths. And it demonstrates the complex ways in which actors conscientise people, revealing how a 'contract behind the contract' must be brought to the surface (Lambek 2010a). Finally, it questions whether this ability to conscientise people is simply sustaining capitalism by imbuing those in power with an air of sympathy and workers with enough security to assuage the desire to revolt.

Social theory: constructing capitalism

This section will explore three empirical claims central to the postliberal argument: that the capitalist construction of the person is not natural; that capitalism achieves control of personal and social self-understanding such that capitalist myths come to be perceived as natural; and that the consequent shift in self-understanding undermines solidarity.

I begin with what some might consider a necessary apology: for discussing capitalism without a detailed exploration of Marx. I then critique Durkheim's exploration of capitalism and organic solidarity for failing to recognise the role of myth in sustaining organic solidarity, irrespective of whether the latter is normatively sufficient. I then use Polanyi, Weber, Parry, and Boltanski and Chiapello as a stepping-stone to move away from Marx and into the role of myth in sustaining capitalism. I give detailed attention to the work of Boltanski and Chiapello. Following both Abu-Lughod (1990) and Pool's (forthcoming) exploration of how the particular manner in which people resist hegemony actually points to a deeper underlying and embodied hegemony, I draw on Boltanski and Chiapello to show how the particular discourses and practices used to challenge capitalism in fact reveal the extent to which capitalism has already been embodied. This latter analytic lens becomes particularly important when assessing attitudes towards the 'gig' economy in the section on economic change.

I then develop a central focus on concepts of time as indicating how capitalism shapes the relationship between myth and solidarity. An ontological shift from what might be called sacred time to secular time creates possibilities for capitalist, rationalised time. I then use time as a lens through which to understand the reduction of values into capitalist value, and subsequently the reification of value as a lens for promoting competition.

Finally, by observing how this notion of time has spread beyond work and into self-understandings, I demonstrate how capitalist time has become performed and embodied and how the body thus becomes a key means through which capitalist time is resisted.

The role of transcendence in sustaining capitalism

As explained, I begin with an apology for excluding Marx from the coming discussion. It may seem anathema to leave out a comprehensive reading of Marx in discussing critiques of capitalism. Yet as explained in chapter 3, Marx's treatment of myth as epiphenomenal to solidarity renders his work unhelpful. Although Marx (1844/2009) recognises that the ruling ideas are those of the ruling class, he sees the struggle to shift ideas as an unhelpful distraction from the struggle to alter structural arrangements. As Boltanski and Chiapello (2007: 26) explain, there is a tendency in Marx, as well as amongst some neo-Marxist scholars, to suggest that 'the sole function of ideologies is to conceal the reality of all-powerful economic relations'. This attitude can undermine the way in which myth is central to both the capitalist endeavour and resistance to it. Moreover, although scholarly studies have been undertaken to demonstrate that Marx may offer a more nuanced reading of myth than is often assumed (Toscano 2009), I see no particular merit in treating Marx as a founding figure with whom scholars must engage at the expense of work that more systematically deals with the relationship between myth and capitalism.

Durkheim, I suggest, has a similarly materialist approach. This point is best understood by reflecting on Durkheim's reversed vocabulary with respect to Tonnies. Aldous et al. (1972) have revealed that this is no accident; rather, the young Durkheim read and reviewed Tonnies *Gemeinschaft und Gesselschaft*, and deliberately switched labels in his own *Division of Labour in Society*. For Tonnies, medieval and rural communities are organic, and urban communities mechanical, whereas for Durkheim it is the other way round. Tonnies sees the use of ideas, symbols and practices to represent and unite a community as organic, but Durkheim sees them as mechanical.

Yet Durkheim thinks the division of labour can go too far, creating excessive self-interest, competition and corruption. In the preface to the second edition of his *Division of Labour in Society*, he says that because the division of labour can tend towards corruption, certain rules and regulations are required in the economy so as to ensure that behaviour is geared towards the collective interest:

> Neither political society, in its entirety, nor the State can take over this function; economic life, because it is specialized and grows more specialized every day, escapes their competence and their action. An occupational activity can be efficaciously regulated only by a group intimate enough with it to know its functioning, feel all its needs, and able to follow all their variations. The only one that could answer all these conditions is the one formed by all the agents of the same industry, united and organized into a single body. This is what is called the corporation or occupational group.
>
> (Durkheim 1902/1984: 5)

Essentially, Durkheim calls for organised labour in the form of guilds and regulatory bodies. What is not clear is whether Durkheim's notion of the occupational group is conceived as the fulfilment of, or as a response to the shortcomings of his so-called organic solidarity. Yet more importantly, what Durkheim does not acknowledge is that even if organic solidarity is normatively sufficient, it may require some sort of myth or culture for its underpinning. The question then is by what means capitalism achieves this underpinning. To understand this, I begin by outlining theory that places myth at the heart of capitalism.

Contra Marx, Polanyi (1944/2001: 47) suggests that pre-modern and non-Western economies are hard for the modern Westerner to understand:

> It is on this one negative point that modern ethnographers agree: the absence of the motive of gain; the absence of the principle of laboring for remuneration; the absence of the principle of least effort; and, especially, the absence of any separate and distinct institution based on economic motives. But how, then, is order in production and distribution ensured?

The answer is provided in the main by two principles of behavior not primarily associated with economics: *reciprocity* and *redistribution*.

Whereas pre-modern economies were, and non-Western economies to some extent continue to be predominantly organised by reciprocity, modern capitalist societies are dominated by the profit-motive. Pre-modern and non-Western societies thus demonstrate that reciprocity is no less natural than greed, acquisitiveness and competitiveness. Ryan and Jetha (2010: 100) point out that there is no reason to consider such reciprocity noble. Instead, reciprocity may be considered a perfectly self-interested means of ensuring survival and peace amidst scarce resources. Indeed, perhaps a defining feature of these economies is that the distinction between self-interest and solidarity collapses (Parry 1986). I will return to this point further down, when I suggest that those pushed to the margins of capitalist society similarly construct myths of reciprocity.

It is Weber, in his deliberate critique of Marx evident in the *Protestant Ethic and the Spirit of Capitalism* (1930/2001), who provides the starting point for exploring myth and solidarity in relation to capitalism in the Anglo-Saxon West (Giddens 2001: xviii). Although not a simplistic idealist, for Weber, it was the emergence of Protestantism, and more specifically Calvinism, amidst a particular concatenation of events in the 17th century, that eventually precipitated the rise of modern capitalism. Weber's central point is that the Calvinist stipulation of salvation by faith alone, rather than by one's place in a hierarchy, dissolves the distinction between preacher and laymen, and renders all occupations equally valid (1930/2001: 67). Combining this with its suspicion towards 'feelings and emotions', Calvinism then stresses that faith is demonstrated by 'objective results', namely, through hard work in one's occupation (ibid: 68). Although this formulation may seem like a paradox, Weber explains that 'however useless good works may be *as a means of attaining salvation . . .* they are indispensable *as a sign of election*'; that is, good works are the means 'not of purchasing salvation, but of getting rid of the fear of damnation' (ibid: 69).

Parry (1986) can further illuminate and extend this point. Parry centres his point around the concept of salvation, which he treats as a 'free gift' from God. According to Parry, it is only in the context of an ultimately free gift from God at the end of life that we can make this life entirely a matter of instrumental exchange. Thus for Weber and for Parry alike, it is the concept of salvation associated with world religions that precipitates the shift from reciprocity to instrumental exchange.

Taking this point more broadly, myth has a determinative impact on the kinds of reward and return people expect for their actions (Parry 1986: 467). Polanyi puts the point thus:

> Once the economic system is organized in separate institutions, based on specific motives and conferring a special status, society must be shaped

in such a manner as to allow that system to function according to its own laws. This is the meaning of the familiar assertion that a market economy can function only in a market society.

(1944/2001: 57)

Yet once the capitalist order is in place, Weber claims, it is able to dispense with its mythic elements. People in the past 'wanted to work in a calling; we are forced to do so' (1930/2001: 123). This element of living in an order in which we no longer choose but rather are forced to focus all of our energy in work, Weber calls the 'iron cage', a concept that was only later applied to socialist bureaucracy (ibid).

Boltanski and Chiapello (2007: 9) offer a different picture. It is insufficient to suggest that myth simply falls away, leaving behind purely structural constraints: force alone is not sufficient to explain why people continue to toil in a capitalist economy. Instead, 'people need powerful moral reasons for rallying to capitalism'. It is worth noting that this is the same point made by post-liberals, only turned 180 degrees: for postliberals, force alone cannot inspire solidarity. One way of reconciling these claims might be to explore ways in which Weber's spirit of capitalism has been secularised (Wuthnow 2006). Yet Boltanski and Chiapello demonstrate that the reality is somewhat more complex than this. They explain that the spirit of capitalism is constantly in flux, incorporating in particular those myths by which it is critiqued.

The shifting spirit of capitalism

Thus the questions emerge: What is the spirit of capitalism, who sustains it and how has it evolved?

Defining capitalism as the pursuit of profit above all else, Boltanski and Chiapello note that different myths are required for sustaining capitalism at different levels of society. Whereas capitalists themselves, that is, those who actively reproduce profit as the primary goal of public activity, may make do with myths of 'material progress, effectiveness and efficiency in the satisfaction of needs, and a mode of social organisation conducive to the exercise of economic freedom', those merely living within capitalist societies require myths that 'coincide with [their] moral experience of daily life' and which speak to a common good (2007: 14). Such myths inevitably shift with demographic, religious, political and economic change. These latter myths can actually place a strain on capitalism in the short term, since seeking profit must be balanced against moral criteria, whilst sustaining capitalism in the long term, since they assuage the impetus to revolt.

These moral myths thus form a dialectical relationship with capitalism. For example, the early spirit of capitalism, that with which Weber was primarily concerned, focused on entrepreneurialism. But after the Great Depression, as anti-capitalist ideas rooted in social justice abounded, a new Keynsian spirit of capitalism emerged that emphasised work as a secure and social domain, alongside 'collaboration between large firms and the state in pursuit of social justice' (2007: 18).

Yet by the 1960s, this model of capitalism came to be critiqued on the grounds that it condemned people to a life of 'meticulous forethought, rational management of space and time, and a quasi-obsessive pursuit of production for production's sake' – in other words, to an iron cage (2007: 38). By way of response, a third spirit of capitalism was developed that focused on 'emancipation and the free association of creators brought together by an identical passion and united, on an equal footing, in pursuit of the same project' (2007: 201). In other words, the kinds of horizontal management we associate with Silicon Valley.

Thus two separate critiques of capitalism emerge, which Boltanski and Chiapello designate the social critique, which foregrounds inequality and egoism, and the artistic critique, which 'foregrounds the loss of meaning and . . . the sense of what is . . . valuable' (2007: 38). They suggest that the majority of anti-capitalist myths heretofore have failed to bring the two together, meaning that capitalism is always able to outmaneuver its critics, by assuaging at times its social critics, and at others its artistic critics (ibid: 38). The problem, they suggest, lies in the fact that whereas critiques of inequality are often rooted in liberal myths of freedom, critiques regarding a loss of meaning are often rooted in conservative myths of a holistic community (ibid: 37). As has been demonstrated, postliberal political theory suggests that this bind is actually a product of liberalism itself. In pushing beyond liberalism, postliberalism is thus able to incorporate both critiques. Postliberals suggest that the same factors that lead to capitalist inequality are rooted in a liberal social theory that undermines the possibility of a shared sense of transcendence, shared values beyond capitalist value. Yet the question of whether this position can resonate with a messy religious and nonreligious landscape remains to be seen.

Boltanski and Chiapello further distinguish between reformist and radical critique. Both positions are vulnerable. Whereas reformist critique can often be ignored, revolutionary critique can often be incorporated (2007: 33). By exploring which myths and counter-myths have been adopted, it is possible to identify the particular spirits of capitalism and anti-capitalism at work in a given time and space. In the next section, I will demonstrate ways in which critiques have indeed been ignored or incorporated in the Anglo-Saxon West generally and the UK specifically. In my ethnography, I will suggest that possibilities emerge for moving beyond this impasse, even if my participants themselves never quite manage to formulate such a critique. I will suggest that by adopting a transcendental social framework, people may be able to offer critiques that are ideologically radical, but politically reformist. The notion of transcendence enables people to step outside of the world disclosed to them, thus creating a new basis on which to critique. Yet as Boltanski and Chiaepllo predict, even radical critiques risk being incorporated into sustaining capitalism.

The key insight offered by Boltanski and Chiapello is that perhaps our state of hopelessness is rooted in seeing capitalism simply incorporate our critiques into itself. If we wish for a critique of capitalism to be successful today, we perhaps need to reform Marx. Rather than critiquing either the epiphenomenality of myth, the specific myths of capitalism, or drawing on new myths to critique capitalism, we need to critique the manner in which capitalism flouts normativity, pursuing only profit while shifting the nature of the myths it draws on to justify itself. Its principle has remained the same for the last two centuries even as its spirit has shifted.

My ethnography will thus question whether certain practices actually act as a vehicle for maintaining capitalism by transforming it from within, helping powerful companies to recognise their mutual interest with the disadvantaged. It connects the private good of a company with the common good of a capitalist system. What it does not challenge is how those companies focus on profit over and above solidarity.

Timeless spirits of capitalism

Yet notwithstanding these insights, certain myths can be seen to operate in all capitalist spaces. I will suggest that challenging these myths may serve to challenge the very nature of capitalism, allowing capitalists and those within capitalist systems alike to collectively develop alternatives that authentically speak to a common good.

A key myth in this regard is that of time, which can be seen to operate in all theory discussed so far, as well as being developed in emerging theory in anthropology.

While time is not a key point of analysis in Weber's *Protestant Ethic*, shifts in understandings of time can offer key insights into social and personal self-understandings. Taylor (2007) and Anderson (1983) have both pointed to shifts in ideas of time as central to the rupture between a religious and secular world in the Anglo-Saxon West. Distinguishing between 'higher' and secular time, Taylor (2007: 96) explains that

> Two events very far apart in secular time might nevertheless be close because one of them approaches the time of origins. This Easter Vigil, for instance, brings us back into the vicinity of the original Easter, closer than last year's summer day – although that was closer in terms of secular time alone.

Taylor's point can be extended to suggest that those sharing in these festivities, in the past, present and future, are closer in time to one another than they are to those not partaking within the same secular time. By celebrating Christmas in church, I am closer in time to the earliest celebrants of the birth of Christ than I am to my partner sat next to me, who has kindly come along to keep me company.

If we think of Weber and Parry's constructions of salvation as representing a sacred time that is in a sense beyond secular time, or timeless, we can reconstruct their argument as suggesting that the imagining of a timeless realm allows people to entirely rationalise secular time: this reformulation helps to make sense of Weber's suggestion that Franklin's construction of time as money exemplifies the spirit of capitalism (Weber 1930/2001: 14, 104). This rationalisation of time leads to the undermining of the sacred and timeless, since within rationalised, secular time, excessive contemplation of the timeless is specifically 'a waste of time' (ibid; see also Taylor 2007: 59). Taylor explains that in purely secular time, events are entirely chronological and homogenous.

> We have constructed an environment in which we live a uniform, univocal secular time, which we try to measure and control in order to get things done. This "time frame" deserves, perhaps more than any other facet of modernity, Weber's famous description of a[n] . . . iron cage.
>
> (ibid: 59)

Yet for Anderson (1983), secular time can create its own possibilities for imagined communities. When one reads a newspaper for instance, the date on the top not only brings a concatenation of disparate events from across the world together into a single moment, but the mass production of that newspaper creates an awareness that other people are simultaneously sharing in the event of reading. Taylor (2007: 392) extends this idea to the market economy, which people imagine as 'sustained by common action in secular time'. Thus even within the entirely rationalised understanding of time, a new possibility for myth is created in which people are sharing a moment across great geographical differences.

Taylor (2007: 720) moreover suggests that there may be a human need for higher time, demonstrated in the way that secular people push against a purely secular idea of time, seeking to 'gather together the scattered moments of meaning into some kind of whole'. In particular, Taylor (2007: 714–715) stresses that 'narration is one way of gathering time. It shapes the flow of time, "de-homogenises" it, and marks out kairotic moments, like the times of revolution, liberation, 1789, 1989 . . . And so we can gather time by commemorating'. In my ethnography, I will suggest that this ability to narrate, or construct myths, is thus key to challenging purely secular, and indeed capitalist time.

Bear (2015: 155) moreover stresses that even within a purely secular understanding of time, capitalism's rationalised and short-term approach to time is resisted by actors seeking this-worldly permanence or stability of work:

> It is certainly true that . . . informalized workplaces are brutally driven by the volatile, short-term cycles of the marketplace described by

Arendt. Yet this temporality stimulates rather than limits ethical assertions and creates longings for permanence. These ethics . . . draw on concepts of nature, ritual and kinship to project large-scale productive processes. In addition, men build a sense of common humanity based on the durable products of labor. So, in short, time is certainly experienced as an acute problem in contemporary austerity capitalism, as Arendt would have expected. Yet this experience provokes ethical claims built from the experience of labor and its durable products or res publica. These are human responses to the contradictions of current forms of capitalism that contribute to instabilities and inequalities or may even lead to a rejection of these.

Based on these thoughts on time, the section on economic change will explore how understandings of time have shifted alongside shifts in the economy. This analysis of time will also be drawn on to discuss how my participants resist capitalism. As already stated, I will suggest that by adopting myth, actors are able to construct transcendental social frameworks that offer potentially radical critiques of capitalism. I will suggest that these possibilities are integrally bound up with ideas of time. The transcendental social points to ways of living together that are perceived as timeless, that is, beyond secular and capitalist time. Yet people actually need to find secular time to reset and reimagine the kind of world they wish to inhabit.

Myths surrounding time are intricately entwined with myths of value. I have already stated throughout the book that for postliberals, the stress within liberalism on the impossibility of shared transcendence primes people perfectly for the idea that the only ideas held in common can be ideas concerning material wellbeing. And since capitalism appears as the best system for improving material wellbeing, liberalism primes people for capitalism. To put this idea in terms of value, the insistence that there can be no universally shared values (which is distinct from the universal right to explore one's own values) precipitates an imaginary whereby the only shared value is capitalist value – values are reduced to value. The rationalisation of time feeds into this idea, since time spent can only be justified in terms of the production of value. To reinvoke Franklin, time is money. Time spent without generating profit is not generating value or meaning either. My ethnography will stress just how caught within this system people are. People struggle to be involved in developing solidarity because they feel pressured to invest their time in generating profit.

Embodying the spirits of capitalism

While the theory discussed thus far is suggestive of how this analysis can be applied to the capitalist system as a whole, and to capitalists, it is equally important to explore how ordinary people adopt this imaginary, and in so doing become complicit in its development.

The most obvious place to look is work itself. For Sennett, the world of work in the new capitalism is characterised by uncertainty. The result is that people can only ever make short-term plans. Yet it is the specific nature of certain values that they are characterised by long-term planning: values such as trust, loyalty, embedding oneself within a community, forming relationships (1998: 26). The demands of work thus increasingly impinge on our social lives not only by giving us less time, but also by making us think of time differently. It might be suggested that capitalist time forces us to think in terms of long-term commitments, such as saving for a mortgage or pension. Yet this kind of long-term planning itself further reduces the amount of time available for forming relationships. We cannot develop ourselves as characters with a long-term story that is embedded in the story of a community. Our myths become highly personalised accounts of our own struggle, and we are connected to others only insofar as we imagine them, since we have little time to form real bonds with such people as partaking in a similar struggle. What is more, we are forced to rationalise even our leisure time, seeking to get the most out of our time, from our increasingly limited holidays, weekends and evenings.

Skeggs (2011, 2014) has demonstrated how the rationalisation of leisure time fits neatly with ideas of social and cultural capital, which become a means by which the middle classes incarcerate themselves in an instrumental relation to their own lives. Every activity, including leisure activity, must be one of improving one's lot. We construct an iron cage around our own lives. It is in this manner that Williams suggests that capitalist hegemony saturates 'the whole process of living' (1977/2009: 110).

The use of the term social capital further points to how the social realm is instrumentalised. Amidst increasing workplace instability and decreasing leisure time, people's relationships to others come to be treated as processes of exchange. People develop "networks" of "contacts". We come to regard those within our imagined community as only valuable insofar as they contribute to either the capitalist system *per se* or else our own strategy to succeed within that system. This aspect in particular seems to speak to Durkheim's notion of organic solidarity. Leaving aside the question of whether we can call such behaviour solidary, what needs to be stressed is that clear myths are required to sustain this supposedly organic solidarity: of capitalist time, value and social interaction.

From this consideration of how capitalist understandings of time and value come to saturate the whole process of living, we can glean another angle on our current inability to envisage an alternative to capitalism. It is not simply that on a political level, capitalism seems to outmanoeuvre its critics, but that there is no longer the time, and no longer the alternative values in our own social and personal lives, to resist the status quo.

Skeggs (2011: 505) stresses that it is not only the world of work in which capitalist understandings of time and value are cultivated. Instead, the notion that a person is only valuable insofar as they contribute to the capitalist system 'is promoted across British government policy, political rhetoric [and] popular culture'. Adorno and Horkheimer (1962/1993: 14–17) go as far as to suggest that popular culture actually champions submission to hopelessness in the face of capitalism. It simultaneously demonstrates the hopelessness of people's situation and champions heroes that deal with this hopelessness with 'exemplary behaviour'. In this sense, 'life in the late capitalist era is a constant initiation rite' into accepting hopelessness (Adorno and Horkheimer 1962/1993: 17). One can develop Miyazaki (2006) to suggest that individuals living within capitalist systems generate similar myths regarding their own lives, that is, of calmly dealing with misfortune and reframing their myths to suit new contexts.

In terms of the Blochian framework developed in chapter 2, the point here is that rather than exemplifying the transcendental social, or ritually assimilating people into its possibility, inspiring people in processes of becoming, popular culture exemplifies and ritualises a capitulation to the transactional social. Yet contra Skeggs, Adorno and Horkheimer, rather than treating the production of these myths as a capitalist conspiracy, it might be better to regard them, and their popularity at the box office, as indicative of the social and personal self-understanding in capitalist societies. We are all complicit in the construction and popularity of these myths.

Spirits of resistance

Yet hopelessness is not the only story. In chapter 2 I identified research into the postsecular that foregrounds how religion challenges purely instrumental approaches to the question of how we ought to live, and I used the transcendental and transactional social and myth as a framework for extending this research to include secular actors. Much of this research deliberately counterpoises religion to capitalism. Baker (2016: 266) suggests that religion offers imaginaries that challenge instrumental self-interest. Cloke and Beaumont (2013: 16) suggest that religion assists people in envisaging the invisible, thus expanding 'the narrow-minded horizon of possibility set by modernity'. Baker (2016: 270) and Williams (2015) point to how religious actors deliberately challenge capitalist logics. Baker demonstrates how religious actors have developed new economies of reciprocity that solidify social relationships beyond religious and religious/secular divisions. And Williams demonstrates how religious actors inspire a sense of service delivery that resist capitalist ideas of time by offering recipients more time than is rationally effective. He further stresses how this inspiration works beyond religious people themselves, inspiring different modes of practice amongst secular actors.

And religion is not the only game in town. Perhaps surprisingly from a materialist perspective, some of the key spaces in which myths of resistance form are amongst those most constrained by capitalism. Much as Polanyi suggests is the case in pre-modern and non-Western economies, a number of anthropologists have demonstrated that in places where capitalism is emerging, '[a]mong the poor, social relations often constitute a much safer "investment" than petty entrepreneurship' (Narotzky and Besnier 2014: 3).

Skeggs (2011), moreover, suggests that amongst the working class in the UK, this same emphasis on values of friendship and family act as a mode of resistance against capitalist hegemony. Skeggs' research in the UK is particularly illuminating because it suggests that even in places where capitalism is supposedly well-embedded, pockets of resistance remain. In particular, working-class women are observed as berating '"middle-class mums" for "shopping their children out" and for not caring for them enough or properly (by going to work full-time)' (503). Skeggs goes on to say that these women 'emphatically did not want to be middle-class, a position they associated with a lack of care for others' (504). More than a mere survival strategy, Skeggs suggests that exclusion from capitalist success leads these women to construct values that deliberately subvert capitalist value:

> [T]heir best chance of value was moral and affective not financial – love. Love was for children (not often for men) and family and friends. Theirs was a revalorisation of relationships made from local, familial sociality where other people were supportive connectivities, not sources for self-accumulation.
>
> (504)

Skeggs specifically refers to how this revaluation resists capitalist time, describing it as 'the *gift of attention over time*' (505). This gift specifically challenges the use of 'time and energy to invest in future employability, economic or cultural property', instead focusing on 'just "being", "with mates", "chit-chatting", and "hanging out"' (505). Skeggs thus begins to show how resistance to capitalist time is embodied in specific rituals and practices such as hanging out. This construction of time with implicit alternative values amongst the working class, moreover, specifically as it is made without reference to religion, perhaps begins to provide possibilities for crossover narratives that can appeal to people of all religions and none.

The capitalist understanding of human nature may have a basis in nature, but so too do ideas of reciprocity and love. Any economic system that wishes to sustain itself without using force to cripple resistance requires myths that sustain and support it. These myths cannot appeal to those in positions of advantage alone, but must also point to a common good that resonates with the realities of the disadvantaged. This section has suggested that the key myths that have sustained capitalism are anti-myths of rationalised time, the reduction of values into value and competition. These myths are imbibed in the workplace and reproduced by policy, politicians and popular culture. Research also suggests that people themselves become complicit in constructing these myths, rationalising even their own leisure time.

Yet I have also pointed to possibilities for resisting the myths of capitalism found in religion and amongst disaffected members of the British working class. Amongst these groups, there appears to be a desire to reconnect economic activity with solidarity, not only ensuring that economic activity itself encourages reciprocity, but also limiting the pursuit of profit in favour of spending time with one's friends and family. Perhaps most striking, these performances of solidarity are not merely socialist, but rather carve out new possibilities for solidarity beyond both the state and the capitalist market, rooted in mutual respect and gift-exchange. Exemplars for alternative ways of being may be far closer to home than we realise.

The question remains, however, of how actors are to inclusively construct these counter-myths in a messy religious and nonreligious landscape that is economically precarious. In the next section, I detail this landscape before exploring my participants' responses in the following section.

Economic policy: beyond capitalism

More than research into the state, research into capitalism has seemed receptive to the role of myth in both sustaining and critiquing capitalism. In this section, I explore the specific ways in which the myths associated with capitalism discussed above have become dominant in the Anglo-Saxon West generally and the UK specifically, paying particular attention to the consequences for those seeking to develop solidarity.

It has already been suggested that the period following the Great Depression led to a different kind of capitalism in which large companies and the state collaborated in the interests of social justice. Yet just as important as the Great Depression was the threat of communism and fascism (Judt 2010; Wall 2008). In the post-war period, countries in the Anglo-Saxon West sought to incorporate the social planning and aesthetic unity associated with communism and fascism partly as a way of assuaging the disaffected. The 1940s, 50s and 60s have thus been characterised as typifying a social democratic consensus, from the New Deal coalition in the US to the founding of the welfare state in the UK. As has already been suggested in chapter 3, both the New Deal coalition and the welfare state were primarily underscored by a Christian myth that stressed a sense of duty to the disadvantaged.

Capitalism as utopian: the rise of neoliberalism

The social democratic consensus was perhaps most formidably interrupted by Hayek. Though much castigated by socialists as encouraging a purely self-interested worldview, Alkire and Ritchie (2010: 4) remind us that Hayek stressed 'the courage to be Utopian' in seeking to restore 'human dignity and freedom'. For Hayek, the worst atrocities of communism and fascism were being mimicked in the creation of the socially democratic state, which emphasised bureaucratic planning over individual autonomy and innovation. Hayek cuttingly described these developments as constituting 'the road to serfdom'. It is this radical faith in reducing the power of the state in order to enable dignity and freedom that many designate 'neoliberalism'. Despite being castigated by many on the economic left as being either amoral or immoral, it is of fundamental importance in understanding the success of neoliberalism that it is a moral narrative, or myth, to do with the liberation of individuals from oppressive institutions.

Remembering Hayek complicates the picture offered by Boltanski and Chiapello. Capitalism is not merely shifting to incorporate new myths that resonate with a disaffected public. It was as much the capitalist-utopia neoliberal thinkers that critiqued the bureaucratic nature of Keynsian social democracy – well before the anti-capitalist reactions of the 1960s. From this perspective, capitalism is not merely reactionary but involves a strong myth of its own. More importantly, from a postliberal perspective, this collusion between neoliberals and anti-capitalist protesters demonstrates less the flexibility of capitalism to incorporating different myths than it does the unity of liberal interests: both neoliberals and the anti-capitalists of the 1960s champion individual emancipation above all else, a narrative that capitalism turns out to be particularly well suited to. Yet as suggested in chapter 2, I will judge the myth in terms of the performances it produces. What liberation means in practice is being in charge of one's own economic destiny: having the right to give all one's time to the generation of profit, and to keep this profit for oneself. All values thus risk being reduced to value. People see themselves as in a competitive rather than solidary relationship with others.

Neoliberalism in practice

Hayek notoriously had a strong influence on British Conservative Prime Minister Margaret Thatcher, who famously, interrupting a moderate speaker at a Conservative Party policy meeting, held up Hayek's *Constitution of Liberty* and proclaimed 'this is what we believe', before slamming the book against the table (Ranelagh 1991). Not only does Thatcher's stress on belief illustrate the importance of myth in developing and sustaining capitalism, but her own performance has served to contribute to the capitalist liturgy. To simply dismiss Thatcher's position as immoral is to leave unexplored the importance of myth in cultivating a capitalism that resonates with people. For Thatcher, 'economics are the method; the object is to change the soul'. Thatcher was seeking to change culture, creating a more independent, self-responsible society or, as she put it, 'there is no such thing as society, only individual men and women' (Thatcher 1987). Although it has been questioned whether Reagan had as strong convictions (Hantz 1996), there is clear ideological parity between Thatcher, Reagan and Mulroney (Savoie 1994).

Two key examples of policy help to illustrate the impact of neoliberalism in the Anglo-Saxon West. The first was in restricting the power of trade unions to call strikes. In so doing, neoliberal governments created a culture in which businesses could reduce wages and increase time spent at work. Milbank and Pabst (2016) suggest that social democrats were complicit in this process, trading off the power of unions for improved social insurance. It is worth noting that governments use opaquely moral narratives when in conflict with unions. In the UK, particularly when in conflict with striking transport employees, the government stresses that they are infringing the rights of ordinary people to go to work. As a result of the weakening of unions, it is now big businesses, rather than states or trade unions, that dictate hours of work (Skidelsky and Skidelsky 2012). The result is that people now have ever less time to spend in contemplation, or with family and friends. A second policy example is the privatisation of major industries with shares being sold to the public. These policies were seen as simultaneously liberating key public services from the yoke of bureaucracy, and as empowering shareholders.

In the UK, a key example of such policy at the level of the individual, still able to generate hostility over 20 years later, is the right-to-buy scheme which saw the mass selling of public housing to tenants at a reduced rate. Much castigated for undermining the power of the state to provide housing for those in need, right-to-buy is still widely regarded by beneficiaries as giving them an economic stake and a sense of belonging in the place they grew up. The point here is neither to morally critique nor support right-to-buy, but to point out the way that it challenged socialist understandings of solidarity not by flouting solidarity altogether, but by developing new myths of solidarity grounded in the right of all people to own property. In the UK at least, rather than distinguishing between capitalists and those living within a capitalist economy, and seeking to limit capitalism in order to assuage the desire to revolt, capitalism shifted to include a larger array of people in the narrative of ownership, self-responsibility and entrepreneurialism, rendering more and more people complicit in the reproduction of capitalism.

Yet the problem is that in equating dignity and freedom with economic value, any policy that increases economic value is regarded as in the best interest of the public. Hence, explains Baker (2016: 264):

> The inexorable logic of the de-regulated market is to put a price on everything, and to prise the individual away from any sense to entitlement or support from anyone or anything else; to instead see themselves as self-standing entrepreneurs; increasingly responsible for creating their own goods and services and increasingly bearing the risk when it all goes wrong.

Perhaps the most radical illustration of the paradox at the heart of this myth of solidarity is understood in terms of personal debt. In an economy underscored less and less by the command of industry, and more by thriving consumerism, successive governments seek to increase consumer spending by making credit cheap (Graeber 2011). Yet cheap credit often drives the disadvantaged into debt. Thus economic policy justified in terms of promoting dignity and freedom places the least advantaged in society into relationships of debt with the most advantaged. It is cruelly ironic that such policy was inspired by warnings against a road to serfdom.

Performances of neoliberal autonomy

It is moreover worth observing the way that the imbibing and embodying of neoliberal narratives has come to influence understandings of time amongst ordinary people. In particular, the capitalist notion of time, not only as rationalised but also as controlled by autonomous individuals has led to an odd situation in which people have begun to willingly opt out of long-fought-for workers rights in the name of autonomy. People enter into contracts no longer as 'employees' with particular rights but as 'workers' with fewer rights or as 'self-employed', with no rights. In some cases, such as with nursing or catering, this means that hours are entirely dictated by the employer, meaning that the worker in reality has no time of their own, instead always in limbo, their time rationalised by the employer. In other cases, such as with taxi services, the worker creates their own schedule, but in reality quickly discovers that they must give up far more time than originally anticipated. This attempt to challenge capitalism by taking ownership of one's time demonstrates not only the depth of capitalist understandings of time, but also the dissolution of solidarity in a capitalist economy. People see themselves as in competition with one another, seeking to produce profit or save money. Rather than collectively bargaining for more rights, people opt out of trades with established pathways to collective bargaining and into supposedly more autonomous jobs, which in reality isolate them not only from 'the boss', but also from those in similar situations that could help. It also worth recognising how those using such services become complicit in this system, choosing cheap taxi rides over solidarity with the collective bargaining power of drivers.

Thus drawing on insights from chapter 2, whereby myths are not judged by their rational content but by the performances they promote, I critique neoliberalism less on the basis of its ideals or of how these are articulated in particular myths, but of the kinds of embodied performances these ideals have tended to promote: under neoliberalism, ideals of individual autonomy and self-responsibility actually tend to place power in the hands of a few, thus decreasing rather than increasing individual freedom; and to distend the connection with those sharing our interests, making it difficult to wrest power back from the few.

Emerging spaces of resistance

Yet as already suggested with the example of HCVS in chapter 3, the dominance of neoliberal policy has also created opportunities for developing new paths to solidarity outside of the auspices of the state. Though it may seem anathema to critics of neoliberalism, it may be the development of just such pathways that neoliberals hoped for, as evidenced in the concept of the Big Society. Though widely treated as an excuse for cuts in public spending, a problem exasperated by the global economic crisis of 2008 and the subsequent dominance of austerity economics, as explained in chapter 3, the central idea behind the Big Society was that communities would be empowered to take control of their own lives and services.

Recent research, to which my own ethnography will contribute, indeed suggests that social actors are ambivalent, rather than wholesale antagonistic, towards neoliberal policies in the social realm. While actors do not wish to endorse neoliberal narratives that they regard as cynical, they nonetheless feel that economic pressures have forced people to be creative, facilitating new possibilities for solidarity. Williams (2015: 192) in particular suggests that in the spaces in which the state recedes, 'religious, secular and humanitarian motivations appear to coalesce around mutual ethical concerns and crossover narratives'. Yet just as these actions seem to coincide with neoliberal policy, they also critically challenge capitalist discourses, as already outlined in the previous section.

In this odd and exciting way, it seems that the same groups that neoliberals see as championing their myths are in fact using their public roles to challenge neoliberal myths. In some sense, I will suggest, the organisations I researched were thus caught in a bind: not wanting to reinforce neoliberal policy, they nonetheless feel a sense of duty to act, and see possibilities for creativity as the state declines. Yet this renewed creativity also facilitates a reimagining of values and practices that suggests a sense of solidarity beyond both the state and the market. It is with these complexities in mind that I turn to my ethnography.

Ethnography: imagining capitalism beyond capitalism

As suggested earlier, the myths associated with capitalism are complexly intertwined with those of resistance. This is not only because capitalism evolves to incorporate myths of resistance. It is also because the *particular* myths employed to resist capitalism demonstrates which myths are already dominant. This is also evident in cases where resistance fails to materialise.

Following chapters 2 and 3, the argument I have been making thus far is that the construction of a religious/secular, mythic/rational binary forecloses possibilities of imagining a different way of living together. In particular, I have suggested that this binary has undermined our capacity to examine the crucial role of myth in sustaining one of the most powerful imaginaries around at present, namely capitalism. By failing to understand how myths shape our social and personal self-understandings, we become complicit in casting capitalism as natural. This not only plays into the hands of a capitalist imaginary, but also undermines our appreciation for the capacity of myth to challenge capitalism from the ground up, namely, by radically altering social and personal self-understandings: how we think about one another, ourselves, and the possibilities of a different way of living together. In particular, I have focused on the myth of time and have explained how capitalist time instrumentalises the way that people create meaning in their own lives and in their relationships with other people and, as a result, diminishes their capacity for developing solidarity.

In the last section, I tried to briefly elucidate how these myths became dominant in the Anglo-Saxon West generally and in the UK specifically. I particularly stressed that processes that resulted in instrumentalisation could be conceived as originating in an altered understanding of solidarity rooted in human dignity and freedom. I suggested that taking such a reading is fundamental to understanding how capitalist myths achieve dominance, namely, by authentically resonating with people. Yet even if these narratives resonate with people, their dominance has resulted in far less freedom than anticipated, in particular leading to increased time at work, decreased time in contemplation, with family and with friends. What is more, where contemplation remains, it may often be focused on how to escape from debt. I also stressed that while neoliberal narratives appear to undermine solidarity, nonetheless some social actors, including many of my research participants, are ambivalent towards neoliberalism, seeing it as both undermining old sources of solidarity *and* presenting an opportunity for new pathways to solidarity.

This section will reveal the complex ways in which my participants variously challenged, submitted to, or wholesale imbibed myths of capitalism, paying special attention to time. I will demonstrate that time provides a key fault line for activists in their relation to capitalism. Ideas of the transcendental social are inherently timeless; they represent ways of imagining roles and responsibilities in the world as it should be that are beyond the constraints associated with the world as it is. I will demonstrate how both religious and nonreligious actors seek out, construct and inhabit a sense of higher time. Yet just as Bloch explains in relation to the transcendental social generally (see chapter 2), Narotzky and Besnier (2014: 3) have pointed out that people's possibilities for imagining a different world are always dialectically related to constraints associated with the world around them. Not only is the search for timeless roles and responsibilities perhaps a direct reaction to a world in which roles and responsibilities are in constant flux, but the capacity to imagine these timeless roles and responsibilities depends on the amount of secular, capitalist time that people have available to them. I will demonstrate ways in which actors simultaneously draw on and challenge secular, capitalist time to carve out time in which they can again reconnect with the timeless.

I moreover question, along the lines of Weber and Parry, whether the search for a world beyond secular, capitalist time, holding faith with the future possibility of such a world, may serve to justify an entirely rationalised approach to time in the world as it is now. This includes exploring Bear's

(2015) suggestion that this process may also go the other way round: inhabiting an increasingly short-term world inspires a reaction against such a world as people reach for permanence. I will develop this suggestion, stressing that this reaction is not necessarily and always naturally occurring, but often requires a myth that is prior to and challenges secular, capitalist time, a 'contract behind contracts', which must be brought to the surface through processes of conscientisation (Lambek 2010a).

I have also stressed in chapters 2 and 3 that some organisations and actors are not as reflexively aware of the way in which their transcendental ideals shape their behaviour, and often find little space or time within work to reflect on these processes. The lack of secular time allotted to the timeless renders people vulnerable to others' myths. I will thus particularly explore how those acting without explicit myths come to imbibe the myths of capitalism, even where the results seem antithetical to their ideals: in particular, they allow for the rationalisation of time, for values to be reduced into value, and come to think of their relationships with others as not only instrumental, but also, in some cases, competitive. Competition is of particular note in that some actors seem to imbibe a capitalist myth that competition fuels adrenaline and makes them more alert and effective.

Notwithstanding the ways in which they challenge secular, capitalist time, my participants are not floating in a parallel world. Instead they are quite specifically operating in fast-paced settings in which highly rationalised approaches to time are fundamental. I suggest that a number of actors come to sacrifice contemplation in favour of devoting themselves entirely to work. In the process, actors often become embroiled in processes of rationalisation, treading a very fine line between creatively challenging and capitulating to, or even sustaining capitalism. I close this section by drawing on Boltanski and Chiapello (2007: 19) to ask whether actors are challenging capitalism in the short term only to provide ways of sustaining capitalism in the long term.

Christians on the Left (CotL)

As explained in the introduction, CotL is rooted in Christian socialism, with its aversion to competition, and its promotion of friendship, reciprocity and empowerment. In chapter 2 I explained how these roots were used to develop a sense of solidarity. Although these roots seemed to jar with CotL's affiliation with the British Labour Party, chapter 3 explained that CotL uses its positional power to develop relational power. I said that CotL simultaneously faces inwards, campaigning to transform conventional politics, and outwards, seeking to change people's lifestyle choices. Here I will explore how myths employed at CotL relate to capitalism. I will briefly explore CotL's theological vision in relation to capitalism before focusing on two campaigns that exemplify CotL's working relationship with capitalism: 'Sunday Trading' and 'Put Your Money Where Your Mouth Is'.

CotL's specific theological stance contradicts ideas often associated with world religions generally and Christianity in particular. Contrary to my earlier suggestion, one might read Marx on the one hand and Weber and Parry on the other as theoretically coinciding. For Marx, myth is a distraction from this-worldly justice. The idea of salvation in the next life helps people to cope with the difficulties associated with a capitalist word. For Weber and Parry, salvation directly legitimates capitalism, since the possibility of an entirely non-instrumental future allows for the complete instrumentalisation of the world around us. CotL deliberately pushes against this understanding of salvation, and challenges others to do the same. The mantra Ralph often used to explain this point was of moving away from 'escapeology' and towards 'eschatology', that is, from faith as 'buying an escape ticket' to faith as 'the transformation of every dimension of human life'. In chapter 2 I referred to CotL's performative evangelism, whereby myth is primarily spread via performances of public duty. Whereas other researchers have counterpoised performance to theological abstraction, here we see that performance is counterpoised to salvation. Not only is Christian faith not a necessary prerequisite of solidarity – it is not a sufficient prerequisite. Performances of public duty alone are the means by which others are judged and solidarity is developed. This insight is key to understanding the following analysis of CotL campaigns in relation to capitalism.

In the build-up to the London Olympic Games in 2012, the coalition government proposed to temporarily suspend the Sunday Trading Act for the duration of the games. The Sunday Trading Act 1994 stipulates that while small shops are allowed to open without restriction, stores over 280 square metres are restricted to opening for six hours between the hours of 10am and 6pm. In its campaign against the suspension, CotL put together a briefing document, sent to all MPs, and particularly to CotL members. I was asked to make personal phone calls to CotL's 44 MPs, explaining the CotL position and asking for information on which way they would vote.

The CotL position was that the suspension of the Sunday Trading Act would:

> place additional pressure on workers and families on what is still seen as the traditional day of rest, religious observance, worship and a day to spend quality time with family members and close friends . . .
>
> Whilst we need to take seriously the economic challenges we face, Christians on the Left does not believe that society and relationships should be subordinated to economic imperatives. The ordering of our economic life should sustain family life and the common life. We should be supporting Sunday's long established unique and sacred place, not squeezing it out of existence. We affirm that we can renew the economy without compromising the day of rest and family time.

CotL's position on the Sunday Trading Act perfectly exemplifies an understanding of time that is counterpoised to capitalist time. In prior times, I have suggested, the possibility of timelessness legitimised the rationalisation of time in the world as it is. Within secular time, this concept was marked by keeping Sunday as separate, allowing the rationalisation of time within the rest of the week. Excessive time spent in contemplation in the rest of the week was considered idle. Yet here capitalist time comes to threaten even Sunday. While CotL recognises the need for increased productivity in the British economy, they are unwilling for such productivity to come at the expense of worship and quality time with family and friends. The campaign demonstrates how the contemplation of timeless roles and responsibilities requires carving out space within secular, capitalist time. It demonstrates an awareness that time is a key battleground in giving people the space to consider alternative values.

CotL's message need not appeal to Christians alone. Their stress on spending quality time with family and friends provides possibilities for crossover narratives which prioritise a particular type of performance. In this sense, the CotL campaign particularly speaks to Skeggs' (2011: 505) observation of the importance amongst working-class people of creating space for the gift of attention over time, exemplified in "hanging out". In this way, as suggested earlier, resisting capitalism is primarily embodied in performances of slowing down time, even flouting capitalist time to be with family and friends. Beyond the idea of keeping Sunday special, it is moreover worth noting how a number of CotL's practices discussed in chapters 2 and 3 are rooted in an idea of slowing down time amidst the fast-paced world of Westminster politics: praying, chatting, having lunches, offering the gift of attention over time. This slowing down of time often frustrates younger CotL activists who feel that time must be used preciously in order to "get things done".

Yet the campaign also demonstrates a way in which CotL appeals to people via what Anderson (1983) designates an 'imagined community' within secular time. CotL appeals to an idea of sharing a day away from work, in which some will worship while others simply spend quality time with family and friends. When asked to explain why we must all have the same day away from work, Dave explained that the demands of an economy in flux mean that unless a single day is kept separate by everybody simultaneously, possibilities of spending quality time with family and friends will be undermined. Yet it must be noted again that this campaign faces simultaneously inwards to politics and outwards to how people live their lives. Keeping Sunday as separate is only worthwhile if people spend the time wisely.

This point became particularly salient in an impromptu discussion with Ralph regarding how little time people have available to them to be involved in developing solidarity.

> I think it's really challenging, I think that space [in which people have no time to develop solidarity] is where an awful lot of people are who know in their guts they want to be involved in something but it's not

very easy to be so. And actually to be honest they're so economically stretched and they've been sold the lie that to be relaxed and actually me-time is sat in front of a flat screen TV on a very comfy couch . . . that actually that's the way – you know, work so hard, or so many hours to make the bills pay . . . right me-time's actually gunna be this. . . . gradually that – I've seen it – that habit can be broken that me-time actually can be time with others in the community, that can be time where you're giving and sharing and actually that can be just as life-giving.

According to Ralph, people have been 'sold a lie' that time spent in front of a TV 'on a very comfy couch' is 'life-giving'. From this perspective, simply giving people more time is insufficient; they also need to be conscientised to recognise that time spent 'giving and sharing' can be just as life-giving. But, Ralph asserts, this can be done.

The 'Sunday Trading' campaign failed. Part of the reason for this failure might be put down to the interconnection between capitalist myth and the kind of person that becomes an MP. Ralph insists that 'you can hide behind the word freedom but actually sometimes freedom means the people with the most money get to say the most'. What is more, this influence of money in politics is hard to fight, since it is usually those with some sort of money in the first place that are able to run for public office:

> A lot of folks do not feel they have the finances or the resources to be involved in politics . . .
>
> [I]t's a kind of very precarious place to be . . . you don't know if you're going to get a job at the end of . . . quite a long job application process. And it's a process that requires a lot of money and a lot of funding to fight a campaign. And it would also potentially mean taking quite a lot of time off work so people would have to work part-time . . . A lot of the folks who are involved in . . . grassroots work are not being paid in sums that allow them that freedom.

This financial issue was particularly evident with Simon. Having decided he was called to be an MP, Simon left his job and fought a number of elections. Now in his forties, he had moved out of his home in London and was living with his parents in Sheffield. When not campaigning, he would oscillate between Sheffield and London, one week living with his parents, the next week sleeping on a friend's sofa. And Simon himself was only able to make these sacrifices because he had substantial savings to rely on.

Again, time becomes fundamental: those without appropriate earnings do not have the time to campaign on issues that matter to them. The point being made here is more subtle than a capitalist conspiracy between big business and politicians. Instead, the suggestion is that in a capitalist world, only those with money have the time to be involved in politics. The result is that the alternative ideologies of the disaffected struggle to find voice in politics.

This analysis speaks well to our current situation of hopelessness. Caught in the iron cage of capitalist time, we are unable to find the time to challenge the very understanding of time that constrains us.

Notwithstanding the interconnection between big business and conventional politics, CotL stresses that all people are complicit in and responsible for challenging capitalist practices that undermine solidarity. Like the 'Sunday Trading' campaign, 'Put Your Money Where Your Mouth Is' simultaneously faced inwards to politics, and outwards to how people live their lives. The campaign simultaneously pressured government to separate retail and investment banking, reinstate shareholder liability, and tax bankers' bonuses, and encouraged ordinary people to change their pensions, investments and bank accounts to more ethical companies. Campaigners recognise that their demands reduce potential profit, both for companies and for individuals. They are explicitly appealing to people to prioritise solidarity over profit. And by facing inwards and outwards simultaneously, they are stressing that change cannot take place in politics alone, but must also take place at the level of the individual.

Pressure at the level of the individual demonstrates how CotL recognises the need to work within the capitalist system to transform it. By encouraging ethical investment and ethical consumption, they are hoping that companies will shift their practice to suit a conscientised consumer demand.

By facing simultaneously inwards and outwards, 'Put Your Money Where Your Mouth Is' speaks to our current state of hopelessness. The campaign suggests that hopelessness is not merely derived from the negligence of big companies or of politicians, but of individuals: the fault, dear Brutus, is not in our stars but in ourselves, that we are underlings. CotL seeks to restore a connection between politics and lifestyle (see Stacey 2017c). They point to the connection between the ethics of companies we deplore and our own ethics: consumers can only force companies to prioritise solidarity over profit if they themselves prioritise solidarity over profit, moving their money to more ethical companies which may offer a lower rate of return – a difficult thing to do when they are already struggling financially. As Eric, a CotL member and an adviser to a senior Labour MP put it, the campaign to make individuals move their money 'draws on the idea in the gospel of Matthew that where one's treasure is, one's heart is'. As much as campaigning for policy changes, CotL appeals to people's hearts, asking them to perform myths of solidarity in their everyday practices.

All facets of CTL's campaigns draw on biblical messages to inspire shared action. What emerges here is the importance of drawing on what Durkheim would call mechanic forms of solidarity, based on shared values and traditions, in order to inculcate a sense of organic solidarity, that is, solidarity based on reciprocity within a capitalist system: a 'contract behind contracts'. Drawing on shared myths is central to conscientising people and inspiring performances that challenge the status quo. It is moreover clear that particularly in relation to time, CotL's campaigns offer possibilities for cross-over narratives that appeal to people of all religions and none.

The major shortcoming of both of these campaigns is in the failure to influence legislative agendas on the one hand, and in the relatively low appeal of a campaign framed in a Christian myth on the other. Yet it must be stressed that if the particular framing is limited, CotL's focus on time provides inklings of a crossover narrative that, as the following case studies will demonstrate, has much resonance outside of the Christian community.

Hackney Council for Voluntary Service (HCVS)

In chapter 2, I explained that while HCVS staff showed a number of secular motivations for action, the idea of equality held preambles of a transcendental social basis for action whereby an imagined future is used to negate and transform the present. Notwithstanding this potential however, I observed an unreflexive relationship with myth that undermined the possibility of connecting transcendental ideals with practices. Thus chapter 3 explained that in the absence of a clear and fleshed out vision, HCVS found itself not only susceptible to co-option by the state, thus becoming imprisoned in an iron cage of bureaucracy, but also itself participating in the construction of this cage, placing parameters around grassroots groups without seeking to empower them. While this trend by no means defined all of the organisation's activities, that it had made its way into certain areas relatively unchallenged suggests that the scope of its influence is arbitrary and no clear line is being drawn as to what constitutes a compromise of HCVS' ideals. I suggested that the construction of a religious/secular, mythic/rational binary forecloses the possibility of employing myth to challenge the status quo. Here I extend this analysis to capitalism, suggesting that by neglecting myth, secular actors can become complicit in breaking down resistance to capitalism.

James, who had formerly worked in the private sector, suggests that capitalism is unfair:

> I'd prefer a more equal society where professionals are rewarded per-haps according to how they contribute to society, whether it's teachers or medics or nurses or the charity sector in comparison to people in the corporate sector, but in terms of the reality of how society is, I'd prefer to work in the not-for-profit sector as it's something I'm motivated by in terms of the fact that it ties in with the kind of belief systems I have, rather than take the higher salary and be less motivated.

James envisages a society of each according to her contribution to society, conceived in terms of helping people, rather than each according to the price allocated by a market.

Just as at CotL, staff at HCVS struggle to get by within a capitalist system. None of the staff have salaries in the highest tax bracket. And living in the same area as they did, I was well aware of the difficulties of getting by. The majority of salary goes on mortgage, if one is lucky enough to own a home, or rent if not, and bills. If one has children, the cost of living can be more difficult still. Capitalism clearly has a strong impact on the charity sector; the low wages associated with the sector put a number of people off working in it. Even for those who do work in the sector, it is often the case that they have worked in business beforehand, seeking to make enough money to live on before joining the charity sector. This was most obvious in John, who drove a 20-year-old Mercedes, which had clearly once been top of the range, but for which now only the faded hood ornament indicated its former glory. John told me:

> We [recently] did a piece of research because there was a huge turnover of people in my position. So we did an analysis of all the people across the 33 London boroughs, and where they came from, and they were all about my age, and they had previous careers that they'd . . . done for like 20 years or something, and then came into the voluntary sector. And one of the questions was why they didn't come into the sector in the first place and they said . . . they couldn't afford to come into the voluntary sector. . . . You have to experience life and what's more worthy, money or the knowledge and the ability to sort of work to make change.

There appear to be two factors at work here. On the one hand, having worked in the private sector previously creates a financial buffer, allowing people to live a comfortable life with a relatively low income. On the other hand, people awaken to the idea of a more worthy life lived working to make a change, and then make the transition into socially engaged work. A number of the staff at HCVS find themselves playing the capitalist system: they need to earn enough money from jobs they are less interested in before they can afford to take jobs in the charity sector. As James suggested, for the most part they get by with the energy provided by the knowledge they are working in something they believe in.

Notwithstanding these critiques of capitalism rooted in direct experience of financial difficulty, HCVS does little to alter structural conditions. The main work of HCVS is to assist social enterprises in getting off the ground. The result of this neglect of structural conditions is a King Midas effect, whereby the organisation is forever rolling back the tide: they are working with the effects of inequality, while structural conditions continue to produce new problems. They are seeking to gain as wide as possible an opportunity in a society that remains unequal and divided in outcome. This neglect is reflected in the way that, as employees in an organisation, HCVS staff, and particularly managers, seem to reproduce capitalist myths.

Since HCVS is not tackling structural arrangements, when those arrangements shift, so too do the practices of the organisation itself. In my time at the organisation, there was a shift towards neoliberal governance. As a result, I observed the slow adoption of capitalist myths and associated practices. The most obvious creep towards the adoption of capitalist practices is the move towards selling services that had previously been free, in particular, surgeries for those seeking to set up social enterprises. These surgeries were regarded as fundamental to HCVS' role in empowering grassroots groups. The kinds of groups and people that came into the offices were obviously disadvantaged themselves: often poorly dressed, under- or overweight, lacking in sufficient language skills, lacking in the kind of flair and discourse associated with success. They were the most motivated members of the most disadvantaged groups, seeking help to establish enterprises that could serve those groups, as well as the wider community. And they needed a lot of help, often more than John himself appeared capable of offering. When money from public funds failed to materialise, these individuals often gave up their own money. John was allotted 30 minutes to speak with each group, but always offered far more, often up to two hours. The suggestion then, that these individuals could afford to pay for training, was anathema to John.

> I don't like it . . . I don't like it because it's going to already cause problems that can't afford anything anyway. And the community groups that are . . . or the number of people coming together to deliver services, they're already working . . . a lot of them already work and this is something that they do on the side. Okay? So now they're going to have to find the money to do this effectively, whereas . . . the way this country's going or anywhere at the moment, you know how, people are just, they're not even talking to each other, you know leading these isolated . . . isolation is massive, you know? Statistics show that so many people are living on their own and they're not communicating and they're not living within a support structure. And this is just gunna get worse. So it's fuelling that I fear. You know, and really when these people, these individuals who work anyway, and then come together, and make things, areas where they live, their work, a little bit better, that could be supported by funding, you know?
>
> What's happened here is that our concentration's gone on to generating income, to sustain some of the work that's needed. And the level of time that's devoted to generating income that enables us to do the work is getting greater, and the time that's spent working with community groups, and the concentration on actually enabling change, is, is lessening.

John demonstrates a deep emotional struggle with the shift towards capitalist practices. He demonstrates an in-depth awareness of how solidarity is undermined by capitalist ideas of time, value and the practices associated with these ideas. He is also concerned about a lack of support networks that will enable people to cope. He demonstrates an awareness of how capitalist ideas of time undermine the possibility of developing secure networks. He is also worried about how serving capitalist ideas of time and value mean that there is less time available for what Skeggs calls the gift of attention over time, and he deliberately challenges capitalist time by giving people more time than they are allotted (see also Williams 2015: 197).

In the face of his failure to convince senior management that this shift will compromise the principles of the organisation, John is 'always thinking that I'm gunna leave'. I have already referred to how staff get by with low incomes on the energy provided by the knowledge they are working in something they believe in. But, as explained in the previous section, when political climates change, so too do the practices on the ground. In these moments, the ideals are shaken, and staff become far more conscious of their sacrifices, as if the black and white romance suddenly turns to colour, and the inadequacy of the material objects surrounding them becomes clear. In moments such as these John would suggest that he simply could not 'afford to go on like this'. The room would feel uncomfortable, as we each began to notice signs of deprivation, from his old but well-maintained clothes, to the plastic jar of fish-shaped snacks that he refills from industrial-sized bags and always offers to guests. I would remember in these moments that, like those he is helping, John too is a motivated individual from a disadvantaged group. Despite this discomfort however, John was not leaving. He still felt tied to his initial motivations for joining HCVS, especially as these were recalled with each new service user, even if he knew these motivations were being compromised in practice.

Yet managers see good reasons for operating more like a business. Notwithstanding his earlier critique of capitalism, James tells me:

> I think some people think . . . my gut feeling is that some people think we need to be a bit more business-savvy, and maybe it's not necessarily a bad thing because it will maybe improve quality . . .
>
> It's always been a bit of a difficult thing so sometimes with free training for example, people don't always appreciate that . . . when there was free [training], people might, you might get 20 people who book onto the training but then only 10 people show up on the day because it's not any financial loss to them, so it's a bit of shame: the finance becomes so dominant in the relationship.

Organisations can feel like they are wasting money if those they are trying to help choose not to show up. They figure that by charging money they will be tying their beneficiaries into a contract and incentivising them to show up. Having this capitalist logic at work on the front line ensures that services are not wasted. This attitude exemplifies the reduction of values into value, whereby payment is the key means of demonstrating interest. As with the state, despite strong criticisms of capitalism, staff may fail to notice the ways in which they are reproducing capitalist narratives. Yet it is worth noting that whereas capitulation to the bureaucratic management seemed widespread, capitulation to capitalism seems to be contained to the management. This difference between frontline staff and managers suggests that face-to-face contact with deprivation creates an awareness of the negative consequences of charging for services. It may also suggest that the disempowerment associated with financial resources are more direct and easier to recognise than those associated with bureaucracy.

A number of HCVS staff are critical of capitalist inequality, yet rather than directly challenging the system, they think of ways of working with it. This may mean accumulating a little private wealth before coming to work in charity, it may mean focusing on the symptoms of inequality, or it may mean changing the practices of the organisation itself so that rather than being provided for free, services are sold. While some staff were extremely critical and uncomfortable with this change, even threatening to leave, the management itself seemed comfortable with the shift, even suggesting that the introduction of charges would ensure greater responsibility on the part of service users. There is a lack of recognition here that the nature of the community being created changes with the economic context. What was a gift becomes a supply for a demand, the intensity of which is measured by the willingness to pay a fee. In this context, community is something that develops in a contractual, supply and demand relationship.

It needs to be remembered that there are pre-contractual grounds for these contractual behaviours. As explained in chapter 2, frontline staff are not primarily motivated by holding onto a job, even if this need has come to shape their practice. Managers do not offer services *because* these make money, but rather feel forced to charge for them on account of limited funds. Frontline staff and managers alike are motivated by personal grievances, sympathy, their own happiness derived from serving others; they are motivated by equality and by practices associated with this. What is more, they appear for the most part aware of how their motivations are undermined by the adoption of capitalist logic. The problem lies in the fact that even as they are aware of these influences, they are not challenging them. This leads to a much broader question about why it is that we can be fully conscious of our values being undermined and yet capitulate nonetheless. Particularly on the part of senior staff, capitulation to capitalist logic is seen as the only way of keeping people in work. Again, there is a sense of hopelessness amidst the advance of capitalism. The question for those instituting these neoliberal reforms is: How long will these pre-contractual ideas hold out in a context that seems antithetical? How long will hope hold out against hopelessness?

Faith-based Regeneration Network (FbRN)

In chapter 2, I explained that although FbRN staff had a strong sense of the connection between myth and solidarity, as members of FbRN they had imbibed modern binaries such as religious/secular and religion/politics and could not conceive of how a multi-faith vision might be used to inclusively develop solidarity in a messy religious and nonreligious landscape. Chapter 3 demonstrated that, as with HCVS, this lack of imagination as to the possible connections between myth and solidarity in a complex landscape was reflected in a failure to reimagine the role of the state, leading Gary to call for more, rather than less bureaucracy. Here I suggest that as with HCVS, the lack of a clear myth leads to an odd situation in which actors clearly unhappy with capitalism nonetheless reproduce hegemonic capitalist myths in their public orientation.

Perhaps reflecting their lack of imagination in connecting either their personal faith or a multi-faith ideal with public reality, members of FbRN actually drew primarily on socialist myths in critiquing capitalism. For Dominic for instance, there is a direct relationship between the downfall of the Soviet Union and the 'rampant capitalism' that has arisen over the last 20 years. He suggests that the Soviet Union provided a symbol that an alternative was possible. Despite what Dominic calls the Soviet Union's 'moral bankruptcy', it nonetheless stood as a political exemplar that could inspire imaginations of a different way of relating to one another economically. Today, however, 'individualism, materialism and capitalism' are the 'universal values'. Yet if the Soviet Union acted as a beacon of an alternative, faith is perceived as only playing a role in the private realm, encouraging personal responsibility. Unlike at CotL, where there is a deliberate attempt to connect political values with lifestyle choices, at FbRN, deliberately established to reflect the role that faith might play in developing an active public sphere, faith is only perceived as challenging capitalism at the level of the individual.

This lack of a public critique of capitalism is not for want of distaste with capitalism. Gary too draws on what he calls 'old-fashioned socialist' myths to critique the way in which government policy has shifted to create a capitalist environment whereby grants, shaped largely by the applicant, are replaced with contracts, shaped largely by the commissioner, and where organisations are forced to compete with one another:

> Everything is going to contracts, often private sector contracts, even in areas that you might imagine would be better served by nonprofit: a social enterprise or a charity . . .
>
> Our relationships with central government have been distorted over the last two years by the changing funding relationship. So . . . although they still talk the language of collaboration, that faith communities and faith community organisations collaborate, actually by their kind of drip feeding, and holding out little bits of money here, little bits of money there, what they're creating is a quite small marketplace, quite a competitive marketplace, where we are competing against each other. And so organisations that would naturally work together are even quite suspicious of each other, because we're not sure what they're doing in relation to bits of money.

Gary's position is well established in policy. In the 1990s, neoliberalism crossed party divides, with New Labour bringing ideals of capitalism into sectors that seemed impervious to full-scale privatisation, in particular the NHS:

> Out of a perception that public services remained inflexible, bureaucratic and often of poor quality, the aim was to drive up productivity. In the development in the 1990s of "quasi-markets" in health, for example, with purchaser/provider splits, and compulsory competitive tendering, the state in effect became the sponsor and champion of market activity in public services.
>
> (Mayo and Moore 2002: 1)

This philosophy soon came to infiltrate the social realm too. As third way socialists and subsequently Red Tories promoted the dissolution of state-funded social services, they legitimised their actions in the language of drawing on and generating social capital. In particular, as already made clear in chapter 3, successive governments looked to faith communities as 'repositories of resources – staff, buildings, volunteers, networks, money – which could be deployed to the social good' (Dinham 2012: 577). Here then, we see solidarity being treated as a resource from which to reduce the need for the state and, in so doing, increase individual freedom – from taxation as much as from state intervention. Most recently, neoliberal policy has come to influence the way that faith groups are engaged, with policy makers encouraging competition between groups to deliver key services.

For Gary, competition between organisations leads to suspicion where collaboration might be the norm. This demonstrates a paradox at the heart of policy reawakening to the role of faith in developing solidarity. Though faith communities are lauded for their ability to work collaboratively in the interests of solidarity, they are being forced to compete with one another in ways that undermine collaboration. What is more, as the state slowly reduces funding and encourages these groups to bid for funds from private sector organisations, there is increasingly less time to spend on those practices that offer a unique understanding of solidarity.

Yet notwithstanding this critique, much as at HCVS, FbRN can be seen to reproduce myths of capitalism in its practices. Although Gary is extremely critical of cuts in public spending, his attitude towards the new neoliberal policy context is ambivalent. Of particular note, already mentioned in chapter 3, is the way that FbRN reproduces myths of financial incentive by suggesting that government can use funding criteria to encourage inclusivity amongst faith groups.

Gary moreover anticipates an interesting future in a neoliberal funding context. For one thing, he suggests that there are some things the organisation can do without money. When setting up the organisation in the first place, there was a strong view amongst most of the people round the table that . . . until we got funding, there was a limit to what we could do. And I was the minority there . . . I will take . . . all the credit for saying we got kick back from a particular government fund and you know "oh we'll have to wait another year" and I said "we don't, we can just do stuff" . . . we're all connected with our own organisations, we've all got resources even though we're currently not paying anybody.

From this perspective, developing a network of people with ideas is more important than receiving funding, which is regarded as an added bonus. Groups respond to a lack of funding by creatively developing networks of shared action. Yet the discussion of undertaking activities to get the organisation off the ground in expectation of funding is one thing, while what to do in the absence of any obvious sources of funding is quite different. When discussing the future, Gary began to sound more like a social entrepreneur:

The question becomes, do any of these organisations, do we, fill a niche, and I think we do, so if one source of funding has come to an end, of course it's worrying . . . but at the same time there are of course interesting opportunities. The question is, could we become more of a front line involved directly in or with community organisations rather than the sort of behind the scenes resource that we have been. And yes we could, and so could other organisations in a similar sort of boat, but there is an issue about whether we have enough time to actually keep us going through a kind of transition.

As with HCVS, when state funding dries up, Gary turns towards the language of capitalism. He suggests that the organisation needs to 'fill a niche' which funders will be attracted to. In this context, community becomes an answer to a need that has been identified and which funders recognise. There is no talk of how faith groups can collaborate to challenge hegemonic capitalist myths. Moreover, the question of having 'enough time' is really one of having enough funding. Again, Gary reproduces the idea that time is money, with the gift of attention over time being conditional upon having funding.

Even where they are extremely critical of capitalism and the spread of capitalist logic into all areas of government policy, organisations have to be willing to negotiate a capitalist system if they wish to be successful in contemporary society. FbRN demonstrates that even those with a strong socialist background can find some area of agreement with an agenda of government cuts, whether this is found in the simple point that community work does not necessarily require money, or in the turn to capitalist logic in thinking about the organisation's survival. Strikingly, it is this socialist myth that is key. Members of FbRN still see the fall of the Soviet Union as the end of a viable alternative to capitalism, and fail to see possibilities arising out of either mono-faith or multi-faith myths. As stressed in chapters 2 and 3, there is a marked absence of a multi-faith theology that is able to offer a clear vision of what the public sphere ought to be like, to draw in members around that vision, and to inspire solidarity. Without funding, there are no internal resources to draw from.

London Citizens (LC)

Thus far we have seen how a Christian organisation develops a strong critique of capitalism, developing a dual practice of campaigning for policy change and seeking to persuade individuals to enact small changes in lifestyle. We have seen how a secular organisation operates within a religious/secular, mythic/rational binary, and in so doing neglects the role of myth in sustaining and challenging capitalism. As a result, the organisation's practices were seen to reproduce capitalist myths. And we have seen how a multi-faith organisation, full of individuals that are personally critical of capitalism, nonetheless operates within binaries of religious/secular and religion/politics, and as such fails to voice an alternative to capitalism. In this sense, it seems we are faced with a stark choice between myths that are powerful but fail to resonate widely and dispensing with myth altogether. In this case study, I present the beginnings of an alternative.

Chapter 2 has suggested that without drawing on any particular tradition, LC is able to cultivate the idea of "taking the world as it is to the world as it should be" as a generalised transcendental framework which negates the everyday world, and thereby empowers actors to transform it. This mode of the transcendental social, very thin in content, is powerful in a diverse society because it is able to draw in people of very different religious and ideological backgrounds. It is also sensible, since rather than setting up members for disappointment, it allows them to focus on small, winnable goals.

Chapter 3 then explained how the idea of the world as it should be is reflected in the search amongst LC members for a purer idea of politics, devoid of the self-serving attitudes and bureaucracy associated with conventional politics. While stressing that LC's relationship with the state was actually quite pragmatic and often convivial, I explained how important it was to maintain a distance and keep activity at grassroots level, thereby ensuring the kind of effervescence, ritual and leadership development that drew people in initially. I also explained that while they did not work within the state, rather than always antagonising the state, they recognised its power and, like other traditional institutions, hoped to make that power less positional and more relational.

In this section I explore how LC's ideas interplay with capitalism. I will show that as with the state, LC is heavily critical of capitalism, and often regards itself as working against big businesses. But again, this oppositional relationship will often give way to behaviours that are more pragmatic and convivial. I suggest that using a broad and reflexive transcendental social frame allows LC to easily navigate between the world as it should be and the world as it is. Yet I also suggest that the elusive nature of the world as it should be, alongside the reification of the world as it is as a capitalist, instrumental and competitive world, leaves LC in an ambivalent relationship with capitalism. Staff at LC often reproduce myths and adopt practices that seem to sustain capitalism, both in the organisation itself and in the wider society it interacts with.

As with CotL, the idea of the world as it should be speaks directly to ideas of time. The world as it should be is an imagined space of timeless roles and responsibilities not subject to the constraints associated with the world as it is. As detailed in chapter 2, the idea of the world as it should be is introduced in training sessions. These sessions provide a liminal space in which people of different religions, races and incomes are asked to collectively imagine a different way of living. Yet as with CotL, facilitating the collective imagining of the world as it should be is by no means an attempt to distract people from the world as it is. Instead, the process is deliberately designed to call on people to act within the world as it is. Imagining the timeless is a device designed to inspire people to act differently within secular, capitalist time. At LC, a transcendental social framework allows people to move from reformist critique to radical critique by stepping outside of the world disclosed to them and creating a new basis on which to act.

It is moreover the case that these training sessions do not only construct a different myth around time, but also sit within a different time. Returning to Taylor's understanding of higher time, these training sessions themselves step outside of secular, capitalist time, pointing vertically towards the world as it should be. These training sessions are thus closer in time to one another, and to great inspirational events, such as the moments when people realised they would become activists, than they are to the days and hours immediately preceding or following. The initiates are closer in time to other initiates in years past than they are to, say, the security guard at the door, or their colleagues and friends elsewhere in the city. As organisers tell stories of these inspirational events, attendees are transported into a realm in which secular, capitalist time collapses.

I have explained one such event in chapter 3, explaining how a concatenation of various myths brought together in a single ritual created a sense of belonging that cut across differences of religion, race and class. The build-up to these events demonstrates a manner in which LC activists navigate between sacred and secular, capitalist time. Though these events are closer in time to other effervescent moments than they are to the days and hours immediately preceding or following, these days and hours are highly rationalised. The events themselves are meticulously organised to ensure that they do not extend beyond the advertised time. The coming together within these events of various community leaders of different religions, races and classes requires numerous one-to-ones (see chapter 2), whereby community leaders are lured into the LC agenda. One-to-ones are arranged to be no more than 15 minutes, to account for the busy schedules and short attention spans of hard-working people in a capitalist system. The collecting of musical instruments, technical equipment and refreshments is written into a schedule, with tasks allocated and expected times of completion recorded.

This awareness of how busy people are extends to both advantaged and disadvantaged in society. When I asked Aaron what the greatest inhibition to solidarity is, he paused for a number of seconds and said:

> Time. People are working long hours, often working two jobs, which take up their weekends too. On top of that they've often got kids to look after. They might be single parents. They have to work long hours just to survive. So when you ask them on top of that, can you help with this, and it's not just about handing money over but getting involved . . . time is always the biggest problem.

For Aaron both the way that time is rationalised within a capitalist system, and the way that it is valued, undermine people's capacity to be involved in developing solidarity. Time at work is not being valued equally, so that, for example a cleaner earns far less in an hour than a banker. This is particularly problematic, since the people that LC most needs to involve in their campaigns, namely, those that are suffering, are those with the least time available to do so.

This critique is employed directly to work with the world as it is. Theo told me that in a campaign for the living wage, whereby businesses are encouraged to pay their staff enough to live on that job alone, corporations were told by the organisation that 'the Living Wage is great for business too. It makes employees more productive, makes them spend less time off sick'. The ability of LC to speak to the capitalist system in this way raises questions as to whether capitalism is being challenged in the short term to be sustained in the long term (Boltanski and Chiapello 2007: 19). LC helps powerful companies to recognise their mutual interest with the disadvantaged. It connects the private good of a company with the common good of a capitalist system. What it does not challenge is how capitalism as a system is directed towards the generation of profit, rather than solidarity.

Just as time is used in this way to conscientise businesses, it is also used to conscientise ordinary people, encouraging them to campaign together on issues of shared concern.

Emily explained how the enormous inequality one observes in London, especially in North London where she worked, can cause real difficulties for the way the organisation operates. This did not mean that the rich were not sympathetic to the plight of the poor, just that it was hard to find issues of shared interest, issues that aggrieved people from all income strata to a similar degree.

> So what we've found with a social care campaign, social care for the elderly, is we've been able to bring together care workers, so a lot of

migrant women working really hard jobs, really long hours; lots of middle-class families who are unable to afford private care, and even if they can afford private care, they still end up with low-paid care workers; families are really struggling to find good quality services for their loved ones. And initially there's a bit of a blame culture around "the staff they don't speak English, they're not trained properly". And actually bringing those people together has been amazing because what we've been able to hear from both sides is how difficult it is to be a care worker, how much pressure they're under, and also how much they want to provide good care for the families, and how difficult it is, and why. And that's enabled us to build this really interesting coalition between families of the cared for, and care workers, and now we're starting to relate to care providers and care commissioners, and the campaign is completely across the income spectrum, the class spectrum, the ethnicity spectrum and the religious spectrum.

By highlighting the time pressure that care workers are under, to provide a certain amount of care within a certain amount of minutes, to work as many hours as they could in order to provide for their own families, Emily was able to develop a broad coalition across differences of religion, ethnicity and class. The example of care is of particular note because it recalls Skegg's (2011) idea of the gift of attention over time. Much as at HCVS, the neoliberalisation of care services entails the rationalisation of time spent with service users, allotting a set time in which to perform functional tasks. This rationalisation is seen to undermine the concept of care.

As at CotL, this ability to develop solidarity around time is suggestive of an imagined community within secular time that recognises the time pressures of the other. Yet it is worth stressing that the imagined community in itself does not seem to produce sufficient solidarity. It is only through the conscientising practices of dedicated organisers, often involving bringing people from very different backgrounds together to meet face-to-face, that this sense of solidarity can develop.

One of the keys to LC's strength is thus found in its ability to successfully navigate between the world as it should be and the world as it is. Yet this same ability could at times lead to the reproduction of capitalist myths. One manner in which this can be seen is in the use of employees' time. Senior organisers recognise that a market society devalues social action in terms of the wage a person can receive for her labour. As with all of the case studies, the result is that social action is by and large a middle-class pursuit, since young people from poorer backgrounds have to earn enough money to support their extended family.

We have one member of staff from East London and he's got a lot of family pressure to be a high earner because he's the eldest son, his mother relies on him, she doesn't work, he needs to give some of his salary to her, so he took a massive risk by coming to work with Citizens because he's a kid from East London kid, could be, you know, could be a banker, could be a lawyer, could be earning three times what he earns at Citizens.

While middle-class activists may find their earnings supplemented by parents, those from poorer backgrounds not only have to make do without this luxury, but also need to earn enough to support other family members. There is no time to supplement this income elsewhere. Organisers often work from as early as 7am and until midnight. Yet senior organisers have to strike a balance between this recognition and the demands of the world as it is. Senior organisers are constantly worried about balancing "getting the most" out of the time of junior organisers without "burning them out".

Reflecting points made by Bear (2015) time also places a limit on how long one can organise for: organising is said to be 'a game for young people', involving long hours, constant travelling, and requiring of people that they have few obligations of time to partners or children. This inability to invest in relationships reflects similar points made by Sennett (1998) and Skeggs (2011). Perhaps ironically, in seeking to develop solidarity in society, and to create more time for overworked people, LC organisers are seldom able to spend quality time with friends or family. 'One day I'd like to go to the cinema, or maybe have a beer with my friends', quipped one organiser to me with a hint of sarcasm. This quip implies a deliberate recognition of competing with the culture industry for people's attention, and to define one's life in contradistinction to a life lived in pursuit of entertainment. But in a culture in which entertainment is the dominant means of whiling one's leisure time, the quip also implies a culture of competition around the absence of time for leisure.

That organisers devalue their own leisure time in this way may well feed into their attitude towards others. Theo told me that one way to work around people's stress that they were too busy was to say 'we like busy people. Busy people get things done'. This attitude seems worrying because it further exploits those who have little time to be involved. Yet it also speaks to a Protestant work ethic that says being busy implies productivity. And yet placing pressure on individuals in this way also demonstrates how, like CotL, LC works both inwards and outwards, seeking to transform conventional politics and big business by asking individuals to resist secular, capitalist time, creating spaces in which they can give their time to a common cause.

Notwithstanding that the lack of time organisers themselves have is based on their giving time to activism, it speaks to further ways in which myths of capitalism and associated practices were adopted within LC. In my time volunteering with LC, I worked with a number of other volunteers surviving on lunch and travel expenses alone – a practice that again prioritises middle-class actors with networks of financial support.

LC also reproduces capitalism in its organising practices. A large source of LC's funding comes from "dues", that is, annual payments from member institutions. LC thus operates within a market of its own: they rely on institutions "buying" their services, which they encourage to do using sales tactics that appeal to self-interest. The discourse used to strategise about bringing on members can be described as either cynical, realistic or rationalised, depending on how one wishes to look at it. Theo explains:

> It's quite, I wouldn't say manipulative, but it's quite down in the world as it is. To say that is not to say that we are not social animals and we're not social animals and cannot be altruistic; it's just that people's actions are determined by what their own interests are. So sometimes being altruistic is in a person's self-interest. And that's not to say if you're self-interested, that's a bad thing, because it's a matter of survival. It sounds Darwinistic, and if people don't get the context, it seems rather sharp and rather dramatic.

In one sense it looks as though LC is taking a capitalist anthropology for granted, understanding that to operate in the world as it is, they need to start with people's self-interest. Yet two points are worth noting. The first point is that, as with the example of the vicar offered in chapter 2, the idea of self-interest is extremely broad, and could even include altruism itself. The second point is that Durkheimian organic solidarity suggests that people will fall into relationships of mutual self-interest almost harmoniously, instinctively. But the LC method involves deep reflexive practice, understanding the place of self-interest, analysing 'what makes that person tick', and subsequently conscientising that person. This formulation of self-interest pushes through a self-interest/solidarity binary, and indeed a self/society binary. The object at LC is to conscientise people into seeing self and society as one and the same. This conscientisation process is primarily mythic and performative, aesthetic and emotional, drawing its strength in particular from emotive stories. Thus LC begins to challenge a capitalist division between self-interest and solidarity by developing a sense that there is no isolated self because how we choose to act has consequences for those around us.

Still, one might question whether this creates the kind of pseudo-*sittlichkeit* discussed in chapter 3: a community held together only by the self-interest of its individual members. Three questions emerge: First, is this the kind of community we are seeking? Second, what happens when a given individual or institution feels its self-interest is no longer served. Does it occasionally sacrifice its needs for the greater good? Third, what if a small group can create a community of self-interest that serves them but no one else? In terms of the individuals within the organisation, Theo suggested that in his time at LC:

> There was a lot of tension. I don't know if it was because of being run by the idea of self-interest. It might have been the competitive nature of all the people at a young age trying to do well. So there was a competitive

aspect to it which sometimes was unhealthy. But at the same time it framed some great leaders within the organisation.

Here, operating on the basis of self-interest in a competitive setting undermines solidarity but also inspires great leadership. As an insider, drawn in by the ideas and actions of the organisation, I equally found myself drawn in by competitiveness. As suggested in the case of FbRN, this competitiveness often led to feelings of suspicion towards fellow organisers. Yet competition is seen as a driver of virtuous behaviour. Theo would tell me about monthly meetings in which organisers would account for the work they had done:

> The nature of the competition was: monthly meeting, 20 organisers, you want to be the one to come in with the most institutions, the most one-to-ones, and it's a very, almost harsh culture. Where . . . it's almost as tough as banking where you're like "these are my numbers". You want to prove to everyone else that you're the best organiser. And the way it was done through monthly meetings, you had to show up and you had to deliver. It wasn't turf-wars but competition to say, "I'm the biggest, I'm the best".

For Theo at least, the competitive nature of these meetings is exhilarating; it leads to harder work on the part of all of the organisers. While my own observations attest to this, I would also point to a sense of resentment and jealousy between young and ambitious organisers. Reflected on society as a whole, the question is whether an approach so rooted in competition as a means can ever produce solidarity as an end.

LC demonstrates that it is possible to be heavily critical of capitalism, and the inequalities that it leads to, whilst nonetheless recognising that one must work with the structures that be and people as they are in order to bring about change. Its strategies of developing a sense of relational power, of using this relational power to pressure companies to change, and of helping disparate communities to discover a shared self-interest offer a kind of reflexive 'organic' solidarity. These community structures perhaps do not naturally form in a diverse capitalist society, but with the conscientising activities of devoted organisers, they can be brought into being and thrive.

Yet drawing on chapter 2, we might also suggest that 'mechanic' forms of solidarity are also drawn from in order to reinforce the 'organic' solidarity – there is what Lambek (2010a) calls a 'contract behind contracts'. A broad and reflexive approach to the transcendental social encapsulated in the idea of the world as it should be, articulated in myths that exemplify both the world as it should be and the world as it should not be, are cultivated, a general and undefined imagined community formed, such as can provide the social imaginary or shared background necessary for agreement on particular issues.

Still, LC can also be seen to reproduce capitalist myths to do with the rationalisation of time demonstrating productivity, prioritising self-interest, payment as indicating participation, and competitiveness. Here we might suggest that the world as it should be is underdeveloped, and perhaps that LC could do more to draw on the alternative values provided by the religious and secular groups with which it works. Yet this apparent reproduction of capitalist myths needs to be reconciled with the fact that LC only works with the world as it is, which in this case means recognising the dominance of capitalist myths as they influence even their own members, in order to work towards the world as it should be. By being involved in LC, organisations and individuals are drawn into a different world in which reciprocity becomes key. One member recognises another, albeit often through the medium of paying a due or increasing an employee's wage, and this recognition creates a bond inspiring the other to work hard. LC organisers appeal to people in the world as it is, a world of rationalised time, self-interest, profit and competition, in seeking to draw them into the world as it should be, a world of reciprocity and solidarity.

Conclusion: capitalism for our time

In chapter 2, I suggested that the construction of a religious/secular, mythic/rational binary undermined both the capacity of religious organisations and individuals to reflexively navigate plurality and the mythic qualities of secular action. In particular, I stressed that myth is primarily performative and therefore that rather than judging myths on the basis of their rational content, it would be better to judge myths on the basis of the performances they produce.

Chapter 3 extended the religious/secular, mythic/rational binary to understandings of the state. I suggested that in the face of diversity, modern de-transcendetalised ideas of the state have become dominant. And I suggested that those without strong myths often find themselves co-opted into and reproducing the iron cage of bureaucracy. I moreover stressed that by shifting from ideas of the state as constructing shared myths to ideas of the state as facilitating myth sharing at the grassroots, it was possible to reimagine the state as a curator of solidarity.

In this chapter I have shown that the religious/secular, mythic/rational binary equally creates problems in relation to capitalism. I suggested that unlike the state, capitalism de-transcendentalises on the basis of efficiency: pondering over the world as it should be is not simply problematic in a diverse society; rather, it is a waste of time in any society. Yet I also stressed that capitalism is sustained by it is own myths. Thus as with the state, I explained, neglecting the power of myth renders people susceptible to the myths of capitalism. Having a strong sense of the transcendental social, which I here linked to the construction of timeless roles and responsibilities, articulated in myths and embodied in performances, allows people to develop critiques of capitalism that are ideologically radical, but politically reformist.

One of the core arguments of capitalism, at least under its neoliberal guise, is that by reducing the size of the state and facilitating free markets, individuals will achieve a new freedom that will facilitate stronger bonds within families, between friends, and within and between communities and nations. Yet the manner in which capitalism rationalises time means that it undermines the possibility of these bonds forming. Partly the point here is that the capacity to imagine timeless roles and responsibilities is interrupted by an approach to time as always moving forwards. The very idea of timelessness loses its value. People are pressed to keep up with the times. Yet this failure of the imagination is also down to the lack of secular, capitalist time people end up having in a capitalist system. Far from saving time for leisure, family and friends, rationalisation spreads into all spheres such that any time spent not developing one's financial, social or cultural capital feels like a waste of time. Reduction in funding and the rationalisation of time place limits on people's ability to resist capitalism. Those forced to devote the majority of their energy and time to survival simply do not have enough time to resist their constraints.

A number of organisations were seen to adopt these myths and practices. I stressed that while CotL had clear ideas of the transcendental social, articulated in myths and embodied in performances that presented a clear challenge to capitalism, their approach would struggle to resonate with people in a messy religious and nonreligious landscape. This failure to resonate was also linked to an excessive focus on conventional politics, rather than working on the ground alongside people of all faiths and none.

As a secular organisation working on the front line, HCVS were ostensibly better placed to challenge capitalism. Yet their adoption of a religious/secular, mythic/rational binary led to an unreflexive relationship with myth, and rendered them susceptible to myths of capitalism, often leading them to reproduce capitalist myths and practices.

As was demonstrated in chapters 2 and 3, FbRN were seen to similarly adopt a religious/secular, mythic/rational binary, alongside a religion/politics binary. The result was that although staff were personally critical of capitalism, they had not developed public discourses or practices that could challenge capitalism, and indeed, like HCVS, often reproduced capitalist myths and practices.

In the cases of both HCVS and FbRN, these shortcomings need to be linked to observations from chapter 3: an unreflexive relationship with myth can also mean difficulty in inspiring communities of volunteers, which means that following funding agendas is a matter of survival.

At LC, rather than adopting capitalist myths in response to pressure, the organisation was seen to adopt capitalist myths and associated practices as a means of working with the world as it is towards the world as it should be. This approach could not be more different from the 'prefigurative' politics advocated by Graeber (2009: 235). I hope I have sufficiently expressed my ambivalence towards the LC approach – on the one hand seemingly effective, on the other socially unsettling. If these are to be the means, what will ultimately be the ends? A question requiring further research is thus which of the two approaches, the prefigurative or the pragmatic, is more effective in the long term.

One of the core ways in which capitalism was challenged was through embodied resistance to capitalist time, exemplified in agitating for greater leisure time for workers, and by resisting the rationalisation of time by embodying the patience required to offer the gift of attention over time.

Yet in a number of cases throughout the ethnography, although people are aware of not having enough time to spend as leisure, with friends, or in developing solidarity, this awareness rarely flourishes into a critique of capitalist understandings of time. Unlike chapters 2 and 3, where my participants develop emergent critiques of society, which I am able to draw on and generalise into a theory, here there is an almost ubiquitous failure to translate oppression into wholesale critique. This suggests that in relation to transcendence and the state, it is capitalism that has become most deeply ingrained and embodied. As suggested at the beginning of this chapter, the particular manner in which people resist demonstrates the underlying hegemonic forces that shape their self-understanding. But this becomes all the more poignant in the failure to resist.

It is moreover worth questioning whether the types of resistance offered by my participants really do challenge capitalism, or if instead they are challenging particularly oppressive practices, and, in bringing businesses, governments and individuals together to reform, they are potentially sustaining capitalism in the long term.

Perhaps a more significant question to ask is whether capitalism reformed is really capitalism at all. By conscientising businesses, governments and individuals to collectively construct common concerns, these groups are developing practices that not only constrain the ability to make profit, but also hold it to account. Boltanski and Chiapello have suggested that capitalism as profit-making always survives even as its spirit shifts to incorporate critiques. Yet perhaps these shifts in spirit are more than mere smoke and mirrors. Perhaps capitalism and critique are in an ongoing dialectical relationship whereby businesses, governments and individuals must constantly be conscientised to reform. Certainly, returning to insights from chapter 1, we might suggest that better than communism, a new mutualist capitalism might ensure that businesses are always held to account by shareholders from across the income spectrum, who are forced through compromise to reach a common ground. Or perhaps, reacting too strongly to the spiral of hopelessness, I have become caught in a spiral of hope. Against such a characterisation, the next chapter will draw on these findings to offer practical steps for reform.

5 Imagining solidarity
Conjuring a world to come

This book opened with a problem, simple in content but seemingly unassailable: how are we to collectively search for the kind of shared beliefs and practices so fundamental to solidarity amidst radical diversity of belief and practice? I suggested that answering this question is fundamental to substantively addressing the needs of people rejecting, sometimes violently, the status quo: from the US to Europe, and from the Middle East to India; from the post-political to the anti-political; from neoliberalism to neo-anarchism.

In the first chapter, I stressed that postliberalism offers an essential critique of our current political situation. Postliberalism stresses that it is specifically liberalism, and not its betrayal as so many other researchers, politicians and journalists seem to suggest, that has inspired the rise of reactionary forces across the globe. Rooted in a pessimistic attitude towards the possibility of a collective search for transcendence, liberalism champions either the state or capitalism as the only means of reconciling people to one another. The result is to empower bureaucrats and capitalists at the expense of ordinary people, leaving the latter with no legitimate public outlet for their transcendence needs and thus creating a vacuum to be filled by radical alternatives. Yet I also made clear that if the postliberal critique of liberalism makes for essential reading of our current situation, the postliberal alternative falls short. It tends to oscillate between a revalorisation of a Christian heritage that fails to speak to most people in the Anglo-Saxon West, let alone the rest of the world, and entirely secular rationalisations that undermine its own emphasis on rediscovering transcendence. This approach, I suggested, reproduces the same religious/secular, mythic/rational binary that envelops liberal political theory.

Chapter 2 offered the beginnings of an alternative. It suggested that emphasising the mythic nature of both religious and secular ideas of solidarity could challenge the religious/secular, mythic/rational binary. At first, this emphasis on myth seemed to simplistically support the postliberal narrative, suggesting that the world is full of irreconcilable notions of transcendence, articulated through myths, that one must opt to hold faith with without having rational criteria for doing so. Yet I suggested a number of reasons for being more hopeful. First, I stressed that the beholders of myths were quite capable of acknowledging that their myths were just some amongst many approaches to solidarity. Second, I demonstrated that myths can be rationally judged – just not on the basis of their content. Instead, myths are judged on the basis of the performances they promote. Third, I suggested that it is possible to create spaces in which people collectively search for solidarity by exploring one another's myths in action.

Chapter 3 drew on these ideas to explore ways of rethinking the role of the state in a diverse religious and nonreligious landscape. If postliberal political theory revalorises a Christian approach to politics that no longer resonates with people, liberal political theory suggests transcendence can be put to one side in favour of politics of material progress. Both approaches, I suggested, placed too little faith in the power of ordinary people to collectively search for solidarity in a diverse religious and nonreligious landscape. Such faith is core to how activists imagine and sustain themselves, providing a potential metanarrative across religious and ideological differences. Instead then, I conjured an idea of the state as a curator of safe and inclusive spaces for sharing myths.

Chapter 4 further explored how these ideas might offer opportunities for rethinking capitalism. In particular, I stressed that the idea of time, particularly the gift of attention over time, might also provide a potential meta or crossover narrative between religious and nonreligious people, allowing them to consider what ways of living and interacting with others might be considered timeless, as well as considering ways in which the present economic system distorts these ways of living. The chapter also stressed, however, the extent to which people have imbibed a capitalist understanding of time.

In this chapter, I seek to bring these ideas together into an alternative political theory that I call imagining solidarity. It must be stressed that at this point I go beyond explorations of lived realities to make normative suggestions. But more than postliberal political theory heretofore, I anchor these suggestions in the lived realities I have brought to life in the course of this book. Where helpful, I introduce new ethnographic insights to develop arguments.

In terms of myth, I make key suggestions as to the kinds of characters we need to be cultivating in order to enable people to construct new myths of solidarity together. In order to avoid reproducing a religious/secular, mythic/rational binary, I deliberately make suggestions that can be applied to religious and secular actors alike. I develop these suggestions in contradistinction to current work coalescing around the idea of the postsecular. I do so on two levels. First, a focus on developing certain types of character with certain types of virtue rules out hard and fast rules as to what kinds of discourse are acceptable in what kinds of sphere. Instead, the focus is on what kinds of characters and performances are acceptable – an idea I have previously called performative postsecularism (Stacey 2017a). Second, I stress that whereas work coalescing around the idea of the postsecular offers the humble aim of breaking down distinctions between the religious and secular, my aim is to cultivate solidarity. To put it simply, I am not merely seeking peace but justice.

This discussion will also impinge on the state. A focus on developing certain types of character with certain types of virtue means offering organisations the power and space to creatively cultivate these characters. And within organisations, it means similarly empowering people. I thus offer a new grounding for the legitimacy of the state and of public action generally. For postliberals legitimacy is grounded in the ability to uphold solidarity rooted in a particular notion of transcendence. For liberals legitimacy is grounded in the ability to improve security and wealth. My alternative is to base legitimacy on the state's ability to empower organisations and individuals to creatively cultivate transcendent ideas of solidarity through the sharing of myths. While these conclusions are made for all institutions, I also offer a single institution to be considered in addition, rather than as an alternative. I call for the development of solidarity centres that act as exemplars for other organisations.

Finally I turn to capitalism. My key stress here is to draw on time as a crossover narrative that can bring religious and secular, capitalist and worker together in solidarity. I suggest that the state should empower businesses that are devoted to revaluing time, offering employees time to spend with family, friends and developing solidarity. Similarly, businesses should empower employees to use their own time creatively. Alongside these broader suggestions, I also make the specific suggestion that businesses should be incentivised to make their practice solidary at its core, rather than merely through paying tax, in particular by linking up with solidarity centres.

People that myths are made of: on cultivating the right kind of character

Postliberals have thus far paid too little creative attention to developing the rights kind of characters in settings of all religions and none. I would speculate that this shortcoming arises from the same tension discussed in chapter 1. Postliberals draw inspiration primarily from a Christian myth. But in recognising plurality, they pass their inspiration through a secular prism, on the other side of which are only rationally construed recommendations for government and business. By way of an alternative, chapter 2 demonstrated that it was possible to think of ways in which myth could be creatively and inclusively developed in pluralist settings.

In demonstrating this alternative, it was necessary to fundamentally challenge the covenant put forth by Habermas (see also Stacey 2017a). Habermas' response to the continuing power of religion in the public sphere is emblematic of what I call an accommodationist approach, whereby researchers, policy makers and practitioners assume that the hegemony of a secular public sphere is both legitimate and sufficient in cultivating solidarity, but wish to make the latter accommodating to people of all religions and none. By way of an alternative, I suggest a contributionist approach, whereby the potential of different transcendent ideals and the myths through which they are articulated, including where these challenge secularity, are explored as if from the perspective of the beholder of those ideals. It is this suggestion that leads me to offer performative postsecularism as an alternative model, the constituent characteristics of which I will now detail (see also Stacey 2017a).

Key characteristics for solidarity in the messy religious and nonreligious landscape

The first characteristic that needs to be briefly re-emphasised is performativity itself. I have tried to stress throughout the book that myth must be judged less in terms of its discursive content than in terms of the performances it produces. This is not only a means of acknowledging the contribution of religion in the public sphere, or merely of shifting our understanding of secular people to explore the mythic elements of their actions. Instead, the point is that myth *is* a performance: the telling of stories that inspire both the story-teller and the listener to embody a different way of living. As I have put this point elsewhere, myth does not represent identity but rather is constitutive of identity (Stacey 2017a). It is not that rationality is useless; it is absolutely fundamental to articulating what is important in life. This book is testimony to the value I place in rationality. Otherwise, I might have reverted to my childhood dream of poetry. But neither is it that the rational must be supplemented with the aesthetic. Instead, this principle must be turned on its head: the aesthetic is fundamental. It is to be supplemented with the rational. The human endeavour is, to misquote Anselm, myth seeking understanding – and not the other way round.

The second characteristic I want to emphasise is reflexivity. Contra Habermas, I do not use reflexivity to imply the ability to translate one's transcendent ideals into a secular language. Instead, reflexivity is simply a matter of awareness as to the way that one's transcendental ideals inform one's beliefs and actions. Unless and until social actors can be aware of the ways in which transcendental ideals (such as that of a God that can intervene in the world, that of humans as fundamentally flawed, or that of each individual being a self-contained rational unit) shape their beliefs and actions (by inspiring them to pray in the face of desperation, by inspiring them to develop political safeguards against corruption or to develop economic systems that appeal to individual self-interest), they will only be as free as the transcendental ideals they unwittingly imbibe.

Transcendental ideals are brought to life through myths: stories of great events or people that, against the odds, embody transcendental ideals in the everyday world. These myths can be true or false in terms of rational or empirical verifiability – whether they are or not is beside the point. Their truth, rather, is found in their resonance with people: whether they inspire a different way of living. Once people recognise that the truth of myth is in the performances it inspires, they are better equipped to reflexively embody myths and performatively challenge the injustices of the world they see around them.

In chapter 2, I demonstrated that reflexive awareness as to the transcendental ideals one harbours and the myths through which they articulated and performed can inspire an energetic and confident approach to public action. And I also demonstrated that a lack of such reflexivity could lead to a sense of disillusionment. In chapters 3 and 4, I demonstrated how a strong sense of reflexivity could enable people to withstand external pressures from the state and capitalism, while a lack of reflexivity led to people imbibing the myths of the state and capitalism, often leading to the adoption of beliefs and practices that undermine their core ideals.

Here it is worth reiterating a point made in chapter 2. The problem with Habermas' emphasis on rational translation, itself more advanced than most other liberal political theory, is not merely, as other critics have suggested, that it places unequal constraints on religious and secular citizens. Rather, the problem is that it paradoxically leads secular actors to imagine and mythologise a realm of pure rationality, thus underestimating and under-valuing a key aspect of motivation, namely, transcendental ideals and the myths through which they are articulated and performed. This leads people to be unaware of both negative and positive consequences of the myths they unwittingly imbibe.

Reflexivity feeds into the third characteristic: humility. Once people open up to the ways in which transcendental ideals shape their beliefs and actions, it becomes much clearer that those assumptions themselves cannot be rationally or empirically proved, but only held faith with. Here it is worth returning to the complicated discussion in chapter 1 regarding Milbank's postulation that reason can only take us so far; the rest is faith. From a liberal perspective, this position seems to close off dialogue. But if our deepest transcendent assumptions are always matters of faith, then the only way of opening up to those with different transcendent assumptions is recognising that there is no rational basis for choosing one assumption over another. Instead, rationality can only lie in the kinds of performances one's assumptions promote. This ability to recognise the fallibility of the rational means that there is always something that transcends even our own transcendental ideals, since these are merely the necessarily flawed constructions of people.

In chapter 2, I articulated this different approach to plurality as the transcendent frame – an inversion of Taylor's immanent frame (2007: 3, 539–593). Rather than seeing faith in something transcendent as one option among others, 'and frequently not the easiest to embrace', religious actors positively engaged in pluralist settings tended to construct an outlook in which 'everyone has a faith' (Ibid: 3). By suggesting that everyone has a faith, actors not only legitimised their own positions, but also recognised the legitimacy of others' positions and worked with those others to further explore their faith.

This finding also has implications for social scientific theories of secularisation (as the decline in belief and practice) and sectarianism as responses to religious plurality (Berger 1967: 144–174–5; Bruce 2006: 37). It is not always the case that actors become simplistically weaker or stronger in their faith in response to plurality. Rather, some actors are able to maintain their faith while humbly opening up to regard it as just one narrative that leads to solidarity. To put this another way, rather than people recognising that their apparently objective worldview is in fact subjective, or else radically withdrawing from the world, my participants responded to plurality by, on the one hand, projecting their worldview onto others, 'everyone has a faith', and, on the other hand, and in order to do so, allowing their apparently objective worldview to stretch and incorporate those with apparently very different beliefs.

This suggestion also provides some quite ground-breaking revelations as far as social movement theory is concerned, even if perhaps not so groundbreaking for the sociology and anthropology of religion. Since the cultural turn in sociology, research is beginning to demonstrate the determinative role of culture and religion in social grievances (Wald et al. 2005). What the literature has not observed, however, is how deeply religious groups may engage in flexible social construction of their theology to suit the situation on the ground. Wald et al. rightly point out that religious groups may act in ways that are not 'utility maximising', but they treat religion as determinative and immutable. They do not observe how the process works the other way too, with theologies being related reflexively to allow for elasticity, and thereby inclusion of more members (Wald et al. 2005: 126). In this way, theology and utility are in constant dialogue.

It must also be stressed, however, that this stretchiness can go too far, leading to a snap: not in the transcendent ideal or in the myth through which it is articulated, but in its ability to predict the actions of those it apparently envelops. As CotL slowly expanded its vision it was able to grow in its membership and apparent influence. But as a result of its expanding to include members with very different ideologies and interests, being part of CotL is no longer a good predictor of how members might respond to or vote on various political and social issues, with the result that on the crucial vote as to whether to go to war in Iraq, CotL convinced less than a fifth of its parliamentary members to vote against the war. On this basis, nuance is required in social movement literature, as analysed by Benford and Snow (2000: 618–619), which suggests that 'the more inclusive and broad collective action frames are, the more likely they are to function as or evolve into "master frames"' from which a broad base can be mobilised for a cause.

This complex relationship between being open to alternative ideals on the one hand, and keeping a set of principles strong enough to predict moral conviction and action on the other, is complicated to reconcile. Part of the answer inevitably comes from drawing people together to focus on specific issues that cause suffering. These issues, the stories of suffering around them and the stories of overcoming then become mythic content that fills the generalised transcendent framework. Part of the answer comes from the third characteristic I want to emphasise: imagination. Once we recognise that the truth of a myth is found in the performances it inspires, we can open up the imaginative capacity of people to engage with, imbibe and explore different myths.

Those people engaged with religious and secular others on a daily basis, encountering their myths and seeing the kinds of performances they promote are best able to imaginatively incorporate those myths into their own lexicon. In chapter 2, I demonstrated this point auto-ethnographically. I suggested that in my time around humble Christians at CotL I soon became inspired by their transcendental ideals and the myths through which they were articulated and performed. I also spoke of how secular organisers at LC came to adopt the myths of various religious participants.

The point of being imaginative in this way is that we need not merely think of elasticity as the only approach to plurality. Instead, any organisation can incorporate a potentially infinite amount of ideals and myths, provided they are able to suspend their disbelief and judge ideals and myths less in terms of their discursive content than in terms of the performances they produce.

The final characteristic that needs to be emphasised is thus solidarity itself. Solidarity is the virtue that brings all of the others together. Unless all of the other characteristics are tied together in the aim to develop characters bound by a mutual desire to uphold one another's dignity, then they remain merely "the heart of a heartless world", epiphenomenal ideals that linger in people's minds without having any real impact on political or economic structures. It is for this reason that I have never been entirely comfortable when hearing participants suggest that "many paths lead to God", worrying that this may imply a personal relationship with the divine rather than a philosophy of public responsibility. Transcendental ideals need to be performed if they are to influence change.

The kinds of spaces in which these characteristics can flourish

The next question is in what kinds of spaces these four characteristics of reflexivity, humility, imagination and solidarity are brought to the surface. From one perspective, it might be suggested that the best we can do is to empower people to act entirely independently. But this is to be caught in the liberal myth that liberal freedom is utterly unconstrained. As stressed in chapters 2, 3 and 4, liberal freedom not only comes with caveats, such as an individual's ability to act according to rational criteria and to contribute to the capitalist system, but also leaves people constrained by those most effective in controlling the levers of power: our freedom is constrained by the political and economic options made available to us.

While I will leave detailed analysis of the kinds of organisation required for emphasising these characteristics to the next section, a few components need to be highlighted here. As might be expected, the organisations best able to emphasise these characteristics are those that are themselves placed in situations in which reflexivity, humility, imagination and solidarity were most required.

In my fieldwork, four points were significant. The first was that organisations whose transcendental ideals were significant in their practice were more likely to have been challenged in those ideals and thereby to have developed a level of reflexivity. It was for instance seen that members of CotL required no encouragement to go straight to the transcendental basis of their actions, and had clear answers as to their feelings about other ideals. It was also seen that when CotL opened up a democratic process for questioning transcendental ideals, the myths through which they were articulated and performed and the particular practices they promoted, members were at their most empowered and enthused. On the other hand, HCVS were unclear on their ideals, indeed of the value of discussing ideals, of the organisation, of its members, and of the people it worked with. Partly this stems from being part of hegemonic secular culture wherein one's ideals are rarely challenged and thus rarely brought to the surface. I found that a key source of disillusionment amongst members was the feeling that they were not involved in identifying the worldview and values of the organisation. This disillusionment was most palpable when shifts took place in national and local fundraising frameworks, and consequently in the organisation's policy. Members felt that the ideals that drew them to work for the organisation in the first place were being undermined, and that they were being hypocritical in their practice. This finding fits with research from Chatterton and Pickerill (2010: 481), who suggest that a lack of attention to the values driving action can lead to fragmentation and individualism.

In relation to CotL, FbRN were less clear on their transcendent ideals as an organisation, and focused instead on the value of giving space to all faiths. I suggested this led to an odd paradox whereby even as people saw the value of their own ideals, and of others' ideals, in challenging secular hegemony, they were not clear on the place of their organisation in this same process. Perhaps a mirror image of FbRN, LC found itself cultivating a shared sense of transcendence, even as many of its members were unclear on their own transcendent ideals.

The second point is that provided transcendent ideals are significant in their practice, an encounter with actors with different ideals is more likely to trigger reflexivity and confidence. For CotL members, this encounter took place through work with non-Christian politicians. For HCVS, because transcendent ideals were very rarely made explicit, critical encounter with other ideals was unlikely. For FbRN and LC, this encounter was far more frequent and explicit, and led to reflection and action not only on *that* there could be parity between religious and secular beliefs, and therefore productive encounter, but also on the discourse and methods that would make these encounters viable and creative.

At LC in particular, reflexivity seemed to be most powerful. And this is specifically because LC's relationship with faith is full of juxtapositions: its founders have a faith background, but it counts amongst its key members mainly secular organisers; it has no explicit position on the power of faith in the public sphere, but the majority of its affiliated institutions are churches, mosques and synagogues. As discussed in chapter 2, these juxtapositions are creatively reflected in LC's method for cultivating solidarity amongst new members: a training process through which members are asked to explore 'taking the world as it is to the world as it should be'. Members are asked to think of some words that they associate with the world as it should be. They are then asked to think of projects that they can implement in their own institutions that will help to bring about this world.

The point to remember here is that the idea of the world as it should be is an imaginative concept that does not require fully fleshing out or ultimate consensus. As Aaron put it, 'we're not all thinking about the same world. I don't know if we're even thinking about a world. Because we've not experienced that world'. Far from stating how the world should be, LC seeks to engage members in a process of imagining how the world should be. Moreover, at the same time as encouraging members to engage with their own deepest values, by writing out suggestions on a board, critical discussion is encouraged, in order 'to show this diverse group of people that there's enough in common in the way the world should be that they can act together'.

Yet what is interesting in LC's taking this theoretical exploration as a starting point is that they studiously avoid fleshing out the world as it should be in any detail. Three reasons are offered for this: the first is a neo-Marxist consideration, shared by the majority of actors with which I worked, religious or secular, that excessive discussion around transcendence is a distraction from this-worldly justice; the second reason is that people worry fleshing out the world as it should be in any detail will lead to division along religious and ideological lines; the third reason is that excessive focus on the world as it should be will undermine the small, winnable goals an organisation has to focus on if it is to achieve the kinds of successes that will inspire further action.

The way in which LC treads this fine line between constructing a shared notion of transcendence and avoiding fleshing out that vision provides a fitting response to the problem of creating stretchy ideals while nonetheless keeping focus on core aims. The power of this method also suggests an additional finding: that the process of socially constructing an imagined world may be valuable *in itself* as a means of cultivating solidarity. The performance itself has power. This finding also speaks to the debate, outlined in chapter 3, between Weber and Durkheim regarding the relationship between the state and solidarity. Whereas Weber stressed the importance of a conviction politician, accountable via democracy to the people, a top-down approach, Durkheim stressed the importance of cultivating civic engagement and debate amongst the people, an approach corroborated by the findings here (see also Palumbo and Scott 2003: 376–377).

The third point is about the kind of encounter. Since I have been stressing the importance of understanding different transcendent ideals and the myths through which they are articulated and performed experientially, although it is fundamental, as I have been arguing, that ideals are discussed, it is equally important that having been discussed, participants have the chance to see one another live their myths out in practice. I have already made clear that this point was recognised by all of my participants, religious and secular. Moreover, just as this experiential encounter is important for mutual learning, it is also important for ensuring that encounter creates real chances for solidarity – not just as an idea or unfulfilled desire but as a set of practices.

This kind of deep reflexivity displayed by LC points to a final and fundamental factor for understanding the relationship between myth and solidarity in diverse religious and nonreligious settings. I have said that people with clear transcendental ideals and myths through which these are articulated and performed are able to embody these ideals in their own lives, acting as exemplars for a different way of living in a complicated world. And I have said that the process of performing the construction of a shared transcendental framework can inspire solidarity so that people holding very different myths can nonetheless learn to imaginatively incorporate one another's myths into their actions through a process of *bricolage*. Similarly, a system of positive feedback emerges whereby as soon as people begin to believe in the possibility of solidarity, and to act it out in their own lives, these actions themselves become the myths that others are inspired by. I have earlier suggested that liberalism becomes a self-fulfilling prophecy such that when people are conceived of as selfish, and polities and economic systems are constructed on this basis, so people respond to incentives, becoming the people that politicians and policy makers imagine them to be. The result can be a sense of hopelessness in which it is no longer clear how to imagine a sense of solidarity. Perhaps the answer is simple: people need to begin to act differently, juxtapose themselves to the world they see around them, and new myths will follow. People must actively conjure a world to come, themselves become the characters that myths are made of.

It is with this hopeful idea of a world to come that I turn to back to the world as it is, exploring the structural arrangements necessary to create spaces for inclusively developing myth and solidarity.

A state of anarchy: curating spaces where mythic characters can flourish

In chapter 3 I claimed that the chief shortcoming of sociological theories of the state is a lack of attention to transcendent sources of solidarity. In a move familiar to that ascribed to Habermas in chapter 2, and recapped in the previous subsection, it is as though having emphasised the importance of a shared religious outlook, all of the thinkers explored, from Weber through Durkheim and Freire, move on to suggest that in a modern, pluralist society, transcendent solidarity, however powerful, is simply impossible, and the notion that the state can play a role in cultivating such solidarity is anathema. I agreed that for the state to hegemonically cultivate a single idea of transcendence could only be perceived as an act of violence in a pluralist society. What is more, if people themselves are not involved in constructing the ideals by which society is shaped, they will always feel alienated from them. Yet I closed chapter 2 by suggesting that it might be possible to simultaneously maintain the importance of transcendent solidarity, while imaginatively moving beyond past ways in which such solidarity had been constructed. And in the previous section, I offered my alternative. Here is not the place to rehash those arguments. Instead I want to use this section to pick up from where I left off in the conclusion of chapter 3: offering a new vision of the relationship between the state and solidarity, by casting the former as the curator of performative postsecularism. As explained in the introduction, I begin by offering general ideas of the state before turning to present an ideal institution.

Turning power inside out

The first characteristic of a state that curates performances of the postsecular is that it focuses on turning power inside out. In chapter 3 I stressed that although globalisation has created a situation in which companies often have more money than states, still states are often the only institutions with enough power to challenge injustice. It was moreover stressed that only the state has the power to implement initiatives across the country. I also demonstrated that activists across the spectrum, from those working within the state to those often challenging the state, still imagine the state as embodying solidarity. Yet if the state is still lauded in ideal terms, in reality the state is often perceived as failing to live up to these lofty ideals. The state imposes agendas and disempowers activists.

I first came across the idea of turning traditional power inside out in my work with CotL. Initially there appeared to be a contradiction in their work. On the one hand, they saw state legislation as key to challenging practices that undermine solidarity. On the other hand, CotL stressed that communities and people are responsible for one another. This confusion cleared up when I realised that CotL see the state as engaging existing institutions in the process of social change. This includes but is also more than the Hegelian notion of the state using carrot and stick to make institutions and people more civil. CotL are critical of the notion of state-implemented social change enacted in isolation because it creates a disconnect between lifestyle and policy. They encourage politicians and the wider public to live out socialism. As a politician, voting on left-wing agendas does not abrogate the responsibility to live a socialist life. Crucially, this includes empowering the wider public. CotL reimagines what it means to be a politician: not just manipulating the levers of positional and institutional power, but also empowering and inspiring others to act. Likewise, as members of the public, it is hoped that we will respond to this call.

The idea of turning power inside out, then, is of recognising the power of positions and institutions, and yet working from these positions and within these institutions to develop new leaders such as will empower more people to become politically engaged. The perfect example of this is CotL's 'Labour Neighbours' campaign, which encouraged Labour MPs and organisers to regard themselves not only as politicians representing their constituents through legislation, but also as community organisers, encouraging local people to become more involved in their local issues.

HCVS demonstrated what happened when people were not empowered in this way. Lower-level staff become disillusioned, taking a very pragmatic approach to ideas such as equality and diversity, explaining to grassroots activists that they had to consider equality and diversity in order to get charitable status and receive funding. Moreover, with no experience of empowerment themselves, lower-level staff were seen to place stringent policy requirements upon community volunteers.

Notwithstanding these issues, the co-optive power of the state was seen more positively with FbRN. The state played an important role in embodying the collective narrative and associated principles that the wider population expects to be upheld in the public sphere: intolerance towards intolerance and collaboration across difference. Putting aside debates as to whether the state is a carrier of vicarious religion or of vicarious secularity, as the state it may be seen as an important carrier of whatever ideals we so choose, enforcing this negatively through law, as well positively through funding. This function may prove to be more, not less important as people begin to reject hierarchies. The state can no longer draw on an already agreed upon myth from which to inspire solidarity. Instead, it can only hope to encourage certain practices and disparage others.

And yet it turns out that this is anyway the best approach. The state may embody a shared narrative, but it has not got the people power to cultivate that narrative. Instead, it must empower organisations and individuals to develop their own ideals and myths. Moreover, the most effective organisations and individuals were those able to cultivate and maintain their own myths and associated practices. From this perspective, it may be that mere utility encourages traditional power to turn inside out and reflect the full diversity of the religious and nonreligious landscape.

One manner of envisaging turning power inside out is demonstrated by LC, which works with existing institutions to become more relational in their approach. As one participant put it, 'our job isn't to create new institutions; our job is to make existing institutions more relational'. What this means in practice is training leaders of powerful institutions to engage with those they deem to represent by sitting down with numerous individuals, listening to what they perceive to be central social problems, bringing these individuals together, and asking what can be done together to solve these problems.

Yet the method offered here can only be seen as a preamble of performative postsecularism. In both cases, a predefined way of relating to the world is taken as a given, after which actors are invited to be involved. Truly turning power inside out would require that people in power are open about and critical of their own transcendental ideals, and invite others to reflect on their ideals; only then will it be possible to cultivate the kind of transcendent solidarity that leads to a mutual sense of responsibility and action.

By in this sense curating spaces for performative postsecularism, the state is able to safely navigate any responsibility not to promote either religion generally or any particular religion or ideology. More importantly for the purposes of this book, the state is able to navigate key contradictions: First, the state is challenged in its core understanding as the monolithic power through which the public sphere is shaped, without being dispensed with altogether. Rather, the state becomes instrumental in challenging its own monolithic status: the state working itself out of a job becomes the guiding principle. Second, the state is able to balance bureaucratic fairness, ensuring that the same inclusive processes are available in all geographical areas, with ideals of engagement and empowerment.

Bringing actors from the outside in

Part of the work of making existing institutions more relational involves changing the kinds of people that are put in positions of power: replacing bureaucrats with curators. Thus the second characteristic I want to emphasise is bringing actors from the outside in.

Again, the focus on bringing actors from the outside in began with CotL, who focused on those politically engaged but disillusioned with conventional politics. This focus became a key aspect of CotL's work. Yet CotL staff quickly discovered that persuading those on the outside, the disillusioned, remains difficult.

CotL staff spend a large portion of their time cajoling people to become more involved in conventional politics. They make clear that a number of decisions inevitably do get made in 'dull' or 'smoke-filled' 'committee rooms', resulting in legislation, and suggest that they are not trying to change the room, but the people in it. CotL undertake this work in two ways, one formal, the other informal. The formal process is the 'Future Candidates' scheme, whereby politically engaged people deemed capable of standing for office are tutored by CotL staff to become proficient public speakers and campaigners. Those involved in this scheme are asked to find 10 people that would support them in their efforts. Once they have found these 10, each of the 10 is asked to find five more. The idea behind this strategy is to develop candidates as relational leaders who derive their power from the ability to motivate political engagement.

The informal process involves encouraging politically engaged people to attend events, partake in campaigns, and meet with MPs. Through this process, it is hoped that people will no longer see politicians as part of a 'different class', to which ordinary people do not have access. Over time, those involved in this process come to see and believe, as one member put it, 'I could do that, and probably better than him'.

Though CotL was the only organisation working directly within Westminster, the practice of bringing activists from the outside in finds support amongst other organisations, for whom keeping close working relationships with positional power was vital to their survival.

As demonstrated in chapter 3, HCVS engaged in educating grassroots activists in the hegemonic narrative. In chapter 3, this practice was treated as evidence of the impracticability of hegemony, since it incites cynicism. Yet here it can be suggested that this cynical approach is a method of inducting grassroots activists into the discourse that will bring them funding. As with CotL, HCVS staff are confounding perceptions of inaccessibility by showing those on the outside how to navigate the discourse and practices of those on the inside.

CotL's approach is not dissimilar from that of LC, albeit the latter operate at a lower level. The aim of LC is to bring politically engaged people into processes in which they can influence change. The key process through which they do this is leadership development. LC first identify potential leaders when undertaking one-to-ones (see chapter 2). They then invite these potential leaders to play a small role in a public action: usually, this involves giving 'testimony', whereby an individual tells the story of suffering that has led them to be involved in the action. Following this speaking role, potential leaders are tested in their ability to bring more people to future events.

Whereas Gupta (2006) has suggested the need for academics to recognise the blurred boundaries between state and civil society, my ethnography of political activism shows that this course of action is not only insufficient, but potentially counterproductive. Placing too much emphasis on the state as ephemeral can make it a slippery target. Instead, it may be better to pinpoint oppressive structures and, rather than blurring theoretical boundaries, blur the boundaries between the people, discourses and practices on the inside and those on the outside. The point may be to simply render the state, its discourses and practices, accessible to and subject to critique by those that feel alienated. It is true that what counts as the state is often socially constructed, but simply pointing to this fact will not change the relationship between the state and the people. Instead, the state needs to be considered permeable.

These two characteristics of turning conventional power inside out and bringing actors from the outside in become the new grounding for political legitimacy. Based on this suggestion, we do not need to dispense with the traditional levers of power, but rather with traditional understandings of power. The new basis of political legitimacy becomes the ability to empower a collective search for transcendent solidarity through the sharing of myths. But this new position does entail a reimagining of what counts as the state; namely, the state indicates any institutions founded on collectively pooled resources for common activities, of which parliaments and bureaucracies are just one manifestation.

Based on these points, I now turn to present an ideal case study. Drawing on collectively funded bodies such as the BBC (up until the recent Conservative government reforms) or universities (until the increasing centralised control that has been witnessed in the UK over the last 30 years), I envisage a collectively funded body, free from government control, that is designed to promote a collective search for transcendent solidarity rooted in the sharing of myths. This body would consist of multiple regional and local solidarity centres designed to inclusively cultivate solidarity.

These bodies would need to receive core funding from central government to reflect the important role the state still plays in developing solidarity: challenging companies, making initiatives available and sustainable across a nation, and reflecting people's sentiments that the state remains an important source of legitimacy for myth and an important carrier of solidarity. Regarding the role of myth in particular, I have already stressed that the state plays an important role in upholding appropriate practices by using funding as an incentive. The state can, for instance, make funding dependent on inclusivity.

Yet core funding should be limited to infrastructure, a lead organiser, and short-term funding for additional organisers. All other funding, for paying organisers in the long term and for campaigns, must come from the organising work itself. This is for two reasons. First, chapter 3 demonstrated that by maintaining a distance from the state, organisations can be more effective in developing solidarity. The connection between myth and solidarity needs to be discerned through face-to-face interaction, rather than at the whim of political trends. Without this safeguard, organisations will be in the same position as HCVS and FbRN, meaning that they never have the requisite stability or independence for long-term campaigns. Based on this model, organisations do not derive their legitimacy from government but from their ability to engage ordinary people and to agitate for change. Moreover, it may often be that the particular causes selected by a solidarity centre involve agitating against the government.

This latter point about potential conflict between solidarity centres and governments means that setting up such centres would require a brave and bold government. Chapter 3 has already shown how many times a government has sought to develop similar institutions. Starting with the best intentions, these schemes quickly descend into patron-client relationships. But it is just such a bold choice that is required in our current political situation. With increasing fragmentation between a liberal elite unwilling to hand over power and a reactionary populace that seems to further justify this instinct, dramatic political change is required.

The second reason for stipulating that organisations must raise their own funding from organising work is that we need to move away from a republican model of representation whereby, outside of being directly involved in conventional politics, the highest end of political engagement is writing to an elected representative or voting. In chapter 4, it was demonstrated that LC have two criteria for including an institution in their work: that they pay dues, and that they are actively engaged in campaigns. By stipulating that institutions must pay dues, they are drawn into a reciprocal relationship. Dues are not treated as payment for a service, but as placing a stake in the organisation. By stipulating that organisations must raise their own funding for organising work, a government would be imposing a new understanding of political legitimacy, derived from the ability to empower a collective search for solidarity.

This point about dues speaks to the question of membership. Individual members would primarily have to be institutions in order to recognise the power that already exists within communities. Solidarity centres should seek to involve as diverse an array of institutions as possible within their area to reflect the diversity of the religious and secular institutional landscape: churches and mosques, synagogues and gurdwaras, trade unions and universities, local government and activists.

But we live in a time of decreasing trust in institutions. Thus a second stipulation of member involvement would be that they themselves seek to turn power inside out, and bring the disaffected in. This would force solidarity centres to think imaginatively about the institutions they include, seeking to represent a whole geographical community by involving as many individuals as possible. For example, solidarity centres might think outside of institutions directly engaged in campaigns for social justice but which are nonetheless core to solidarity, such as social movements, sports clubs, theatres, pubs, cafes and friendship groups. By focusing on these alternative spaces, solidarity centres can reconnect with the ways in which solidarity flourishes outside of conventional politics, as well as reconnecting these isolated and esoteric pockets of solidarity with a larger whole.

It is worth noting that the resources for these solidarity centres are already available in the UK in the form of CVSs, as well as in Canada in the form of neighbourhood houses. These institutions, long-established in the social landscape, are currently at risk, either of closing down entirely, or else of being co-opted into a neoliberal model of service delivery. By reimagining CVSs as solidarity centres, they can both become key focal points of ideas of solidarity and rediscover ways of surviving that are rooted in developing a reciprocal relationship with the community.

The opening context of this book is an increasing disconnection between liberal elites and ordinary people, one of the results of which, I claimed, is the rise of reactionary movements that reject conventional politics. I also claimed that at the core of this disconnect is a pessimistic attitude towards the possibility of a collective search for solidarity amidst radical diversity of belief and practice. In chapter 3, I suggested that seeking a new meta-myth that might inspire solidarity would be to neglect the widespread rejection of hierarchy, particularly where these hierarchies are realised in conventional politics. Yet I also demonstrated that by reimagining the state as a curator of performances of postsecularism, it might be possible to simultaneously respect the continuing role of the state in embodying solidarity, while empowering ordinary people in a collective search for solidarity.

While the practical suggestions I have made in this section may be disappointing to those seeking complete revolution, I suggest that these steps are more rather than less revolutionary than movements currently rejecting conventional politics. First, as already suggested, these apparently pragmatic steps are based on a revolution in understandings of the way the state is legitimised: no longer either as the champion of a single notion of transcendence, or as the driver of improvements in security and wealth in the absence of such a notion, but rather as the enabler of ordinary people in a collective struggle for solidarity. Second, I cannot conceive of a suggestion more idealistic than that politicians and policy makers are called upon to empower bodies that may challenge their privileged position as creators and instigators of policy at all levels. First, politicians and policy makers are called upon to ensure positional power gives way to relational power. A favourite story amongst organisers at LC is when Glasman suggested to then British Prime Minister Gordon Brown that he was not leader because he did not have any followers. Second, politicians and policy makers are called upon to enable social scientific construction of policy to give way to local and collective explorations of appropriate solutions. Lord Philip Gould entitled his memoir *The Unfinished Revolution* to indicate how social scientific reasoning had not yet become the fundamental basis of politics in the UK. He may not have realised it, but Gould was in fact talking about the unfinished revolution of liberalism. While there is still time left, before the last of those with positional power have become convinced of this method; before the connection between politics and lifestyle, politicians and ordinary people becomes utterly sundered; before the rejection of conventional politics altogether and the retrenching in religion, race, nation, gender and class become the only options, we need to think again.

The solidary economy: rediscovering time

Chapter 4 suggested that liberalism's religious/secular, mythic/rational binary had been imbibed to the extent that it was no longer possible to see the myths at work in sustaining capitalism. Sharing as they do the same pessimism as to the possibility of a collective search for transcendent solidarity, left liberals are well primed to reproduce the idea that capitalism is rooted in the natural state of humankind: the individual pursuit of security and wealth. Moreover, the collapse of the Soviet Union helped to further reproduce this idea. Despite its acknowledged moral and economic bankruptcy, the Soviet Union stood on the horizons of people's imagination, allowing them to think that an alternative was possible in which people were motivated by collective rather than individual improvement.

I stressed that in fact, capitalism is sustained by myths. Moreover, these myths are often morally powerful. It is not simply, as postliberals suggest, that losing the possibility of a shared sense of transcendence leads to the prioritisation of security and wealth as a kind of lowest common denominator. The rationalisation of time and the improvement of security and wealth are strong moral drivers inspiring solidarity. Yet I also pointed out that even judging capitalism on its own terms, it tends to disempower large groups of people.

In particular, I suggested that capitalism distorts perceptions of time, as well as reduces the amount of time people have. To explain this point, I suggested that we might conceive of the transcendental social as based on timeless roles and duties. And I said that capitalism undermines this timelessness in two ways: First, by rationalising time, capitalism creates a situation in which timeless roles become harder to imagine. Second, by restricting the amount of spare time people have, and by encouraging them to value even that time in terms of generating capital, capitalism leaves increasingly less time to consider the timeless. As a result, people slowly come to frame their social engagements and relationships in terms of capitalist improvement: they contribute to cultural or social capital. So not only does our perception of time become distorted such that anything timeless loses relevance, but we no longer have enough time to consider what is really important.

I also suggested that the restriction of time itself is insufficient as a means of conscientising people. Instead, deliberate processes of conscientisation need to be developed whereby businesses, their workers and the wider community collectively engage in a search for timeless roles and duties. And in the absence of the Soviet alternative, new exemplars need to be developed that inspire people.

Although the restriction of time itself is not sufficient to conscientise people, I suggested that the notion of timelessness itself might provide a crossover narrative, a starting point for the cultivation of transcendental ideals and myths through which these ideals are articulated and performed, that appeal to people of all religions and none.

These suggestions require that states and businesses alike create time and space for these processes and exemplars to emerge. This section thus explores avenues for the changes required. As with the previous section, I begin by offering general points for the economy as a whole, before moving to make specific suggestions.

Making time for the timeless

The first point is to reconceive of the rationalisation of time as a means of creating enough time to consider timeless roles and responsibilities. Businesses that promote this new conception need to be championed. This means creating structures that encourage workers to reflect on timeless ideals; creating time within the working day for considering the timeless ideals at which the business itself is aiming; and offering time for workers to spend with friends, family, and in the community.

Creating structures that encourage reflection on ideals is partly, as postliberals have suggested, a matter of giving workers a stake in the company by making them shareholders, a move which also entails that workers have a democratic role within the direction of the company. But there is nothing to say that this act alone will improve the overall direction of a business, since workers themselves may be just as much motivated by the pursuit of profit as are their managers.

Thus these structural changes need to be supplemented with deliberate processes for considering the timeless ideals towards which a business is aiming. To avoid superficial and self-serving reflection, these processes need to be embedded in the constituencies a business serves, and in the communities in which it is located. Drawing on suggestions from the previous section, a business needs to treat itself as a state: legitimised not merely on the basis of the pursuit of profit, or, following social democratic ideas, on its tax returns, but also on the basis of its ability to empower people in a collective search for solidarity. The central question for a business becomes, what does it contribute to solidarity? The answer to this question needs to be discovered through the curation of inclusive discussions as to the timeless ideals being served. Thus the concept of shareholders needs to be broadened to include not only workers, but also clients and affected members of the public. This suggestion relies on the recognition that mutual conscientisation is fundamental to organic solidarity. It is meaningful interaction between people in very different positions of power that creates an awareness of shared needs – not mere exchange within a market. This point becomes especially pronounced given that in a global economic system, market exchange is itself increasingly faceless, and thus depends ever more on an element of trust.

The notion of including clients also confounds the capitalist treatment of money as the closure of a covenant, a service rendered and paid for. Instead, the buyer enters into a reciprocal relationship where she too becomes complicit in and responsible for the actions of a company. While this idea may seem worrying to business owners, it could be conceived as a means of sustaining capitalism, albeit a very different idea of capitalism, in the long term by assuaging the desire to contract out, or boycott. It also places more rather than less responsibility on consumers, because, as with those refusing to partake in conventional politics discussed in the previous section, they are confronted with the burden of changing, rather than merely rejecting the status quo. Finally, treating consumers as shareholders offers grounds for hope. Boycotting goods can often feel like an interminable process that squeezes our standards of living and requires endless research into whether the brand we switch to is really any more ethical than the brand we are boycotting. Instead, consumers can keep their standards of living and their aesthetic preferences provided they take responsibility for the consequences.

Alongside these shifts internal to businesses, workers need to be given more time away from work. This means giving them the time to do so: time to spend amongst family, friends, and in their community. Chapter 4 demonstrated that the rationalisation of time has influenced individuals' understandings of time to the extent that they rationalise even their leisure time. Only by generously giving workers time away from work can it be expected that they will have the energy and clarity to meaningfully contribute to the search for timeless ideals.

Reconceiving businesses as more than mere profit creators is a shift that must happen on the part of businesses. But reconceiving businesses as more than mere taxpayers requires action on the part of the state. Reducing the tax burden on businesses that embed their practice in the pursuit of timeless ideals is fundamental to giving businesses the time they require to pass on to their workers. While speaking of tax incentives may seem like resorting to purely rational motivations, current tax arrangements are a specific denial of solidarity, since they are handed out without regard for social contribution.

Yet beyond such incentives business leaders themselves need to recognise the advantages of exemplary practice. Boltanski and Chiapello (2007: 38) have spoken of the difficulty of instigating ethical change amongst businesses. While ethical compromises serve capitalism in the long term by assuaging the desire to revolt, they often damage individual businesses in the short term as they wait for other businesses to follow suit. One crucial point here is that both states and civil society actors need to place pressure on businesses that fail to contribute to solidarity. But a more fundamental answer to this worry is that when a business empowers workers, clients and affected members of the public, it also calls on them to work hard for the benefit of the business. I say that it "calls on them" because this is not merely a social scientific point but a normative one. As individuals we are all already complicit in the ethical and unethical aspects of the economy. If a business takes steps to imbed itself in solidary practice, this calls for reciprocal solidarity in terms of hard work, consumption of its products, and goodwill for its plans within a community.

These reflections on reciprocity between businesses, workers, clients and affected members of the public speak to more specific suggestions. I thus turn to reflect on the relationship between businesses and solidarity centres.

From consumer to shareholder

I have already suggested that a key part of the work of creating structures that encourage businesses and their workers to reflect on their ideals is broadening the concept of shareholders to include workers, clients and affected members of the public. The process of reflecting on timeless ideals thus becomes embedded in a missional, as well as a geographical community. One means of achieving this end is to link businesses with the solidarity centres envisaged in the previous section.

This might happen in two ways with mutual benefits. First, as already suggested in the previous section, solidarity centres would primarily build membership in the form of institutions. Members pay dues, which, rather than payment for a service, is treated as entry into a reciprocal relationship. For solidarity centres, this would provide a vital source of funding. For businesses, this relationship would give them real power within a community, potentially giving them a stake in questions of worker pay, education, and the security and prosperity in a community necessary to improve the quality of life of their workforce. It would also improve relations between the business and the community. I also suggested that a key criterion of membership must be a commitment to turning power inside out and bringing activists from the outside in. Not only could solidarity centres thus help in the practical work of reforming businesses from within, but also businesses could assuage activists by showing a willingness to collaborate. For larger firms, if the head of corporate social responsibility became the key contact with solidarity centres, then this could be a relationship with real power for mutual advantage.

Solidarity centres could also provide a clear link between giving workers more time and ensuring that that time is spent contributing to solidarity. Workers could be given time off specifically to work with solidarity centres. For solidarity centres, this would provide a vital source of people, often people with a particular expertise. For businesses, this would relieve the burden of corporate social responsibility. It would also provide businesses with the security of knowing that they are themselves less likely to be the target of campaigns. Since solidarity centres would operate according to community organising principles, the workers will have a direct influence on the issues around which solidarity centres campaign. This would also ensure that corporate social responsibility is directly related to improving issues on which the business itself impinges, rather than the current disconnect whereby a business will sometimes provide workers for causes unrelated to their practice.

It is moreover worth noting that connecting teams of workers with solidarity centres may serve to offer teambuilding experiences that are directly linked to issues relevant to the business, and that currently businesses pay extortionate rates for.

By linking corporate social responsibility with solidarity centres, governments will have a clear indication of when a company is deserving of a tax break, since solidarity centres themselves might be asked to confirm the vital role of a particular business in their work, as well as improvements in business practice. Businesses too will have a clear idea of when worker time has been spent wisely.

It is of course worth noting that, as with the state, once businesses directly empower solidarity centres, they may find that conflicts of interest arise. It might be the case, for example, that solidarity centres are campaigning for a living wage, which a particular business is failing to pay to all of its workers. Yet the very point of linking businesses with solidarity centres is that these conflicts can be resolved amicably. Trust is placed in ordinary people to collectively search for a common good without needing to resort to the state, and without simply accepting that the market resolves all issues.

Solidarity centres also speak to the declining power of trade unions mentioned specifically in chapters 3 and 4, and drawn throughout my ethnography. In a world in which one rarely stays with a single trade, let alone a single company throughout one's working life, solidarity centres can draw on a sense of solidarity rooted in shared ideals in shared spaces, helping people to build relational power with people from other trades to agitate for better working conditions.

As with the previous section, anti-capitalist activists may feel disappointed with my pragmatic suggestions. Yet as I argued there, my suggestions here might be considered more rather than less revolutionary than the mere rejection of capitalism. In the absence of a Soviet alternative on the horizon, indeed perhaps I should say with gratitude *because* of the loss of this alternative, we are forced to think of alternative exemplars for a different way of living. It is far easier to simply imagine a polar opposite than to think of practical ways in which we can convince people to change their behaviour. Moreover, and fundamentally for the purposes of this book, I have stressed that the socialist alternative fails because it shares with capitalism a pessimistic attitude towards the possibility of a collective search for transcendent solidarity, instead merely opting for a different basis, namely collective rather than individual ownership, on which to reach for the same end, namely improvements in security and wealth spread as widely as possible. Socialism must be imposed by the state. Daring to be human, daring to place trust in businesses and people to collectively search for transcendent solidarity is far harder. Thus if my suggestions seem to be smaller, more pragmatic, less hopeful and indeed less significant than socialists might hope for, it is because the reimagining of human possibilities on which they rely are in fact much bigger, and much more hopeful.

Conjuring a world to come

We live in challenging times. But a mood for change is in the air. Putting aside normative questions as to the ideals reflected by the rise of reactionary politics across the globe, we can take inspiration in recognising that people are willing to act. Decades of lamenting that people are disengaged is being disproved. But much to liberals' dismay, this new energy is turning against them. Too little have they realised that the rejection of conventional politics might have been the result of liberalism itself.

Indeed, so deeply rooted is the hegemony of liberalism that even as ordinary people rise up against them, liberals take this as a sign that their ideals have not spread far or deep enough. The apparent violence underlying anti-immigration rhetoric is merely evidence of the underlying violence amongst purportedly educated people. Far from finding ways of empowering ordinary people, the liberal answer is to further restrict access to politics: we need education restrictions on the right to vote.

We can go on like this. History suggests we probably will. Crisis after crisis, liberalism finds a way to re-emerge. A flicker of hope is followed by politics as usual. The emergent liberalism prior to the Second World War came back with a vengeance just as soon as fascist and socialist alternatives seemed to evaporate from the horizon. The neoliberalism of the 1990s and early 2000s prior to the 2008 economic crisis re-emerged just as soon as protestors could be cleared from public spaces and forgotten.

The problem with reactionary movements of both right and left is that they fail to put faith in ordinary people to come up with pragmatic responses to their problems. Hence these movements bubble up, reach a crescendo and disappear. Rather than an outright rejection of conventional politics or of capitalism, a deep reimagining of what ordinary people are capable of is required with associated steps.

At this time in which the political and economic structures are again being called into question, those that want real, long-term change need to resist the sprinting frenzy of reactionaries and instead commit to the long marathon of imagining and slowly realising timeless ideals. If fear of fascism and socialism gave rise to the great synthesis of the welfare state, an ideal that has become sacred across Europe, there is hope that fear of the current reactionary movements across the globe can inspire at least the pragmatic suggestions made in this chapter.

Conclusion
An awareness of what is missing

This book has sought to take readers on a journey: from the dangerous and divisive political climate that faces them at present, back in time to the theological and philosophical roots of this climate, through the ambiguities and ambivalences involved in ordinary people's struggle to develop solidarity amidst this climate, to quite practical reforms that might serve as the beginnings of a different politics. But much is missing, both in terms of research that I would have liked to draw on, and research that people like me, at the crossroads of theology, philosophy, sociology, anthropology and activism, ought to undertake. In the following, I will subdivide my discussion of what is missing into sections broadly representing the trajectory of the book: the Anglo-Saxon West, theology, religion, the state and capitalism.

Anglo-Saxon West and beyond

While I have tried to show the ways in which ordinary people collectively search for solidarity in the Anglo-Saxon West, showing the ineptitude of either Christian or liberal narratives, my ethnographic work has been limited to London, UK. I maintain that ethnographic work is indispensable for bringing to life the complex ways in which transcendental ideals are articulated in myths and realised through performance. Yet far more work is required to explore similarities and differences within the Anglo-Saxon West. Partly, this means further research in the US and Canada. I am currently undertaking such comparative research in Vancouver, Canada. But particularly given the importance I have attributed to the way that specific discourses shape self-understandings, further research is also required beyond the English-speaking world, in particular in settings such as France, Germany, the Netherlands and Scandinavia.

More work is also required to explore the possibility of a collective search for solidarity in places where liberal theories and practices are spreading. Partly this means that further research is required into those countries being pulled into the fold of liberal hegemony but caught on the border between this and other traditions, in particular the countries of Southern and Eastern Europe. These countries will also be important for pushing beyond (post-)

Protestant contexts, considering in particular how ideas concerning solidarity have been shaped, in Southern Europe by Catholicism and corporatism, and in Eastern Europe by Orthodoxy and Soviet socialism. Yet it is also important to push beyond broadly (post-)Christian contexts to where the ideals and practices of liberalism are merging with very different ontologies, polities and economies, and where similarly reactionary and anti-liberal forms of politics are emerging: in Turkey, the Middle East, India and the Philippines, amongst others. If Christianity on its own cannot be the answer in the Anglo-Saxon West, it certainly cannot be the answer in these settings. It is moreover worth noting, as I have suggested in chapter 2, that the approaches I have identified display (post-)Christian tendencies, and so too, as a result, do my findings: there remains a strong focus, for instance, on the importance of cultivating shared beliefs in order to facilitate action, notwithstanding my attempts to show how deeply these are embedded in performances. It is worth exploring whether these same ideas apply elsewhere.

It is also worth stressing that while providing a geographical context is crucial to developing deep understandings of people's motivations, it is important not to excessively reify the Anglo-Saxon West as ontologically, politically or economically distinct. Of special note, for instance, is the way that the transcendental framework I have been advocating, and which has required such careful work to construct so as not to reverse secular hegemony and impose a pseudo-religious identity on secular people, has a cognate in the already well-established concept of *dharma* in South Asia. Pool (2016) has strictly precluded the possibility of translating *dharma* to 'religion', instead preferring the term 'an ethics of justice and order' which impinges on both social and personal self-understandings, and potentially provides the basis for ethical renewal across religious differences, since each religion has its own embodiment of *dharma*. Yet notwithstanding the unifying potential of the concept of *dharma*, in a postcolonial context, secular reifications of the religious/secular binary are dominant, such that even those living in rural settings will themselves consider it problematic to possess a *dharma* in the absence of a religious worldview. To be both ethical and atheist seems improbable.

Beyond extending the research to different places, it is also worth extending to different constituencies. A key example here is unlocking how to cultivate a collective search for solidarity amongst people who are apparently disengaged from politics. A central inspiration for this book is research suggesting a decline in political and social engagement of all kinds. This would mean undertaking research beyond the usual institutions we associate with engagement, exploring sports clubs, theatres and pubs. Most crucially of all to my mind, we need deep ethnographies of place within the Anglo-Saxon West. This would require a turn in current academic culture. At least as far as the relationship between religion and solidarity is concerned, anthropologies of place are too often associated with research in other places. This not only reifies a religious/secular binary, but also a West and the rest dichotomy. Globalisation results both in forms of homogenisation, in particular the spread of liberal hegemony, and heterogenisation, since liberalism takes on locally specific forms (see for example Appadurai 1996). Given this idea, there is anyway less value in the idea of the West and the rest, and reifying this distinction serves to devalue the intricacies of all cultures (see also Laidlaw 2014). It is moreover the case that when anthropological methods are brought home, this often means merely replicating these methods within particular institutions, most prominently in religious institutions. This approach may itself further reproduce the religious/secular binary, reifying such institutions as what might be called 'the other within'. I thus suggest a move from anthropologies of particular groups of people to anthropologies of place. Something similar has already been advocated (Low and Lawrence-Zuniga 2003), but the anthropology of place has yet to reach maturity in the Anglo-Saxon West, particularly where this means including people of all religions and none in an overarching framework of study, to come to an understanding of how various interpretations of globally circulating ideals and myths are coming together in a certain place and mingling with other, more local ideals and myths.

Especially if we are seeking to understand the lives of those relatively disengaged from institutions, we can only do this by researching a city, a town, a village, and the ways that people engage with one another. Of course, it is not as exciting to undertake research in Scunthorpe or Detroit as it is in the Amazon, but such work is essential, particularly if we are to have a nuanced understanding of the findings we develop elsewhere. A particularly good example of this work comes from Miller (2008), who explores the presence or absence of the sacred amongst people living on a particular street in London, and from Engelke (2012), who though focusing on a single organisation, shows particular interest in its interactions with the wider town in which it is based. Numerous authors are also beginning to hone the interaction between religious and secular actors in particular spaces, most notably through the concept of 'geographies of postsecular rapprochement' (Beaumont and Baker 2011; Cloke and Beaumont 2013; Williams 2015).

Speaking of anthropologies of place is also helpful in reminding us of how transcendental ideals and the myths through which they are articulated are shaped by place. Block (2016: 9) has suggested that 'scholars of religion often neglect the category of space', since 'it may be surprising that so apparently private, and perhaps culture-transcendent, an aspect of life is heavily influenced by where one lives'. Challenging these assumptions must be key to future work. By locating research in a place, we can become more aware of what is shared between people of all religions and none (Knott 2009).

As a more nuanced understanding of differences of place emerge, so a more global perspective will follow. This aspect is key: in a world in which both politics and businesses are going global, so too must our understanding of how solidarity is constructed. It will moreover be fundamental to stay true to one of the core points of this book: we cannot, even with the most thorough research, seek to extrapolate from research to politics without consulting, involving and empowering the people on the front line already acting. If politics and businesses are going global, so too is the social imagination. Thus before simply proclaiming ideas for a global politics, it will be important to explore the sources of global solidarity already developing amongst ordinary people.

Theology and beyond

This book has contended that although potentially global, in its current form the postliberal analysis is limited to the Anglo-Saxon West. It is also limited by a lack of creativity in engaging with the multifarious ways in which people in liberal settings draw on transcendent ideals, articulate these through myths, whether of Jesus, Muhammad, or of a parent or an old friend, and live out these myths in the world they see around them. Drawing on Christian theologies of the past, postliberalism fails to adequately engage the present.

But postliberalism also rests heavily on a particular assumption about the past, namely, that prior to the onset of modernity, people had a strong sense of solidarity rooted in a Christian understanding of transcendence. In order to make this argument, much more research is required into whether and how ordinary people navigated the ambiguities and ambivalences associated with a collective search for solidarity prior to the onset of modernity. Plurality did not begin with the European Wars of Religion. Christendom was not a homogenous world, and even if it were theologically and politically, the pre-modern church and state were insufficiently developed for their tentacles to reach into every community (Southern 1970/1990: 23). Yet such research itself will always be limited to materials that are available, and perhaps we will never know the answers. It might be worth contending, drawing on research from this book, that postliberals are not trying to hark back to a real past, but rather are conjuring an ideal past from which to derive myths of solidarity. Yet this would be a very dangerous misreading of my arguments. To draw on my arguments to justify the conjuring of an imaginary past by deliberately ignoring the very real struggles of certain groups and individuals would first of all be to ignore my stress on the importance of drawing on social scientific method to engage with lived realities, and second would be to ignore the priority I have given to performance. If there is to be any justification for shifting the rationality of myth from its discursive content to the performances it inspires, then we must be particularly critical and rigorous in our judgement of these performances, in this case asking: How inclusive and empowering was medieval Christendom? Or, perhaps being fair to postliberals, how inclusive and empowering might it have been?

With these shortcomings regarding our knowledge of the past in mind, it is important that we do not repeat the same mistakes in the present, glossing over the way that ordinary people navigate ambiguities and ambivalences associated with a collective search for solidarity, as well as the way that some groups and individuals are excluded. Even and perhaps especially theologians, seeking as they do to make normative claims about how the world ought to be, need to make sure that they are anchoring their ideals in understandings of what is possible in reality. The theologian might reply, drawing on the research available on this book, that they are merely constructing transcendental ideals that might enable people to journey from the world as it is to the world as it should be. But if this is the case, theologians need to recognise that they do not have a monopoly on the imagination. One of postliberals' key criticisms of liberal political theory is not merely that it constructs a realm of belief-independent rationality, but that it assumes only certain elites are capable of safeguarding this world. If this critique has at its heart an ethics, rather than merely an ontological conjecture about the way we imagine, then postliberals need to recognise that they are reproducing elitism by setting themselves up has the safeguards of transcendence. This book has moreover tried to show that if we wish to find a sense of transcendence that will actually serve as a source of solidarity in the precarious religious and political climate before us today, then it is amongst those actively engaged in developing solidarity that we will find it.

There are numerous examples of the much more creative theological work I am advocating here, work that places normative arguments into a hermeneutic relationship with lived realities, of which two are particularly significant. Baker et al. (2015) offer an understanding of Christian theology that prioritises performance. They do so by drawing on numerous case studies of Christians developing solidarity across religious differences. Rooting his own work in a long case study of London Citizens, Bretherton (2015) demonstrates how religious and secular actors alike can offer lessons for a more engaged theological approach. If theology is to have any resonance today, it needs to engage with the ethno-theologies or theology-in-use of ordinary people by at least drawing on ethnography, if not actually undertaking ethnographic research (see also Scott 2005; Fountain and Lau 2013). Put simply, we need to spend time with and learn from the people whose minds and lives we want to change.

Religion and beyond

I have throughout suggested that reflexivity is rooted less in the ability to translate one's motivations into a secular language than in an ability to understand how one's ideals are articulated through myths that impinge on performance. This point is particularly controversial and divisive if used to suggest that religious organisations and individuals are better at reflexivity than secular organisations and individuals. This is not my intention. Instead, as I hope is made abundantly clear in my discussion of FbRN, and more so when this is compared with my discussion of LC, my point is that there is not so much a religious/secular distinction as a postliberal/liberal distinction.

Those that consider it dangerous and divisive to invoke ideals and myths in plural spaces quite naturally spend less time reflecting on these ideals and myths, and so become liable to disillusionment, or else to adopting discourses and practices that jar with their own ideals.

That the secular group with which I worked, namely HCVS, tended not to hold a reflexive relationship with their ideals cannot be simplistically generalised to secular groups or individuals generally. As my discussion of FbRN demonstrates, religious actors can be similarly lacking in reflexivity if they do not have the conceptual means of transporting their private faith into public critique. And as my discussion of LC illuminates, secular individuals can have deep ideals, and powerful and reflexive relationships with these ideals, the myths through which they are articulated, and the performances of solidarity thus inspired. Yet while much research is available into how religious organisations and individuals develop solidarity in wider society, and while only a small imaginative leap is required to see how such research can be translated into my theoretical framework, far less research is available into how secular actors develop solidarity (Baker 2013; Bretherton 2015; Cloke and Beaumont 2013; Wood 2002). Partly as a result, policy makers in the Anglo-Saxon West have often focused funding on religious groups when seeking to develop solidarity (Beckford 2012; Clarke 2006; Dinham 2009, 2012; Wuthnow 2006). Work with secular actors is on the horizon, however. Lori Beaman is currently undertaking work on environmental activism, and my own work in Vancouver focuses specifically on using methods developed in this book to explore the transcendental ideals and myths of secular actors.

That reflexivity is rooted less in the ability to translate one's motivations into a secular language than in an ability to understand how one's ideals are articulated through myths that impinge on performance also speaks to research into ethics, particularly recent research in anthropology. Rather than deriving solidarity from rational reflection, my participants draw ethical potential from myths. Rather than the hard and fast rules of deontology or consequentialism, my participants prioritise the development of characters with particular virtues.

Indeed, it should in particular be stressed that where ethical action is taken from hard and fast rules, such as when ideals are derived from policy frameworks, both moral energy and the capacity for reflexivity seem to be undermined.

These insights particularly speak to recent debates in the anthropology of ethics, which discourage too sharp a distinction between Eastern and Western subjects, developing a straw man of the Western, Cartesian bounded self, and which we might extend to discourage too sharp a distinction between religious and secular subjects (Laidlaw 2014). Even if Cartesian thought is dominant in theology, philosophy, politics and policy (a point that is itself contestable), people on the ground do not seem to display a Cartesian self (see also Cannel 2013). Instead, the ethical subject is formed through social relations. This point becomes particularly stark when we reflect on secular subjects, who draw on stories both of great historical figures and of family members and friends whose lives they seek to embody or live in honour of, rather than developing rational frameworks which are subsequently applied in a social realm from which the individual always remains aloof.

It is thus particularly by engaging with how secular actors in the Anglo-Saxon West develop solidarity that we can begin to push through distinctions between the West and the rest, and between the secular and the religious. Such research will not only help politicians, policy makers and practitioners to avoid unwittingly sowing the seeds of division, but will also, more importantly in my view amidst the dominance of secularity at both political, organisational and individual levels, enable people to develop more engaging frameworks for solidarity.

The state and beyond

It perhaps seems unfashionable to talk about the role of the state today. The social democratic consensus of the 1960s has given way to a neoliberal consensus. The role of the state is radically called into question by both left and right (Judt 2010). Even those who still hold onto the state are confronted with what has been called the progressive's dilemma: how to maintain egalitarian ideas about social justice as well as a relatively open attitude towards migration and migrant integration (Kymlicka 2015). The power of the state increasingly pales in comparison with global market forces to the extent that it has been suggested ours is a time or interregnum in which the rulers no longer can rule and the ruled no longer wish to be ruled (Baumann 2012). So why talk about states? Why not talk instead of emerging religious, political and social movements confronting local problems with global implications? This book suggests maintaining a focus on the state is important for a number of related reasons. Perhaps most importantly, liberalism has achieved a position of hegemony in the Anglo-Saxon West and is swiftly making ground across the globe. The reification of the state as a means of controlling people as well as filling in for their inadequacies in solidarity is central to the liberal project. Thus thinking about the state, what its role should be, is an essential starting point for reimagining how we ought to live. Second, beyond liberalism, the state, broadly conceived, or as some may prefer "public institutions", are a useful starting point for thinking about what goods must be collectively resourced, which itself relies on deeper questions concerning what is really important in life. Third, in whatever way the world is changing, people seeking to develop solidarity on the ground still regard the state as key to curating the development of a shared sense of transcendence from which to address issues of social justice. Today, this emphasis seems to again be emerging amongst the wider populace, for whom neoliberalism has made it harder to locate sources of accountability, from parking authorities to social care providers. So the question is how to talk about states, broadly defined, in this new complicated time of interregnum.

There is also plenty of research available into the relationship between welfare states and religious belief. Research from Backstrom et al. (2011) and Gill and Lundsgaarde (2004) suggests that countries with strong welfare states tend to have lower levels of propositional belief. There is also plenty of research into how welfare states can, in a neoliberal age, be materially supported by religious groups (Beckford 2012; Clarke 2006; Dinham 2009, 2012; Wuthnow 2006). Far less research is available into how transcendent ideals and the myths through which they are articulated can generate the solidarity necessary for sustaining welfare states, that is, the willingness to pay more taxes or to volunteer. Developing this broader framework is crucial to the question of solidarity at present, particularly in the Anglo-Saxon West where secular identities are on the rise. If we do not wish for welfare to be sustained by the few for the many, then we must move beyond religion to broader frameworks, asking how a shared sense of transcendence can be developed such as might sustain solidarity. This question becomes particularly complex in spaces of radical diversity of belief and practice. This book has gone some way to offering findings that might be applied to the development of welfare, as well as to developing sufficient solidarity that might rule out certain aspects of welfare, encouraging people to act on their own initiative to support one another. But more direct research is required into the myths that sustain welfare, particularly as recipients of welfare increasingly come from other countries and contexts. What myths are already sustaining welfare, and how are these interrupted and expanded to include or exclude new stories and people?

This book also suggests that the next step for academics interested in the relationship between myth, solidarity and the state might be to undertake action research. Stepping out of the academy to engage with ordinary people on the frontiers is the first step towards empowering those people. Perhaps the pinnacle is to cross the fourth wall, the researcher-participant threshold, and become actively engaged in processes of change. As the concept of the state expands, so might academics, particularly in publicly funded universities, take it upon themselves to challenge the monopoly of central government and become involved in developing solidarity.

Capitalism and beyond

Neoliberalism, by the admittance even of the IMF (Ostry, et al. 2016), widely perceived as its chief progenitor over the last 20 years, is the most powerful economic ideology across the globe at present. An abundance of research is today available into how people across the world both resist and reproduce neoliberalism. Why then have I chosen to focus on capitalism? I hope that this book, and chapter 4 especially, has managed to turn this question on its head. If it is fundamental to understand the ideological roots of our current political and economic situation, then how can people ignore capitalism in their explorations of neoliberalism? Chapter 4 demonstrated in particular that it is the widespread imbibing and embodying of capitalist understandings of time, even amongst organisations and individuals that are openly hostile to capitalism, that ensures neoliberal policies always manage to fall on such placid, if not fertile ground. As with the state, thinking about capitalism can help us to question what goods ought to be collectively resourced, how we ought to spend our time and thus what is really important in life.

More research is required, then, into how people resist and reproduce the myths of capitalism. Some particularly illuminating work in this regard comes from the Gens group, which explores the moral underpinnings of capitalism, particularly as this relates to gender (Bear et al. 2015). Research in this cluster has also innovatively demonstrated how capitalist time ties up with understandings of place. Global businesses underscored by a particular understanding of time draw in people in different places across the world, and produce very different results depending on the types of myths already established in those places.

In turning to address these issues, academics need to imbibe some of the insights provided by this book, learning to cut through a religious/secular, mythic/rational binary. There are plenty of resources from within numerous religious traditions, as well as from Marxism, feminism and environmentalism. People from within or else studying these various traditions need to find ways of speaking with one another, developing processes of *bricolage* that bring together various powerful myths. And together they need to speak beyond their closed circles to the wider public. I am currently seeking to bring these various strands together in my own network, Alternative Visions in the Public Sphere (AltVisions)

As already suggested in chapter 4, capitalism easily shifts to incorporate the myths of its critics. For such an elusive target, perhaps real change requires interdisciplinary and inter-sectoral collaboration between academics, politicians, policy makers and activists. Thus as with research on the state, as capitalism achieves a place of global hegemony, perhaps the next step for researchers is to cross the fourth wall and become involved in developing, for example, more ethical business practices or more reciprocal processes of exchange on the ground. A more conventional, though not uncontroversial root comes from the recent work of the William Temple Foundation, which is seeking to develop spiritual capital in business settings, while a more radical path is offered in the direct action of Graeber (2009).

The academy and beyond

I finally want to make a broad call, which I hope speaks to anyone undertaking research in the humanities or social sciences. As already stated, one of the fundamental aspects of the postliberal critique is that our current problems do not stem merely from the construction of belief-independent rationality but also the monopolisation of that realm by an elite. If we as researchers want to begin to address our current political circumstances, a call that seems ever more pressing in the light of recent developments across the world, the first step has to be recognising that research is not for politicians and policy makers alone: it is for the people we care to inspire. As I suggested in chapter 3 in relation to the state, as academics we need to learn to turn simultaneously inwards to the academy, to politicians and policy makers, and outwards to influence the way that ordinary people live their lives. One manner of doing this is established in the research that led to this book: we draw our findings from the insights of ordinary people. Another is demonstrated in my calls for action research, which may provide opportunities for academics to be involved in developing solutions in the real world, rather than simply passing on tools to those in positional power. Another way of doing this is to write and speak for an audience of ordinary people. This does not mean that we must give up on academic writing. To suggest this would be to undermine this entire book, which my non-academic friends assure me is almost impossible to read. Rather, it means that each piece of research might simultaneously produce outputs for numerous contexts. There is much distaste in England currently, as suggested in chapter 5, with the ever-stronger co-optive powers of the Higher Education Funding Council for England (HEFCE). This is an important conflict to consider, since it impinges on broader themes explored in this book, as well as speaking directly to the place of academics in developing solidarity both within and beyond the academy. Discussion often coalesces around the emphasis on impact, which is perceived as forcing academics to spend ever less time on research for its own sake, instead instrumentalising their work to serve policy requirements. This book would suggest that these shortcomings are down to a liberal understanding of the role of the state – to impose a particular way of practicing one's vocation. Impact as an ideal, which we might rephrase as the development of research that has the capacity to empower ordinary people with the tools for leading fuller lives, is not a problem. The problem is when the state decides for itself that this ideal is not already embodied in how we practice our vocation; the problem reaches its apex when having decided this, the state undermines the integrity of academia by turning a tradition of solidarity and collaboration into one of competition for sparse resources. Like the people I have discussed throughout this book, we must learn to resist this kind of co-option by being more aware now than ever of our ideals, more aware now than ever of the myths through which these ideals are articulated, and more aware now than ever of the performances that promote solidarity both within and beyond the academy. We challenge co-option by being better than those that seek to co-opt us.

Bibliography

Abrams, P. (1977/1988) Notes on the Difficulty of Studying the State, *Journal of Historical Sociology* 1(1), 58–89.

Abu-Lughod, L. (1990) The Romance of Resistance: Tracing Transformations of Power Through Bedouin Women, *American Ethnologist* 17(1), 41–55.

Adorno, T. and Horkheimer, M. (1962/1993) The Culture Industry, in T. Adorno and M. Horkheimer, eds., *Dialectic of Enlightenment*, Continuum, New York, US.

Aldous, J., Durkheim, E., and Tonnies, F. (1972) An Exchange Between Durkheim and Tonnies on the Nature of Social Relations, With an Introduction by Joan Aldous, *American Journal of Sociology* 77(6), 1191–1200.

Alexander, J. (2003) *The Meanings of Social Life: A Cultural Sociology*, Oxford University Press, Oxford, UK.

Alkire, S. and Ritchie, A. (2010) *Winning Ideas: Lessons From Free-market Economics*, accessed at: www.ophi.org.uk/working-paper-number-06/ (22 March 2016).

Althusser, L. (1971/2006) Ideology and Ideological State Apparatuses, in A. Sharma and A. Gupta, eds., *The Anthropology of the State: A Reader*, Blackwell, Oxford, UK, pp. 86–111.

Anderson, B. (1983) *Imagined Communities: Reflections on the Origins and Spread of Nationalism*, Verso, London, UK.

Appadurai, A. (1996) *Modernity at Large: Cultural Dimensions of Globalization*, University of Minnesota Press, Minneapolis, US.

Asad, T. (2003) *Formations of the Secular: Christianity, Islam, Modernity*, Stanford University Press, Stanford, US.

Avineri, S. (1972) *Hegel's Theory of the Modern State*, Cambridge University Press, Cambridge, UK.

Backstrom, A., Davie, G., Edgardh, N., and Petterson, P. (2011) *Welfare and Religion in 21st Century Europe: Volume 2: Gendered, Religious and Social Change*, Routledge, London, UK and New York, US.

Badie, B. and Birnbaum, P. (1983) *Sociology of the State* (trans. A. Goldhammer), University of Chicago Press, Chicago, US.

Baker, C. (2009) Blurred Encounters? Religious Literacy, Spiritual Capital and Language, in A. Dinham et al., eds., *Faith in the Public Realm: Controversies, Policies and Practices*, Policy Press, Bristol.

Baker, C. (2013) Moral Freighting and Civic Engagement: A UK Perspective on Putnam and Campbell's Theory of Religious-Based Social Action, *Sociology of Religion* 74(3), 343–369.

Baker, C. (2016) Faith in the Public Sphere – In Search of a Fair and Compassionate Society for the Twenty-first Century, *Journal of Beliefs and Values* 37(3), 259–272.

Baker, C., James, T., and Reader, J. (2015) *A Philosophy of Christian Materialism: Entangled Fidelities and the Public Good*, Ashgate, Farnham, UK.

Baker, C. and Miles-Watson, J. (2014) Exploring Secular Spiritual Capital: An Engagement in Religious and Secular Dialogue for a Common Future?, *International Journal of Public Theology* 2(4), 442–464.

Baker, C. and Skinner, H. (2006) *Faith in Action – The Dynamic Connection Between Spiritual and Religious Capital*, William Temple Foundation, Manchester, UK.

Barnett, C. (2001) *The Audit of War: The Illusion and Reality of Britain as a Great Nation*, Faber and Gaber, London, UK.

Bates, T. (1975) Gramsci and the Theory of Hegemony, *Journal of the History of Ideas* 36(2), 351–366.

Baumann, Z. (2012) Times of Interregnum, *Ethics and Global Politics* 5(1), 49–56.

Beaman, L. (2014) Deep Equality as an Alternative to Accommodation and Tolerance, *Nordic Journal of Religion and Society* 27(2), 89–111.

Beaman, L. (2016) Namaste: The Perilous Journey of 'Real' Yoga, in L. Beaman and S. Sikka, eds., *Constructions of Self and Other in Yoga, Travel, and Tourism: A Journey to Elsewhere*, Palgrave MacMillan, Basingstoke, UK, pp. 101–110.

Beaman, L. (2017) *Deep Equality in an Era of Religious Diversity*, Oxford University Press, Oxford, UK.

Bear, L. (2015) *Navigating Austerity: Currents of Debt Along a South Asian River*, Stanford University Press, Stanford, US.

Bear, L., Ho, K., Tsing, A., and Yanagisako, S. (2015) *Gens: A Feminist Manifesto for the Study of Capitalism*, accessed at: https://culanth.org/fieldsights/652-gens-a-feminist-manifesto-for-the-study-of-capitalism (10 May 2017).

Beaumont, J. and Baker, C. (2011) *Postsecular Cities: Space, Theory and Practice*, Continuum, London, UK.

Beckford, J. (2012) SSSR Presidential Address Public Religions and the Postsecular: Critical Reflections, *Journal for the Scientific Study of Religion* 51(1), 1–19.

Beetham, D. (1994) Max Weber and the Liberal Political Tradition, in A. Horowitz and T. Maley, eds., *The Barbarism of Reason: Max Weber and the Twilight of Enlightenment*, University of Toronto Press, Toronto, Canada.

Bellah, R. (1967) Civil Religion in America, *Daedalus* 96, 1–21.

Bellah, R., Tipton, S., Sullivan, W., Madsen, R., and Swidler, A. (1985) *Habits of the Heart: Individualism and Commitment in American Life*, University of California Press, Berkeley and Los Angeles, US.

Bellah, R., Tipton, S., Sullivan, W., Madsen, R., and Swidler, A. (1991) *The Good Society*, Alfred A. Knopf, New York, US.

Benford, R. and Snow, D. (2000) Framing Processes and Social Movements: An Overview and Assessment, *Annual Review of Sociology* 26, 611–639.

Berger, P. (1967) *The Sacred Canopy: Elements of a Sociological Theory of Religion*, Anchor Books, Garden City, US.

Berger, P. (1979) *Facing up to Modernity*, Penguin, Hamondsport, UK.

Beveridge, W. (1948) *Voluntary Action: A Report on the Methods of Social Advance*, accessed at: https://babel.hathitrust.org/cgi/pt?id=uc1.b4265954;view=1up;seq=7 (10 May 2017).

Bhaskar, R. (1979) *The Possibility of Naturalism: A Philosophical Critique of the Contemporary Human Science*, Humanities Press, Atlantic Highlands, US.

Bhaskar, R. (1986) *Scientific Realism and Human Emancipation*, Verso, London, UK.

Bloch, E. (1954/1995) *The Principle of Hope* (trans. N. Plaice, S. Plaice, and P. Knight), MIT Press, Cambridge, US.

Bloch, M. (2008) Why Religion Is Nothing Special But Is Central, *Philosophical Transactions of the Royal Society* 363, 2055–2061.

Bloch, M. (2010) Bloch on Bloch on Religion, *Religion and Society: Advances in Research* 1, 4–28.

Bloch, M. and Parry, J. (1989) Introduction: Money and the Morality of Exchange, in M. Bloch and J. Parry, eds., *Money and the Morality of Exchange*, Cambridge University Press, Cambridge, UK, pp. 1–32.

Block, T. (2016) *The Secular Northwest: Religion and Irreligion in Everyday Postwar Life*, University of British Columbia Press, Vancouver, Canada.

Boltanski, L. and Chiapello, E. (2007) *The New Spirit of Capitalism* (trans. G. Elliot), Verso, London, UK.

Bradstock, A. (2013) *History of Our Movement*, accessed at: www.christiansonthe left.org.uk/history_of_our_movement (10 February 2016).

Brennan, G. and Pettit, P. (2004) *The Economy of Esteem*, Oxford University Press, Oxford, UK.

Bretherton, L. (2015) *Resurrecting Democracy: Faith, Citizenship and the Politics of a Common Life*, Cambridge University Press, Cambridge, UK.

Brint, S. (2001) Gemeinschaft Revisited: A Critique and Reconstruction of the Community Concept, *Sociological Theory* 19(1), 1–23.

Brown, C. (2001/2009) *The Death of Christian Britain: Understanding Secularisation 1800–2000*, Routledge, Abingdon, UK.

Bruce, S. (2006) Secularization and the Impotence of Individualized Religion, *Hedgehog Review* 8(1–2), 35–45.

Bryman, A. (2004) *Social Research Methods*, Oxford University Press, Oxford, UK.

Bunyan, P. (2013) Partnership, the Big Society and Community Organizing: Between Romanticizing, Problematizing and Politicizing Community, *Community Development Journal* 48(1), 119–133.

Burr, V. (2015) *Social Constructionism*, Routledge, East Sussex, UK.

Calhoun, C. (2014) Religion, Government and the Public Good, *Temple Tracts* 2(2), 32–359.

Cannel, F. (2013) The Re-enchantment of Kinship, in F. Cannel and S. McKinnon, eds., *Vital Relations: Modernity and the Persistent Life of Kinship*, School for Advanced Research Press, Santa Fe, US.

CDP. (1977) *Gilding the Ghetto*, CDP Inter-Project Editorial Team, London, UK.

Chatterton, P. and Pickerill, J. (2010) Everyday Activism and Transition Towards Postcapitalist Worlds, *Transactions of the Institute of British Geographers* 35, 475–490.

Chriss, J. J. (1993) *Durkheim's Cult of the Individual as Civil Religion: Its Appropriation by Erving Goffman*, accessed at: http://engagedscholarship.csuohio.edu/cgi/viewcontent.cgi?article=1098&context=clsoc_crim_facpub (10 May 2017).

Christian Socialist Movement. (2006) *Our Statement of Values*, accessed at: www.thecsm.org.uk/documents/CSMOurnewstatementofvalues_000.pdf (10 February 2016).

Christie, N. and Gauvreau, M. (2001) *A Full-Orbed Christianity: The Protestant Churches and Social Welfare in Canada 1900–1940*, McGill-Queen's Press, Montreal, Canada.

Clarke, G. (2006) Faith Matters: Faith-based Organizations, Civil Society and International Development, *Journal of International Development* 18(6), 835–848.

Cloke, P. and Beaumont, J. (2013) Geographies of Postsecular Rapprochement in the City, *Progress in Human Geography* 37(1), 27–51.

Cohn, N. (1957/1993) *Pursuit of the Millennium*, Pimlico, London.

Comte, A. (1844/1988) *Introduction to Positive Philosophy* (trans. F. Ferre), Hackett Publishing, Indianapolis, US and Cambridge, UK.

Coser, L. (1984) Introduction, in E. Durkheim, *The Division of Labour in Society* (trans. W. D. Halls), Macmillan, London, UK.

Davie, G. (1994) *Religion in Britain Since 1945: Believing Without Belonging*, Blackwell, Oxford, UK.

Davie, G. (2015) *Religion in Britain: A Persistent Paradox*, Wiley-Blackwell, Oxford, UK.

Day, A. (2011) *Believing in Belonging: Belief and Identity in the Modern World*, Oxford University Press, Oxford, UK.

Day, A. (2017) *The Death of Anglicanism's Last Active Generation: Does It Matter?* Oxford University Press, Oxford, UK.

DCLG. (2008) *Face to Face, Side by Side: A Framework for Partnership in Our Multifaith Society*, DCLG, London, UK.

DiMaggio, P. and Powell, W. (1983) The Iron Cage Revisited: Institutional Isomorphism and Collective Rationality in Organizational Fields, *American Sociological Review* 48(2), 147–160.

Dinham, A. (2000) *Another New Deal for What Community? Local People's Experiences of Participation in the Government's New Deal for Communities*, PhD Dissertation, Goldsmiths, University of London, UK.

Dinham, A. (2005) Empowered or Over-powered? The Real Experiences of Local Participation in the UK's New Deal for Communities, *Community Development Journal* 40(3), 301–312.

Dinham, A. (2009) *Faiths, Public Policy and Civil Society: Problems, Policies, Controversies*, Palgrave Macmillan, Basingstoke, UK.

Dinham, A. (2011) What Is a 'Faith' Community? *Community Development Journal* 46, 526–541.

Dinham, A. (2012) The Multifaith Paradigm in Policy and Practice: Problems, Challenges, Directions, *Social Policy and Society* 11(4), 577–587.

Dinham, A. (2014) *Ontologies of Public Policy: How Philosophical and Religious Ideas Shape and Mis-shape Public Policy*, Paper presented at University of Chester AHRC Conference Philosophy, Religion and Public Policy Keynote, 8–9 April.

Dinham, A. and Francis, M. (2016) *Religious Literacy in Policy and Practice*, Policy Press, Bristol, UK.

Dinham, A. and Jackson, R. (2012) Religion, Welfare and Education, in L. Woodhead and R. Catto, eds., *Religion and Change in Modern Britain*, Routledge, London, UK.

Dore, R. (2002) Will Global Capitalism Be Anglo-Saxon Capitalism? *Asian Business and Management* 1, 9–18.

Du Bois, B. (1979) *Passionate Scholarship: Notes on Values, Knowing and Method in Feminist Social Science*, Paper presented at Annual Meeting of the American Association for the Advancement of Science; Symposium on 'Feminism and the Philosophy of Science', Houston, 6 January.

Duncan, C. and Moore, D. (2003) Catholic and Protestant Social Discourse and the American Welfare State, *Journal of Poverty* 7(3), 57–83.

Durkheim, E. (1902/1984) Preface to the Second Edition, in E. Durkheim, *The Division of Labour in Society* (trans. W. D. Halls), Macmillan, London, UK.

Durkheim, E. (1915/2008) *The Elementary Forms of Religious Life* (trans. C. Cosman), Oxford University Press, Oxford, UK.

Eagleton, T. (1991) *Ideology: An Introduction*, Verso, London, UK.

Eisgruber, C. (2006) Secularization, Religiosity, and the United States Constitution, *Indiana Journal of Global Legal Studies* 13(2), 445–472.

Engelke, M. (2012) Angels in Swindon: Public Religion and Ambient Faith in England, *American Ethnologist* 39(1), 155–170.

Faith-based Regeneration Network. (2012) *Keeping It Together*, FbRN, London, UK.

Fitzgerald, T. (2011) *Religion and Politics in International Relations: The Modern Myth*, Continuum, London.

Flyvbjerg, B. (2001) *Making Social Science Matter* (trans. S. Sampson), Cambridge University Press, Cambridge, UK.

Forbes, H. (1987) Harz-Horowitz at Twenty: Nationalism, Toryism and Socialism in Canada and the United States, *Canadian Journal of Political Science* 20(2), 287–315.

Fountain, P. and Lau, S. W. (2013) Anthropological Theologies: Engagements and Encounters, *The Australian Journal of Anthropology* 24(3), 227–234.

Francis, M. and Knott, K. (2015) Return? It Never Left: Exploring the 'Sacred' as a Resource for Bridging the Gap Between the Religious and the Secular, in C. Kutz, H. Riss, and O. Roy, eds., *Religious Norms in the Public Sphere: Proceedings of a Conference Held at UC Berkeley on May 6–7, 2011*, European University Institute, Florence, Italy.

Freire, P. (1970/1996) *Pedagogy of the Oppressed* (trans. M. B. Ramos), Penguin, London, UK.

Frohnen, B. (1992) Robert Bellah and the Politics of 'Civil' Religion, *Political Science Reviewer* 21(1), 148–218.

Fukuyama, F. (1992) *The End of History and the Last Man*, Hamish Hamilton, London, UK.

Gamoran, A. (1990) Civil Religion in American Schools, *Sociology of Religion* 51(3), 235–256.

Geertz, C. (1973) *The Interpretation of Cultures*, Basic Books, New York, US.

Gerteis, J. (2011) Civil Religion and the Politics of Belonging, in J. Go, ed., *Rethinking Obama*. Emerald, Bingley, UK.

Giddens, A. (2001) Introduction, in M. Weber, ed., *The Protestant Work Ethic and the Spirit of Capitalism*, Routledge, London, UK and New York, US, pp. vii–xxiv.

Gill, A. and Lundsgaarde, E. (2004) State Welfare Spending and Religiosity: A Cross-National Analysis, *Rationality and Analysis* 16(4), 399–436.

Glasman, M. (2011) *The Labour Tradition and the Politics of Paradox*, accessed at: www.lwbooks.co.uk/journals/soundings/Labour_tradition_and_the_politics_of_paradox.pdf (28 March 2017).

Gorski, P. (2011) Barack Obama and Civil Religion, in J. Go, ed., *Rethinking Obama*. Emerald, Bingley, UK.

Gorski, P. (2013) What Is Critical Realism? And Why Should You Care? *Contemporary Sociology* 42(5), 658–670.

Graeber, D. (2009) *Direct Action: An Ethnography*, AK Press, Oakland, US and Edinburgh, UK.

Graeber, D. (2011) *Debt: The First 5000 Years*, Melville House Publishing, New York, US.

Gramsci, A. (1971) *Selections From the Prison Notebooks*, International Publishers, New York, US.

Guardian/Reading the Riots. (2011) *Reading the Riots: Investigating England's Summer of Disorder*, accessed at: http://eprints.lse.ac.uk/46297/1/Reading%20the%20 riots(published).pdf (10 May 2017).

Gupta, A. (2006) Blurred Boundaries: The Discourse of Corruption, the Culture of Politics, and the Imagined State, in A. Sharma and A. Gupta, eds., *The Anthropology of the State: A Reader*, Blackwell, Oxford, UK, pp. 211–242.

Habermas, J. (1985) *The Theory of Communicative Action. Vol. 2: Lifeworld and System: A Critique of Functionalist Reason* (trans. T. McCarthy), Beacon Press, Boston, US.

Habermas, J. (2006) Religion in the Public Sphere, *European Journal of Philosophy* 14(1), 1–25.

Habermas, J. (2008) Notes on Post-Secular Society, *New Perspectives Quarterly* 25(4), 17–29.

Habermas, J. (2010) An Awareness of What Is Missing, in J. Habermas, ed., *An Awareness of What Is Missing: Faith and Reason in a Post-Secular Age* (trans. C. Cronin), Polity Press, Cambridge, UK, pp. 15–23.

Habermas, J. (2011) 'The Political': The Rational Meaning of a Questionable Inheritance of Political Theology, in E. Mendieta and J. VanAntwerpen, eds., *The Power of Religion in the Public Sphere*, Columbia University Press, New York, US, pp. 15–33.

Hall, P. (2006) A Historical Overview of Philanthropy, Voluntary Associations, and Nonprofit Organizations in the United States: 1600–2000, in W. Powell and R. Steinberg, eds., *The Nonprofit Sector: A Research Handbook*, Yale University Press, New Haven, US.

Hansen, T. (2012) *Melancholia of Freedom: Social Life in an Indian Township in South Africa*, Princeton University Press, Princeton, US.

Hantz, C. (1996) Ideology, Pragmatism and Ronald Reagan's Worldview: Full of Sound and Fury, Signifying. . .? *Presidential Studies Quarterly* 26(4), 942–949.

Harris, J. (2001) General Introduction, in F. Tonnies, ed., *Community and Civil Society*, Cambridge University Press, Cambridge.

Hauerwas, S. (1984) *The Peaceable Kingdom: A Primer in Christian Ethics*, University of Notre Dame Press, Notre Dame, US.

Hay, C. (1999) Marxism and the State, in A. Gamble, D. Marsh, and T. Tant, eds., *Marxism and Social Science*, Palgrave, Basingstoke, UK, pp. 152–174.

Heelas, P. and Woodhead, L. (2005) *The Spiritual Revolution: Why Religion Is Giving Way to Spirituality*, Blackwell, Oxford, UK.

Hegel, G. (1821/1991) *Elements of the Philosophy of Right* (trans. H. B. Nisbett), Cambridge University Press, Cambridge, UK.

Hervieu-Leger, D. (2006) The Role of Religion in Establishing Social Cohesion, in K. Michalski, ed., *Religion in the New Europe*, Central European University Press, Budapest, Hungary.

Hirschkind, C. (2006) *The Ethical Soundscape: Cassette Sermons and Islamic Counterpublics*, Columbia University Press, New York, US.

Horowitz, A. and Maley, T., eds. (1994) *The Barbarism of Reason: Max Weber and the Twilight of Enlightenment*, University of Toronto Press, Toronto, Canada.

Hunsinger, G. (2003) Postliberal Theology, in K. Vanhoozer, ed., *The Cambridge Companion to Postmodern Theology*, Cambridge University Press, Cambridge, UK.

Ivereigh, A. (2010) *Faithful Citizens*, Darton, Longman and Todd, London, UK.

Jailobaeva, K. (2007) *Civil Society From Liberal and Communitarian Perspectives*, accessed at: www.isn.ethz.ch/Digital-Library/Publications/Detail/?lng=en&id= 145085 (10 February 2016).

Judt, T. (2010) *Ill Fares the Land*, Alan Lane, London, UK.

Kahneman, D. (2011) *Thinking, Fast and Slow*, Penguin, London, UK and New York, US.

Kalberg, S. (1980) Max Weber's Types of Rationality: Cornerstones for the Analysis of Rationalization in History, *The American Journal of Sociology* 85(5), 1145–1179.

Keane, W. (2010) Minds, Surfaces and Reasons in the Anthropology of Ethics, in M. Lambek, ed., *Ordinary Ethics: Anthropology, Language and Action*, Fordham University Press, New York, US, pp. 64–83.

Kelly, J. (2015) *London – Centric*, accessed at: www.bbc.co.uk/news/resources/idt-248d9ac7-9784-4769-936a-8d3b435857a8 (20 August 2017).

Knight, K. (2005) Aristotelianism vs Communitarianism, *Analyse & Kritik* 27, 259–273.

Knott, K. (2009) From Locality to Location and Back Again: A Spatial Journey in the Study of Religion, *Religion* 39(2), 154–160.

Kumar, K. (1991) *Utopia and Anti-Utopia in Modern Times*, Blackwell, Oxford, UK.

Kymlicka, W. (2015) Solidarity in Diverse Societies: Beyond Neoliberal Multiculturalism and Welfare Chauvinism, *Comparative Migration Studies* 3, 1–19.

Laidlaw, J. (1995) *Riches and Renunciation: Religion, Economy and Society Among the Jains*, Clarendon Press, Oxford, UK.

Laidlaw, J. (2014) *The Subject of Virtue: An Anthropology of Ethics and Freedom*, Cambridge University Press, Cambridge, UK.

Lambek, M. (2000) The Anthropology of Religion and the Quarrel Between Poetry and Philosophy, *Current Anthropology* 41(3), 309–320.

Lambek, M. (2008) Value and Virtue, *Anthropological Theory* 8(2), 133–157.

Lambek, M. (2010a) Introduction, in M. Lambek, ed., *Ordinary Ethics: Anthropology, Language and Action*, Fordham University Press, New York, US, pp. 1–38.

Lambek, M. (2010b) Toward an Ethics of the Act, in M. Lambek, ed., *Ordinary Ethics: Anthropology, Language and Action*, Fordham University Press, New York, US, pp. 39–63.

Lambek, M. (2012) Religion and Morality, in D. Fassin, ed., *A Companion to Moral Anthropology*, Wiley Blackwell, Oxford, UK, pp. 341–358.

Lammy, D. (2012) *Out of the Ashes: Britain After the Riots*, Guardian Books, London, UK.

Latour, B. (1993) *We Have Never Been Modern* (trans. C. Porter), Harvester Wheatsheaf, New York, US.

Ledwith, M. (2005) *Community Development: A Critical Approach*, Policy Press, Bristol, UK.

Lee, L. (2015) *Recognizing the Nonreligious: Reimagining the Secular*, Oxford University Press, Oxford, UK.

London Citizens (2012) *A Citizens' Inquiry Into the Tottenham Riots*, accessed at: www.methodistlondon.org.uk/sites/default/files/Citizens-Inquiry-into-the-Tottenham-Riots-REPORT.pdf (10 May 2017).

London Edinburgh Weekend Return Group (1980) *In and Against the State*, Pluto Press, London, UK.

Longino, H. (1990) *Science as Social Knowledge: Values and Objectivity in Scientific Inquiry*, Princeton University Press, Princeton, US.

Low, S. and Lawrence-Zuniga, D., eds. (2003) *The Anthropology of Space and Place: Locating Culture*, Blackwell, Oxford, UK.

Lynch, G. (2012) *The Sacred in the Modern World: A Cultural Sociological Approach*, Oxford University Press, Oxford.

Lynch, G. (2015) *Remembering Child Migration: Faith, Nation-Building and the Wounds of Charity*, Bloomsbury, London, UK.

MacIntyre, A. (1981/2007) *After Virtue: A Study in Moral Theory*, Notre Dame Press, Notre Dame, US.

Mann, J. (2015) *Britain Uncovered Survey Results: The Attitudes and Beliefs of Britons in 2015*, accessed at: www.theguardian.com/society/2015/apr/19/britain-uncovered-survey-attitudes-beliefs-britons-2015 (20 August 2017).

Mann, M. (1986) *The Sources of Social Power: Volume 1, A History of Power From the Beginning to A.D. 1760*, Cambridge University Press, Cambridge, UK.

Marske, C. (1987) Durkheim's 'Cult of the Individual' and the Moral Constitution of Society, *Sociological Theory* 5(1), 1–14.

Marx, K. (1844/2009) Introduction, in K. Marx, ed., *A Contribution to the Critique of Hegel's Philosophy of Right*, accessed at: www.marxists.org/archive/marx/works/1843/critique-hpr/intro.htm (10 May 2017).

Mauss, M. (1954/2010) *The Gift: The Form and Reason for Exchange in Archaic Societies*, Routledge, Abingdon, UK.

Mayo, E. and Moore, H. (2002) *Building the Mutual State: How Local Communities Can Run Public Services*, New Economics Foundation and Mutuo, London, UK.

Mayo, M. (2000) *Cultures, Communities, Identities*, Palgrave Macmillan, Basingstoke, UK.

Mellor, P. and Shilling, C. (1997) Confluent Love and the Cult of the Dyad: The Pre-Contractual Foundations of Modern Contractarian Relationships, in J. Davies and G. McLoughlin, eds., *Sex These Days*, Sheffield Academic Press, Sheffield, UK.

Mendieta, E. (2002) Introduction, in J. Habermas, ed., *Religion and Rationality*, Polity Press, Cambridge, UK.

Michea, J. (2009) *Realm of Lesser Evil* (trans. D. Fernbach), Polity Press, Cambridge, UK.

Michener, R. (2013) *Postliberal Theology: A Guide for the Perplexed*, Bloomsbury, London, UK.

Midgley, M. (2003) *The Myths We Live By*, Routledge, London, UK.

Milbank, J. (1990/2006) *Theology and Social Theory: Beyond Secular Reason*, Blackwell, Oxford, UK.

Milbank, J. (2009) Liberality Versus Liberalism, in J. Milbank, ed., *The Future of Love: Essays in Political Theology*, SCM Press, London, UK, pp. 242–263.

Milbank, J. (2013) A Closer Walk on the Wild Side, in M. Warner, J. Vanantwerpen, and C. Calhoun, eds., *Varieties of Secularism in a Secular Age*, Harvard University Press, Cambridge, US.

Milbank, J. (2014) *Every Bit as Red as Blue: The New Story Told by Blue Labour*, accessed at: http://richardsrobinson.org.uk/2012/07/the-new-story-told-by-blue-labour-an-essay-by-professor-john-milbank/ (10 May 2017).

Milbank, J. and Pabst, A. (2016) *The Politics of Virtue: Postliberalism and the Human Future*, Rowman & Littlefield, London, UK.

Miller, D. (2008) *The Comfort of Things*, Polity Press, Cambridge, UK.

Mitchell, T. (1991) The Limits of the State: Beyond Statist Approaches and Their Critics, *American Political Science Review* 85(1), 77–96.

Miyazaki, H. (2006) Economy of Dreams: Hope in Global Capitalism and Its Critiques, *Cultural Anthropology* 21(2), 147–172.

Mouffe, C. (2007) *On the Political*, Routledge, Abingdon, UK.

Narotzky, S. and Besnier, N. (2014) Crisis, Values and Hope: Rethinking the Economy, *Current Anthropology* 55(9), 4–16.

Norman, E. (1987) *The Victorian Christian Socialists*, Cambridge University Press, Cambridge, UK.

Noyes, J. and Julian, C. (2013) *Rebuilding Britain's Institutional Fabric: The Transformative Role of the Church of England*, accessed at: http://respublica.org.uk/documents/qmw_Crucible_Jan%202014_17_24.pdf (28 March 2014).

Olaveson, T. (2001) Collective Effervescence and Communitas: Processual Models of Ritual and Society in Emile Durkheim and Victor Turner, *Dialectical Anthropology*, 26, 89–124.

Ollman, B. (1977) Marx's Vision of Communism: A Reconstruction, *Critique: Journal of Socialist Theory* 8(1), 4–41.

Ostry, J., Loungani, P. and Furceri, D. (2016) Neoliberalism: Oversold?, *Finance and Development* 53(2), 38–41.

Paley, J. (2001) The Paradox of Participation: Civil Society and Democracy in Chile, *Political and Legal Anthropology Review* 24(1), 1–12.

Palumbo, A. and Scott, A. (2003) Weber, Durkheim and the Sociology of the Modern State, in T. Ball and R. Bellamy, eds., *Cambridge History of Twentieth Century Political Thought*, Cambridge University Press, Cambridge, UK.

Parr, C. (2014) *The 10 Most Highly Educated Global Cities*, accessed at: www.timeshighereducation.com/news/the-10-most-highly-educated-global-cities/2013788.article (28 March 2017).

Parry, J. (1986) The Gift, the Indian Gift and the 'Indian Gift', *Man* 21(3), 453–473.

Pink-Dandelion, B. (2016) *The Curiously Compelling Nature of Non-Doctrinal Religion: Quakers and Secularization*, Paper presented at British Sociological Association Sociology of Religion Study Group Annual Conference 2016 Paper, 12–14 July.

Polanyi, K. (1944/2001) *The Great Transformation: The Political and Economic Origins of Our Time*, Beacon, Boston, US.

Pool, F. (2016) *The Ethical Life of Muslims in Secular India: Islamic Reformism in West Bengal*, PhD Dissertation, London School of Economics and Political Science, UK.

Pool, F. (forthcoming, in press) Religious Conversion as Ethical Transformation: A Study of Islamic Reformism in Rural West Bengal, in P. Berger and S. Sahoo, eds., *Godroads: Modalities of Conversion in India*, Cambridge University Press, New Dehli, India.

Prochaska, F. (2006) *Christianity and Social Service in Modern Britain*, Oxford University Press, Oxford, UK.

Putnam, R. and Campbell, D. (2010) *American Grace: How Religion Divides and Unites Us*, Simon & Schuster, New York, US.

Ranelagh, J. (1991) *Thatcher's People: An Insider's Account of the Politics, the Power and the Personalities*, HarperCollins, New York, US.

Rawls, J. (1971/1999) *A Theory of Justice*, Harvard University Press, Cambridge, US.

Rawls, J. (1987) The Idea of an Overlapping Consensus, *Oxford Journal of Legal Studies* 7(1), 1–25.

ResPublica. (2013a) *The Localism Act: One Year On*, accessed at: www.respublica.org.uk/item/The-Localism-Act-One-Year-On (28 March 2014).

ResPublica. (2013b) *Acting on Localism*, accessed at: www.respublica.org.uk/item/Acting-on-Localism-The-role-of-housing-associations-in-driving-a-community-agenda (28 March 2014).

Robbins, J. (2015) Where in the World Are Values? Exemplarity, Morality and Social Process, *Sociologias* 17(39), 164–196.

Rochester, C. (2012) Councils for Voluntary Service: The End of a Long Road? *Voluntary Sector Review* 3(1), 103–110.

Rowe, A. (1978) Review: The Future of Voluntary Organisations (Wolfenden Report), *Journal of Social Policy* 7(4), 491–493.

Ryan, C. and Jetha, C. (2010) *Sex at Dawn: How We Mate, Why We Stray, and What It Means for Modern Relationships*, HarperCollins, New York, US.

Sandel, M. (2012) *What Money Can't Buy: The Moral Limits of Markets*, Penguin, London, UK.

Sargisson, L. and Sargent, L. (2004) *Living in Utopia: New Zealand's Intentional Communities*, Ashgate, Farnham, UK.

Savoie, D. (1994) *Thatcher, Reagan and Mulroney: In Search of a New Bureaucracy*, University of Pittsburgh Press, Pittsburgh, US.

Schmitt, C. (1922/2006) *Political Theology: Four Chapters on the Concept of Sovereignty*, University of Chicago Press, Chicago, US.

Scott, M. W. (2005) 'I Was Like Abraham': Notes on the Anthropology of Christianity From the Solomon Islands, *Ethnos* 70(1), 101–125.

Sennett, R. (1998) *The Corrosion of Character: The Personal Consequences of Work in the New Capitalism*, W. W. Norton & Co, New York, US.

Shanks, A. (1991) *Hegel's Political Theology*, Cambridge University Press, Cambridge, UK.

Shaw, M. (2003) Gilding the Ghetto and in and Against the State, *Community Development Journal* 38(4), 361–366.

Skeggs, B. (2011) Imagining Personhood Differently: Person Value and Autonomous Working Class Value Practices, *The Sociological Review* 59(3), 496–513.

Skeggs, B. (2014) Vales Beyond Value? Is Anything Beyond the Logic of Capital? *British Journal of Sociology* 65(1), 1–20.

Skidelsky, R. and Skidelsky, E. (2012) *How Much Is Enough?* Penguin, London, UK.

Skopcol, T. (1996) Unravelling From Above, *The American Prospect* 25, 20–24.

Skopcol, T. (2008) Bringing the State Back in: Retrospect and Prospect, *Scandinavian Political Studies* 31(2), 109–124.

Smith, A. (1776/1982) *An Inquiry Into the Nature and Causes of the Wealth of Nations*, Penguin, London, UK.

Southern, R. W. (1970/1990) *Western Society and the Church in the Middle Ages*, Penguin, London, UK.

Stacey, T. (2012) Workers of the World . . . Love One Another? *Telos* 160, 183–191.

Stacey, T. (2016) *Losing Our Religion: Sources of Solidarity in Pluralist Settings*, PhD Dissertation, Goldsmiths, University of London, UK.

Stacey, T. (2017a) Imagining Solidarity in the Twenty-first Century: Towards a Performative Postsecularism, *Religion, State and Society* 45(2), 141–158.

Stacey, T. (2017b) A Post-liberal Idea of the Person: Religious and Cultural Strategies for Persons as People, in B. Wood, ed., *Post-Liberalism, Individualism and Society*, Cambridge Scholars, Cambridge, UK.

Stacey, T. (2017c) Liberalism in Search of Vision: Restoring the Connection Between Policy and Lifestyle, *Radical Orthodoxy: Theology, Philosophy, Politics* 4(1), 172–199.

Stacey, T. (forthcoming 2018) The God-shaped Hole in Post-liberalism: Why Community Development Matters, in N. Turnbull, ed., *Radical Orthodoxy: Annual Review II*, Wipf & Stock, Eugene, US.

Taylor, C. (1960) What's Wrong With Capitalism? *New Left Review* 1(2), 5–11.

Taylor, C. (1992) *Ethics of Authenticity*, Harvard University Press, Cambridge, US.

Taylor, C. (2004) *Modern Social Imaginaries*, Duke University Press, Durham, US.

Taylor, C. (2007) *A Secular Age*. Harvard University Press, Cambridge, US.

Taylor, C. (2011) Why We Need a Radical Redefinition of Secularism, in E. Mendieta and J. Van Antwerpen, eds., *The Power of Religion in the Public Sphere*, Columbia University Press, New York, US.

Taylor, C. (2014) University of Nottingham Firth Lectures, *Philosophical and Theological Anthropology in the 21st Century*, accessed at: www.nottingham.ac.uk/theology/research/firth.aspx(10 February 2016).

Thatcher, M. (1987) interviewed by Douglas Keay for *Woman's Own*, accessed at: www.margaretthatcher.org/document/106689 (30 April 2017).

Titmuss, R. (1971/1997) *The Gift Relationship: From Human Blood to Social Policy*, The New Press, New York, US.

Toscano, A. (2009) *Rethinking Marx and Religion*, accessed at: https://pervegalit. wordpress.com/2009/12/27/rethinking-marx-and-religion-by-alberto-toscano/ (10 May 2017).

Turnbull, N., ed. (forthcoming 2018) *Radical Orthodoxy: Annual Review II*, Wipf & Stock, Eugene, US.

Vanderwoerd, J. (2011) Reconsidering Secularization and Recovering Christianity in Social Work History, *Social Work and Christianity* 38(3), 244–266.

Vanheeswijck, G. (2014) *The Ambiguity of Post-Secular and Post-Metaphysical Stories*, Paper presented at University of Bern, Working With "A Secular Age" Paper. 5–8 March 2014.

Vos, K. (2011) Shareholder Versus Stakeholder Capitalism, in R. Blanpain, W. Bromwich, O. Rymkevich, I. Senatori, and C. Agut Garcia, eds., *Rethinking Corporate Governance: From Shareholder Value to Stakeholder Value*, Wolters Kluwer, Alphen, The Netherlands.

Wald, K., Silverman, A., and Fridy, K. (2005) Making Sense of Religion in Political Life, *Annual Review of Political Science* 8, 121–143.

Wall, W. (2008) *Inventing the "American Way": The Politics of Consensus From the New Deal to the Civil Rights Movement*. Colgate University Press, Hamilton, US.

Ward, G. (2014) *Unbelievable: Why We Believe and Why We Don't*, I.B. Tauris, London, UK.

Warren, M. (1994) Nietzsche and Weber: When Does Reason Become Power? in A. Horowitz and T. Maley, eds., *The Barbarism of Reason: Max Weber and the Twilight of Enlightenment*, University of Toronto Press, Toronto, Canada.

Weber, M. (1919) *Politics as a Vocation*, accessed at: http://anthropos-lab.net/wp/wp-content/uploads/2011/12/Weber-Politics-as-a-Vocation.pdf (25 August 2016).

Weber, M. (1922/2006) Bureaucracy, in A. Sharma and A. Gupta, eds., *The Anthropology of the State: A Reader*, Blackwell, Oxford, UK, pp. 49–70.

Weber, M. (1930/2001) *The Protestant Work Ethic and the Spirit of Capitalism*, Routledge, London, UK and New York, US.

Weller, P. (2006) *Time for a Change: Reconfiguring Religion, State and Society*, T & T Clarke, London, UK.

Wernick, A. (2001) *Auguste Comte and the Religion of Humanity: The Post-Theistic Program of French Social Theory*, Cambridge University Press, Cambridge, UK.

Williams, A. (2015) Post-secular Geographies: Theo-ethics, Rapprochement and Neoliberal Governance in a Faith-based Drug Programme, *Transactions of the Institute of British Geographers* 40(2), 192–208.

Williams, R. (1977/2009) *Marxism and Literature*, Oxford University Press, Oxford, UK and New York, US.

Williams, R. (1999) Visions of the Good Society and the Religious Roots of American Political Culture, *Sociology of Religion* 60(1), 1–34.

Williams, R. (2013) Civil Religion and the Cultural Politics of National Identity in Obama's America, *Journal for the Scientific Study of Religion* 52(2), 239–257.

Wilson, E. (2012) *After Secularism: Rethinking Religion in Global Politics*, Palgrave Macmillan, Basingstoke, UK.

Winch, P. (1958) *The Idea of Social Science and Its Relation to Philosophy*, Routledge, New York, US.

Wood, B., ed. (2017) *Post-Liberalism, Individualism and Society*, Cambridge Scholars, Cambridge, UK.

Wood, R. (2002) *Faith in Action: Religion, Race and Democratic Organising in America*, University of Chicago Press, Chicago, US.

Woodhead, L. (2012) Introduction, in L. Woodhead and R. Catto, eds., *Religion and Change in Modern Britain*, Routledge, London, UK.

Woodhead, L. (2014) *How Public Religion Has Changed Now that the Church and State Isn't the Only Game in Town*, Paper presented at ESA Sociology of Religion Research Network Conference, Belfast Keynote, 3–5 September.

Woodhead, L. (2016) Intensified Religious Pluralism and De-differentiation: The British Example, *Society* 53(1), 41–46.

Worsley, P. (1987) *The Trumpet Shall Sound: A Study of "Cargo" Cults in Melanesia*, Schocken, Jerusalem, Israel.

Wuthnow, R. (1989) *The Struggle for America's Soul: Evangelicals, Liberals and Secularism*, William B. Eerdman, Grand Rapids, US.

Wuthnow, R. (2006) *American Mythos: Why Our Best Efforts to Be a Better Nation Fall Short*, Princeton University Press, Princeton, US.

Index